EASY PREY INVESTORS

EASY PREY INVESTORS

*Why Broken Safety Nets Threaten
Your Wealth*

AL ROSEN AND MARK ROSEN

McGill-Queen's University Press
Montreal & Kingston • London • Chicago

© McGill-Queen's University Press 2017

ISBN 978-0-7735-4819-0 (cloth)
ISBN 978-0-7735-9990-1 (paper)
ISBN 978-0-7735-9991-8 (ePUB)

Legal deposit first quarter 2017
Bibliothèque nationale du Québec

Printed in Canada on acid-free paper that is 100% ancient forest free
(100% post-consumer recycled), processed chlorine free

McGill-Queen's University Press acknowledges the support of the Canada
Council for the Arts for our publishing program. We also acknowledge the
financial support of the Government of Canada through the Canada Book
Fund for our publishing activities.

Library and Archives Canada Cataloguing in Publication

Rosen, Al, 1935–, author
    Easy prey investors: why broken safety nets threaten your wealth/
Al Rosen and Mark Rosen.

    Includes bibliographical references and index.
    Issued in print and electronic formats.
    ISBN 978-0-7735-4819-0 (cloth). – ISBN 978-0-7735-9990-1 (ePDF). –
    ISBN 978-0-7735-9991-8 (ePUB)

    1. Commercial crimes – Canada. 2. Fraud – Canada. 3. Corporations –
Corrupt practices – Canada. 4. Financial institutions – Corrupt practices –
Canada. 5. International financial reporting standards. I. Rosen, Mark,
1973–, author II. Title.

HV6771.C3R68 2017   364.16'30971   C2016-906194-9
                                             C2016-906195-7

This book was typeset by Marquis Interscript in 11/14 Sabon.

For Darlene and Nicole

Contents

Acknowledgments

In 2010, Madison Press Books published our book, *Swindlers*, which covered topics related to the serious shortcomings in Canada's supposed investor protection system. Although *Swindlers* made various references to Canada's then-proposed adoption of IFRS (International Financial Reporting Standards), implementation of IFRS did not occur in Canada until 2011–2012.

Although we predicted in 2010, and earlier, that IFRS was too weak and ill-grounded conceptually to be able to serve as an International Standard, sufficient practice evidence was not yet available in 2010. A follow-up book was needed to show that Canada's lawmakers had deeply erred in permitting IFRS to be utilized in Canada.

Many previously existing flaws in Canada's investor protection system became magnified under IFRS. Astoundingly, IFRS conflicted not only with decades of trying to improve the rights of investors, but it also contradicted Canadian laws and business valuation practices. Excessive power was granted to corporate executives to "cook the books," and mislead investors.

After 2011–2012, it became obvious that major deficiencies in our laws, in absent oversight and in IFRS are combining to play directly into the hands of financial tricksters. In essence, no reliable group in Canada is even trying to protect prospective shareholders and creditors. Our components of a theoretical investor protection system are just not functioning in Canada. The "buck is repeatedly being passed" with nobody willing to admit that a whole new system is needed; the IFRS system has been and is just too flawed to be repairable; it is embarrassing.

Several people encouraged us to write another book because of our lengthy involvement in researching and testifying in Court Cases arising from Canadian financial failures. From our many speaking engagements, we have learned that investors in Canada are still unaware of the absence of basic protections. Contrary and extensive advertising apparently has been misleading them.

Special encouragement to write another book came from Dr R.T. Naylor of McGill University aided by Philip Cercone of McGill-Queen's University Press (MQUP), along with dozens of former students and colleagues. Our assistants, Jodi Cunningham and Hillary Gammon, exerted considerable and valuable effort in researching as well as typing the manuscripts.

Ryan Van Huijstee and the staff at MQUP helped us in many ways as did the editor, Bruce McDougall, and the anonymous book reviewers. The financial analysts and staff at Accountability Research Corporation and Rosen & Associates Limited made several important contributions, as did numerous barristers in Canada and elsewhere.

Thank you to all.

Al Rosen and Mark Rosen

Preface

Investors in Canada are being systematically swindled out of large amounts of their investment and retirement savings. We're not talking about the small numbers of fraudsters who turn up on the evening news. We're referring to a continuous bleed of money, caused by institutionalized inequities that pierce multiple layers of alleged protection. Investors mistakenly believe that their pension plans, mutual funds and other investments are safeguarded, when in fact, they are suffering losses that are monumental compared to individual publicized scams.

Albert Einstein once quipped that "compound interest is the eighth wonder of the world. He who understands it, earns it ... he who doesn't ... pays it." Think of Canada's broken investment safety net as the opposite of receiving compound interest. When specific effects are considered up close, they may seem inconsequential to some, but when viewed collectively over the course of 40 years, the result is a devastating erosion of wealth.

The deterioration of investor protections has accelerated over the last five years in Canada, after our lawmakers permitted an extensive loosening of financial reporting and accounting requirements for public companies. Corporate executives were given increased power to report inflated profits through nothing more than accounting sleight-of-hand. This backward step came after the financial crisis of 2008. When other countries were tightening up regulations as a response, Canada moved in the opposite direction.

This added to another significant and long-standing deficiency. In 1997, a landmark decision by the Supreme Court of Canada essentially handed widespread legal immunity to financial statement auditors who approved misleading financial statements. In essence, investors were told by the Court that they should not be using audited annual financial statements for investment decisions.

Meanwhile, securities commissions maintained their well-established practice of rarely investigating financial statement manipulations, deferring to the financial statement auditors to determine what is appropriate in the financial reporting world. As a result, securities prosecutions have been uncommon, convictions rare, and penalties trivial, serving merely to encourage and inspire further financial deceptions. The wrong people were put in charge of setting the quality of financial reporting standards.

These are three big strikes over the past 20 years, with rarely a positive sign that lawmakers or regulators are taking the situation seriously. Unfortunately, investors have become so accustomed to the weakened system, and the slow drain on their savings, that to many, it's the only reality they have ever known. It would be better to have no guards at all, rather than to perpetuate the false sense of security that exists in Canada today.

In short, investment protections provided by lawmakers, boards of directors, external auditors, and securities regulators have become increasingly weak in Canada through extended neglect and lack of reform, leading to several distinct and problematic issues:

1 Investors continually receive false, misleading, or confusing information from various sources, including the media, investment analysts, and companies themselves. Investors should not be blindly relying on the audited financial results of companies, or many of the investment reports and recommendations produced using those same numbers.
2 Financial reward and motivation systems for remunerating corporate executives are often twisted to benefit select individuals while putting investors at a serious disadvantage. Many of Canada's financial reporting and accounting requirements are phrased in vague terms that are easily exploited by deceitful executives, or just as bad, misunderstood by investors.

3 While Canada's Criminal Code discourages unethical behaviour,
   it does not address or prohibit in sufficient detail many of the specifics common to financial statement manipulation or white collar
   deceptions. As a result, there is a reluctance on the part of public
   prosecutors to pursue cases against swindlers. In the rare cases of
   a criminal conviction, victims recover pennies on the dollar. While
   investors can also try to pursue recourse in the civil courts, these
   proceedings remain prohibitively expensive, and the legal deck
   remains stacked against investors.

4 Canada clings to an archaic governance concept known as self-
   regulation. Despite many years of significant failures, lawmakers
   continue to allow external financial statement auditors to act
   with only minimal oversight. All too often, decisions are made
   by lawmakers and the courts that disadvantage investors while
   benefiting the self-regulated and their clients.

5 The organization that regulates Canada's external auditors has
   adopted, with the permission of lawmakers, a system for corporate financial reporting and accounting called International
   Financial Reporting Standards (IFRS). This has placed investors
   at a major disadvantage, assigning too much power and choice to
   corporate management, and providing them the ability to inflate
   reported profits. Under basic governance concepts, an independent body should be responsible for setting financial reporting
   standards that are reasonable for all. But, in Canada the entity is
   largely under the financial control of the external financial statement auditors, who have repeatedly displayed biases against
   investors, in favour of their paying clients, the corporations.

6 Passing the buck has become second nature in certain Canadian
   financial circles. Our lawmakers surprisingly defer to self-
   regulators, who in turn, disclaim responsibility, and point
   investors in the direction of boards of directors and even to
   executives – the same people they are supposed to oversee and
   help control.

7 Lessons are not being learned from the long series of major corporate and financial reporting failures in Canada such as Bre-X,
   Livent, Nortel, Sino-Forest, Castor Holdings, and Valeant
   Pharmaceuticals, to name but a few. Many of these cases raise
   repeated themes of alleged elementary deceptions that can be

avoided if they are learned and watched for. Yet, the media draws little attention to, and makes scant analysis of, this repeated history of Canadian financial failures, adding to the myopic tendency of investors to miss the big picture and underestimate the longer-term corrosive impact that Canada's weak investor safety net has on their savings.

Investors have little choice but to develop a new approach to protecting their savings. This book provides considerable advice on how to revise your current investment approach to counteract Canada's broken investment safety net.

We introduce you to many of the common financial manipulations that occur in Canada including: accounting deceptions like overstated revenue, profits, assets, and cash flows; common Ponzi schemes disguised within public companies; undue executive enrichment attained through flawed compensation plans; and deceptive numbers used by companies to inflate their performance, which are designed specifically to escape regulatory oversight.

Taken together, the topics discussed in this book not only affect your investments, they also have an impact on the Canadian economy in the form of wasted investment capital and a reluctance by non-Canadians to invest in the country. We believe that these inequities need to be urgently addressed and that reform is essential. However, until the safety net can be repaired, investors need advice and help to avoid becoming easy prey.

EASY PREY INVESTORS

1

Unacceptable State of Affairs

Canadian investors and retirees are known to be ideal victims for stock market and investment shenanigans: they tend to blame themselves for their losses. They seldom pressure governments to correct blatant and repeated deceptive practices. And they turn their money over to companies like Nortel, Livent, and Sino-Forest assuming that their investments are safe in the hands of presumed honest and competent managers.

Despite the prevalent myth that financial manipulation only rarely happens in Canada, this country practically invites fraudsters to prey on its citizens. Contrary to the prevailing myth, Canada has never had a strong investor protection system. In recent years, it has become even weaker. Why? Lawmakers don't want to spend the money to legislate and operate the type of organization required to help protect investors from fraud.

To make matters worse, lawmakers in Canada are bombarded with demands from big business to reduce regulatory red tape, and they often comply with these demands without careful analysis of the consequences. Since the 1980s, the loser has been the Canadian investor.

We see examples of thefts virtually every week. We also see the vast majority of the thieves walk away with their bloated loot bags. By the time Canadian investors realize what has happened, their money has vanished. In the rare case when they recover some of their losses, they usually receive pennies on the dollar.

In too many cases the financial cheat can be a close friend or family member. But the most successful manipulators take advantage of

Canada's loose laws and regulations and its lamentable record in investigating and prosecuting white-collar crime. Dozens of Canadian-based scams would never get off the ground in another country. These cheats also know that the Canadian business media will pay little or no attention to their schemes. For these individuals, Canada is a paradise. Why risk spending part of your life in jail in another country when you can successfully work your fraud scheme in Canada, where the laws are vague and prosecution is rare?

In case you think this sounds far-fetched, let's look at a few of the situations that we'll explore in more detail throughout this book:

1 For several years, Canadians have placed their money in business income trust variations, many of which are nothing more than Ponzi schemes. Under the label of falsely being called income, their own money is given back to them as a return on their investment, or profit.

   Investors believe that they are receiving a high yield, but most of it is bogus. But while the government has taken steps to close tax loopholes associated with income trusts, it does virtually nothing about these partially disguised Ponzi schemes. Meanwhile, sloppy accounting and reporting rules in Canada allow these schemes to flourish to this day.

2 In 2011–2012, Canada adopted a management-controlled financial reporting system called International Financial Reporting Standards (IFRS). While the US generally rejected IFRS, for good reasons, Canada adopted the standard on the premise that it would harmonize Canada's financial reporting practices with the rest of the world. Canadians were told that IFRS eliminated onerous regulations and improved previous Canadian reporting standards; but in fact, it encourages even more misleading financial reporting. Not only have Canadian investors been misled, but financial analysts, bankers, lawyers, lawmakers, and others also remain largely clueless about the way IFRS encourages financial games.

   As we'll discuss throughout this book, IFRS enables corporate managements to exaggerate profits and distort asset values. It undermines investor protection even further by relieving accountants and external auditors of government oversight, which was inadequate to begin with.

Since Canada's governments will not take steps to alert investors to the pitfalls of IFRS, this book will show you what to look for to avoid false promises and questionable ethics in Canadian companies that utilize IFRS financial reporting.

3 The introduction of IFRS into Canada came after a strenuous, yet hasty, push by Canadian financial statement auditors. The main effects of IFRS were to give more financial reporting powers and choices to corporate management, and to reduce external auditors' legal liability. Instead of protecting investors, IFRS has opened the floodgates to looser financial reporting requirements monitored by self-regulating accountants and external auditors. Deceived by overblown IFRS-based financial reports, investors lose more money every year to financial deceptions.

4 Provincial securities commissions and other so-called oversight bodies in Canada raised no objection to IFRS and accepted the judgment of the country's self-regulated accountants and external auditors. Today, when governments consider changes to financial reporting standards and requirements, their consultations extend no further than these self-regulated practitioners. What's wrong with this picture?

5 As we'll discuss in later chapters, dubious companies like Sino-Forest Corporation locate themselves in Canada not by accident but by design. This fact alone should give governments a reason to look more closely at the lack of effectiveness of self-regulation. Why, of all the countries in the world, would these companies choose Canada? To emphasize Canada's feeble system of investor protection, a US organization had to blow the whistle on Sino-Forest, as they've done with similar frauds in the past. In fact, Canadian investors are much better protected by US regulators than they are by regulators in their own country.

6 Some excellent financial analysts work in Canada, but in our experience, the good ones are outnumbered by poorly trained individuals whose research is based on dubious motivations and questionable ethics. When companies issue shares in Canada, underwriters apply considerable pressure to inexperienced

financial analysts to recommend the stock. Relying on these recommendations, investors buy the shares, and the underwriter clears its inventory of hard-to-sell securities. Even without such pressure, many analysts accept a company's published performance figures at face value without looking for widespread deception. With the analyst's blessing, some pension plan and investment managers rely on distorted research to buy overvalued stocks, leaving Canadian investors to suffer the losses when the stock later collapses. With some provinces creating or considering provincial pension plans to supplement the Canada Pension Plan, even more of your money is at risk from white-collar criminals.

7 To make it even more difficult to bring financial manipulators to justice, civil law imposes a two-year limitation period on investors to sue them. (In Quebec, the limitation period is three years.) This gives investors only two or three years to gather enough information, sometimes in complex cases, to pursue their lawsuit. Over that period, each cheat and con artist involved in the case can hire a different lawyer, forcing investors to spend more time and financial resources to pursue their case.

Some investor groups in Canada opposed this two-year limitation, but most big businesses supported it, and once again our lawmakers ignored the investors. Restricted by this two-year limit and left vulnerable to IFRS, Canada's investors must rely more than ever on US laws to protect them.

8 Even if a financial cheat is sent to jail under a criminal proceeding, investors seldom get their money back. They stand a much better chance of recovering their money in civil court, but the cost of pursuing a civil case is high. A class action case can ease the burden on each individual, but such cases face some serious obstacles in Canada. Judges can place a high burden of proof on plaintiffs. Technicalities must be dealt with. Conflicting laws and unexpected Court decisions often prolong such cases until they're abandoned altogether.

9 Buck-passing of responsibility for overseeing securities problems and implementing necessary reforms causes endless problems in Canada. As we'll explain later, IFRS places investors at a huge disadvantage, assigning too much power and choice to corporate

management and allowing them to flatter themselves through their vague reports to shareholders. In reply to one of our letters to Cabinet Ministers in 2016, the federal Finance Minister responded:

I would suggest that you bring your concerns regarding IFRS ... to the attention of the Accounting Standards Board ... (as) the independent body with the authority to establish accounting standards for use by all Canadian entities.

In other words, the federal Finance Minister washed his hands of all responsibility and referred us for resolution of the serious issues that we raised to the very people who were causing many or most of the problems.

We find the Minister's response deeply unacceptable for several reasons:

a The Accounting Standards Board brought IFRS to Canada based on merits that do not and could not exist. In many cases, IFRS enables corporate management to invent their own rules of reporting. Instead of achieving the Standards Board's stated goal of a uniform reporting system throughout the world, IFRS enables thousands of corporate executives to interpret for themselves a compendium of loose guidance and commentary.

b The Accounting Standards Board in Canada cannot possibly be independent when it is largely financed and controlled by Canada's external financial statement auditors. They were permitted by our lawmakers to force IFRS upon Canadian public companies (except those that adopted US requirements), which has caused, and will continue to cause, extensive deceptions and investor losses.

c External auditors have repeatedly displayed biases against investors and have not responded to their concerns. As we'll discuss in the following chapters, investors have sued external auditors for approving financial statements that were soon deemed to be materially misleading. Unfortunately, Canadian auditors in most cases have escaped prosecution and have been unfairly protected by illogical laws and Court decisions.

Considering the reply that we received to our letter in 2016 from the federal Minister of Finance, this situation is destined to continue. Investors' interests apparently are not a government priority and are not relevant to lawmakers. Under such circumstances, why should people bother to invest in Canada?

d As a self-regulating entity, the Accounting Standards Board has repeatedly passed the buck on the adequacy of and legal liability for financial reporting to Boards of Directors of individual corporations. As recently as January 2016 the head of the Standards Board told Canada's Chartered Financial Analysts that oversight of financial reporting was a Board responsibility.

Overall, Canada's governments have continually protected a seriously flawed system that leaves large portions of investors' savings easily vulnerable to predators. As well, the government is not amending legislation to overturn anti-investor Court decisions and restore theoretical protections to investors. Instead, they remain easy prey for swindlers in Canada. Not only do lawmakers deny responsibility for serious losses to investors, they have no apparent plans to reverse this rapidly rising trend in financial deceit.

AHEAD

In our experience, Canada's financial con artists are not very creative. They use the same tired games repeatedly. A main reason is that the deceptions have been successful for them. In the pages that follow, we'll teach you how to protect yourself. We'll show you some of the more popular tricks that fraudsters have used successfully. We'll explain some of the technicalities that you need to know when you look at corporate financial statements. In particular, we'll show you how to recognize companies that inflate their profits and distort their operating cash levels. IFRS allows large amounts of this manipulation by granting unchecked power to corporate management with little or no oversight from regulators or governments.

Investors need to read financial documents with a significant degree of scepticism. Our goal is to show you where to look.

2

Ponzi Schemes

Ponzi schemes succeed when confused investors brag about their wonderful investment and inadvertently draw friends and relatives into the scam. As we'll discuss in this chapter, there are several types of Ponzis. And as we'll eventually explain in detail, they may operate for years, circulating a small amount of cash while borrowing from banks that do not amend their analytical techniques.

Over the years, several public companies listed on the Toronto Stock Exchange and filing audited financial statements have turned out to be nothing more than Ponzis. While their perpetrators walk away unpunished, protected by their companies audited financial statements, investors are left with a fraction of their money, or zero.

In essence, a Ponzi persuades investors that monthly, quarterly, or annual dividends or cash receipts come from the company's *profits* earned on their invested money. In fact, the payments often come from their own money, or from borrowings.

Here's an example: An investment advisor asks for $10,000 and promises a 10% annual return on your money, for five or more years. At that rate, the advisor could indeed pay you $1,000 a year for 10 years out of your own money. But a financial cheat would tell you that the annual payment comes from earned profits from investing your $10,000.

In some cases, you won't discover the deception until maybe 10 years go by. At that point, the fraudster will have paid you $1,000 a year for 10 years, and you will have received back all of your original $10,000 investment. Unfortunately, you will have received no interest on your $10,000, and your original investment will be worthless.

To make matters worse, you have likely paid annual income tax on the $1,000 of fake interest. You also may have re-invested some or all of the $1,000 payment with the fraudster. And you will likely have encouraged your friends to invest in the scheme, as well, acting as an unwitting salesperson for the con artist.

One day, after the cheat has attracted enough money from you, your friends and other investors, your annual cheque for $1,000 will not arrive. When you inquire, you'll discover that the swindler has disappeared with your money and the money of your ex-friends, as well. Once in a while, these cheats are caught. But usually they've hidden a portion of the money offshore and squandered the rest of it on wine, women, and song.

In Canada, authorities seldom take action against such schemes until they receive enough complaints that they can no longer ignore them. Criminal charges may or may not be laid. If a prosecution results, it will take several years, and you will likely recover little or none of your money. But you will have wasted not only your money but considerable time and emotional energy, as well.

Whether the scheme involves a private arrangement or a publicly listed company, a Ponzi scheme works by taking an initial investment and repositioning or relabeling it as faked profit or income. In Canada, this type of financial sleight of hand is not only possible, it's allowed by certain rules governing accounting and financial reporting. Financial manipulators can cook the books to inflate profit and hide losses without breaking serious rules at all.

IFRS makes this possible. IFRS emphasizes balance-sheet numbers and confuses the distinction between profits and income versus your invested principal. This confusion enables a Ponzi schemer to persuade you that the $1,000 you receive each year as a dividend reflects profit earned on your $10,000 investment and is not just a returned portion of your own money. Meanwhile, few investors ever ask a financial cheat where he or she has invested their money, or any other basic questions. As long as they receive their hefty disguised dividend cheque, they simply trust that all's well.

INCOME TRUSTS

Investing in income trusts, large numbers of Canadians have been duped for several years after 2000 by pathetic and inadequate financial reporting, while regulators and external auditors have stood on the sidelines. These group Ponzis have been modified, but are still growing today.

In some cases, scammers get away with a Ponzi by replacing a single letter in their description of payments to investors. Some of these payments they describe as a return *on* capital. Others they describe as a return *of* capital.

A return *on* capital describes an earned profit on invested money. The profit may be real or fabricated, as we'll see. But it's supposed to be a profit, nonetheless.

In contrast, a return *of* capital simply describes a payment to you of some of your original investment. It's not profit. It's your money, coming back to you.

Between 2000 and 2010 business income trusts (BITs) in Canada often confusingly used the words on and of in describing returns to investors. Using contorted accounting and reporting procedures they would calculate faked profits by recording revenue that did not exist, and describing expenses as assets on the balance sheet rather than deducting them from revenue on the income statement.

Several BITs issued payments to investors using money borrowed from banks or raised from sales of more units to the original investors, now better described as victims. Even though the books were being cooked, no crime was being committed, because accounting rules allow for alternatives.

Many BITs advertised misleadingly that their particular financing structure generated a higher return on investment from tax savings. Until the government amended the Income Tax Act, some of these tax savings actually existed. But in most cases the higher faked yields largely came from accounting manipulation.

While the BIT scam unfolded, investors were left on their own. The Canadian news media applauded the high returns available from BITs. Securities administrators remained silent. External auditors issued standard-form audit reports and kept their distance. Provincial and federal governments fretted about lost tax revenues but ignored the shaky ethical and financial foundations of most BITS. They took all the necessary steps to collect the overlooked taxes, but they did nothing to improve financial reporting in Canada. Self-regulation of financial reporting standards continued without a hitch.

At the end of the fiasco, the big losers were Canadian investors. Some people lost their life savings. Several chose to end their life.

The promoters of BITS succeeded for several reasons. Individual investors spread the word about the wonderful returns available from BITS. The news media raised awareness of their high yields. Seniors groups and investment clubs, some of them operated by financial schemers, poured money into BITS. Little was done by lawmakers or regulators either to oversee the schemes or educate investors about the nature of BITS.

Reluctant to question group behaviour, investors seldom made the distinction between returns from BITS based on real profits versus returns that came from their own money. Governments remained silent. Regulators provided no oversight. Since then, little has changed.

PROFITS AND PONZIS

Canada's adoption of IFRS has created serious confusion among investors and has given wide leeway to public companies listed on Canada's stock exchanges to determine what constitutes a legitimate profit. For example, a mining company operating a single mine could use "cash flow from operating activities" to determine their version of "profit." It would base this figure on an honestly prepared Cash Flow Statement. The cash basis of its profit calculation would make sense, because a single mine has a relatively short life. The company will *not* have to replace worn-out equipment, and it will not have to consider depreciation or amortization of its assets in calculating its version of profit. Its profit will be generated as cash from its operating activities, calculated simply by subtracting the *cash* costs of mining and administration from the selling price of ore.

The mining company should tell you that its dividend does *not* come solely from the profit on the sale of ore but from your original investment, as well, being a combination of return of and return on your investment in the mine.

Likewise, a new company that has not reached its efficient operating level could (but typically does not) define profit as sales revenue less cash expenses, ignoring non-cash amortization costs that it will only incur when it reaches more efficient operating levels.

Companies like these have legitimate reasons for defining profit in the way that they do, and they can make their logic clear to investors. But, overall, these companies are exceptions.

Unfortunately, other companies are not so forthright. Unless you approach these companies with caution, you can lose your shirt. These companies may exhibit the following types of characteristics:

1 They have manipulated their reported net income by fiddling with faked or hoped-for revenue and have hidden expenses;
2 They have inflated cash flow from operating activities through games such as temporarily withholding cash payments, letting accounts payable rise;
3 They take advantage of IFRS gimmickry to base profits on imaginary gains arising from nothing more substantial than management optimism. For example, IFRS allows management to estimate and record as profit so-called estimated "value" increases in the "value" of certain real estate property. The company may not have to sell the property or obtain offers from legitimate buyers. Under some circumstances which are explained later, the company can record these increases in estimated values as *current-year income*.

Publicly traded companies in Canada use such IFRS gimmickry all the time, paying high dividends that far exceed legitimate profits. Many of these companies are nothing more than early-stage Ponzi schemes. To pay the dividend, many of them borrow the cash rather than taking it from profits. In these cases, bank lenders do not do their homework and fail to adjust the audited profit figures downward to obtain a more realistic financial picture of the company.

These companies will commonly include marketing, promotion, and development expenses as assets on their balance sheet rather than recording them as expenses. They will then overstate their reported profits accordingly.

When companies publish such manipulated figures, Canadian investors and many analysts, as well, simply accept them as valid. After all, IFRS allows it. It's up to investors to make the mental corrections to avoid holding onto Ponzis-in-progress.

Investors can't simply take the company's word, audited or not. They have to trace for themselves the sources of the cash being utilized for payment of dividends. If they can't find sufficient real cash being generated by the company's operations, they should look for other non-profit-generated sources, such as:

1 Borrowings: Investors should examine the interest rate, collateral, and principal repayment dates involved. Each of these can have serious long-term effects on the company, usually negative.
2 The sale of common or preferred shares: Investors should determine the price per share and the number of shares involved. (How such money was utilized by the company should be ascertained. Was the money used to pay dividends? If so, the Ponzi warning alarm should be ringing.)
3 The sale of plant, equipment, subsidiary companies, and similar assets: Investors should determine whether these sales make business sense or simply contribute to illegitimate profits. Shrinking a company just to generate fake profits eventually leads to bankruptcy.

Typically, investors should heed the warning signs of manipulated profits, overstated operating cash flows and expensive borrowings. Unfortunately, unsuspecting investors tend to focus upon the received "dividends" and then buy more company-issued shares that keep the company afloat.

Investors can recognize a company on the verge of imminent collapse when it has to sell its long-term assets such as buildings, at depressed prices. Typically, these represent the company's best assets. Once the downward spiral begins, it's difficult to turn around.

SUMMARY

In evaluating the health and profitability of a company and detecting problems, investors should focus on four popular, but possibly suspect, measures of success:

1 Income/Profit for each quarter and year;
2 Operating cash flow (or cash flow from sales and services activities of the company), and then ignore or cancel-out techniques used to inflate the figure;
3 Figures that appeal to financial analysts such as "free cash flow" or "adjusted" profit, which we'll explain in later chapters; and
4 So-called "alternate measures of profit" that many companies grossly exaggerate. We'll explain these in later chapters, as well.

Con artists often rely on these four categories to execute their Ponzi and other schemes, as we'll explain in graphic detail in later chapters. Hence, for learning purposes focus first on the four, because manipulations of them are common in Canada.

3

Sino-Forest: Why Us?

Now that we've shown you some of the basic concepts involved in the financial deception of Canada's investment world, we'll explain why financial cheats would likely choose to operate in Canada. As an example, we'll discuss the rise and fall of Sino-Forest Corporation.

We could have chosen any of a number of Canadian multi-million-dollar financial failures that have occurred in recent years, such as Castor Holdings, Nortel Networks, Poseidon Concepts, Confederation Life, and several business income trusts to show that nobody is minding Canada's investor-protection store. With IFRS allowing management even greater freedom to manipulate their audited financial results, such failures will only continue, and will multiply.

To survive as investors, you have to learn to detect the scams before the ultimate disasters occur. You have to regard with scepticism any reassurances that financial reporting in Canada is under control. As we'll show you, such reassurances by Canadian governments and regulators do not stand up to closer scrutiny. Private company failures can be added to the list should any doubt exist that Canada has numerous failures.

WHY CANADA?

Of all the countries in the world that companies like Sino-Forest could have chosen to obtain money, why did they choose Canada to carry out their alleged fraud? Why did a rash of similarly designed deceptions occur in Canada around the same time, such as over 2011 and 2012? Several factors come to mind:

1 Since Canada does not seriously investigate and prosecute white-collar crime, financial manipulators have little to lose by trying out their schemes in this country.
2 Canadian investors are all too willing to buy over-hyped investments, while they remain blissfully unaware of Canada's poor record for prosecuting financial scams and the negligible amounts of money recovered when duplicitous schemes go bad.
3 Canadians place too much faith in favourable assessments by financial analysts of stocks that the stocks' underwriters, who employ the analysts, want to sell to generate a fat fee. In fact, many financial analysts are simply glorified salespeople.
4 As companies return to the public stock market to raise more money, they provide more opportunities for underwriters to collect fees and for their analysts to hype the stock's merits, even if there are none. An ongoing Ponzi scheme has to involve many debt and equity underwritings.
5 Under IFRS, an undeserving company can easily attract investors by manipulating its financial statements to make itself appear much stronger than it is.

SINO-FOREST CORPORATION

Tables 3.1, 3.2, and 3.3 provide condensed financial statements of Sino-Forest Corporation. Notes are not reproduced because the learning process at this stage cannot become overwhelming.

The failure of Sino-Forest Corporation (SFC) in 2011–2012 should have alerted lawmakers, securities commissions, regulators, and investors in Canada to the vulnerabilities of this country's investment environment. But few of them have paid attention. Investors in SFC shares and in mutual and pension funds that held those shares all lost considerable money. Small amounts have been recovered; and legal proceedings are continuing. But investors will never recover most of the money that they lost in this fiasco. They can only hope that they don't get fooled again.

Table 3.1 Consolidated balance sheets (condensed) as at December 31
(in thousands of United States dollars)

	2010	2009
ASSETS		
Current		
Cash and cash equivalents	1,223,352	1,102,366
Short-term deposits	32,101	70,387
Accounts receivable	636,626	282,306
Inventories	61,978	45,978 (B)
Prepaid expenses and other	125,238	54,747
Convertible bonds	–	29,446
Assets of discontinued operations	–	1,531
Total current assets	2,079,295	1,586,761
Timber holdings	3,122,517	2,183,489 (A)
Capital assets, net	113,150	77,377
Intangible assets	139,910	636
Other assets	274,161	115,636
	5,729,033	3,963,899 (K)
LIABILITIES AND SHAREHOLDERS' EQUITY		
Current		
Bank indebtedness	153,959	103,991
Current portion of long-term debt	87,670	–
Accounts payable and accrued liabilities	499,854	250,287
Income taxes payable	10,602	7,346
Liabilities of discontinued operations	3,699	12,156
Total current liabilities	755,784	373,780
Long-term debt	1,659,682	925,466
Future income tax liabilities	63,906	–
Total liabilities	2,479,372	1,299,246
Non-controlling interests	51,540	–
Shareholders' equity		
Equity portion of convertible senior notes	158,883	158,883
Share capital	1,261,300	1,213,495 (Y)
Contributed surplus	11,673	12,200
Accumulated other comprehensive income	314,912	224,148
Statutory reserve	1,988	1,670
Retained earnings	1,449,365	1,054,257
Total shareholders' equity	3,198,121	2,664,653
	5,729,033	3,963,899 (L)

Table 3.2 Consolidated statements of income and retained earnings (condensed), years ended December 31 (in thousands of United States dollars)

	2010	2009
Revenue	1,923,536	1,238,185 (C)
Costs and expenses		
Cost of sales	1,252,023	797,800 (D)
Selling, general and administration	89,712	63,980
Depreciation and amortization	5,145	4,693
	1,346,880	866,473
Income from operations before the undernoted	576,656	371,712
Interest expense	(128,124)	(70,977)
Interest income	10,609	9,691
Exchange losses	(3,086)	(4,958)
Loss on changes in fair value of financial instruments	(4,419)	(417)
Other income	2,932	1,600
Income before income taxes	454,568	306,651
Provision for income taxes	(70,644)	(27,864)
Net income from continuing operations	383,924	278,787
Net income from discontinued operations	8,179	7,583
Net income before non-controlling interests	392,103	286,370
Non-controlling interests	3,323	–
Net income for the year	395,426	286,370
Retained earnings		
Retained earnings, beginning of year	1,054,257	769,557
Net income for the year	395,426	286,370
Transfer to statutory reserve	(318)	(1,670)
Retained earnings, end of year	1,449,365	1,054,257

To avoid getting duped, you first have to realize that no one else will protect you, not governments, not lawmakers, not regulators, and not the auditors of financial statements. We've already discussed the apathy of lawmakers and the tendency of governments to pass the buck. As for the self-regulated auditors, North American studies have shown that they detect only about one fraud in 20.

In the case of SFC, the alleged fraud was revealed not by Canadian auditors, regulators, lawmakers, or analysts. The warning to investors

Table 3.3 Consolidated statements of cash flows (condensed), years ended December 31 (in thousands of United States dollars)

	2010	2009
CASH FLOWS FROM OPERATING ACTIVITIES		
Net income for the year	395,426	286,370 (H)
Net income from discontinued operations	(8,179)	(7,583)
Add (deduct) items not affecting cash	746,474	522,397 (E)
Depletion of timber holdings included in cost of sales	7,919	4,693
Depreciation and amortization	26,555	13,689
Accretion of convertible senior notes	3,573	4,601
Stock-based compensation	4,419	417
Loss on changes in fair value of financial instruments	(2,089)	1,880
Unrealized exchange (gains) losses	(511)	(751)
Other	1,173,587	825,713 (F)
Net change in non-cash working capital balances	(333,502)	(41,196)
Cash flows from operating activities of continuing operations	840,085	784,517 (G)
Cash flows used in operating activities of discontinued operations	(562)	(826)
CASH FLOWS USED IN INVESTING ACTIVITIES		
Additions to timber holdings	(1,358,878)	(1,032,009) (T)
Increase in other assets	(43,331)	(38,041)
Additions to capital assets	(25,240)	(11,649)
Decrease (increase) in non-pledged short-term deposits	21,872	(10,942)
Business acquisition, net of cash acquired of $63,829,000	2,139	–
Proceeds from disposal of capital assets	296	216
Acquisition of convertible bonds	–	(200)
Other	75	–
Cash flows used in investing activities	(1,403,067)	(1,092,625) (I)
Cash flows from investing activities of discontinued operations	1,478	24,120
CASH FLOWS FROM FINANCING ACTIVITIES		
Increase in long-term debt	624,750	460,000
Increase in bank indebtedness	47,962	36,534
Decrease (increase) in pledged short-term deposits	17,255	(13,633)
Issuance of shares, net of issue costs	8,555	652,474
Proceeds from exercise of share options of a subsidiary	3,079	–
Payment of financing costs	(20,328)	(27,591)

Table 3.3 Consolidated statements of cash flows (condensed), years ended
December 31 (in thousands of United States dollars) (*continued*)

	2010	2009
Repayment of long-term debt	(530)	(150,000)
Payment on derivative financial instrument	–	(5,781)
Cash flows from financing activities	**680,743**	952,003 (J)
Cash flows used in financing activities of discontinued **operations**	–	(5,972)
Effect of exchange rate changes on cash and cash **equivalents**	**2,309**	(22)
Net increase in cash and cash equivalents	120,986	661,195
Cash and cash equivalents, beginning of year	1,102,366	441,171
Cash and cash equivalents, end of year	1,223,352	1,102,366

came from the US, where a sharp-eyed analyst finally blew the whistle
on sfc, which was utilizing an old trick. In its last five years of operation, sfc's audited annual financial statements seemed to confirm
that it was a growing organization. Only on closer examination did
the holes begin to appear in sfc's corporate fabric. Since no one else
will do it for you, we will try in this book to explain to you how to
conduct this closer examination yourself.

We will show you how to ask critical questions, and how to evaluate an acceptable response before you make an investment decision. It
is too late to step back from your possible investment in sfc. But in
Canada, it's never too late to learn how to avoid the next case of financial deception. We all know that it will happen again and again, given
Canada's casual attitude.

In the following pages we'll refer to sfc's consolidated balance
sheet and other financial statements reproduced in Tables 3.1 to 3.3.
You might also refer to Appendix 1 (located near the back of the
book), where we briefly explain the basics of financial reporting.

The typical financial report of a publicly traded company includes
at least three parts:

1 A *balance sheet*, which lists assets that the company owns, liabilities that the company owes, and the portion that remains when
   liabilities are subtracted from asset values, often called the

owners' equity. For example, if you acquired a house, it would appear as an asset on your balance sheet. The mortgage on the house would appear as a liability. The difference between the "value" (or dollar figure) of the house and the outstanding mortgage would appear on your balance sheet as the owner's equity.

2 An *income, or profit, or operating statement,* where the company indicates sales revenues and expenses incurred over a specified period. The difference between the two determines the company's profit or loss for the period. An income statement may appear as follows:

Sales revenues	$10,000,000
Cost of products sold (cost of the inventory that was sold)	4,000,000
Gross profit	6,000,000
Operating expenses (wages, etc.)	4,500,000
Profit before tax	1,500,000
Income tax	600,000
Net profit	$ 900,000

3 A *cash flow statement,* which includes three separate categories:
 a *Cash* (or equivalents) arising from the company's *operations* such as buying and selling trees. [See Line G on Table 3.3: SFC's Cash Flow Statements.]
 b Cash acquired by obtaining *long-term financing,* such as by borrowing money from a bank, selling bonds or selling the company's ownership shares to increase owners' equity. [See Line J on Table 3.3: SFC's Cash Flow Statements.]
 c Cash invested in long-term assets such as land, buildings or long-lived trees that will grow over several years in size and value before you sell them. [See Line I on Table 3.3: SFC's Cash Flow Statements.]

For investors, the most critical segment of the cash-flow statement is the cash earned from selling goods such as trees, less the cost paid to acquire the trees and to pay operating expenses such as wages and tree harvesting costs. (Table 3.3, Letter G.) Financial analysts determine the value of a company based more on its *cash* derived from operations than its net profits.

If you look closely at s f c's financial statements, you'll see that they don't make sense. You'll also see that the fundamental nature of s f c's business is unclear. Was it:

1 A tree farm? Trees may take 10, 20, or 30 years to grow before they're ready to be cut down and sold. Until that happens, s f c's income remains minimal.
2 A trading operation? Like a department store that continually buys and sells an inventory of clothing and other goods, s f c could buy and sell trees or logs, continually replenishing its inventory.
3 A combination of the two? If so, in which proportions?
4 Something else?

These distinctions are important. Financial reporting differs from one industry to another. For accounting and reporting purposes, tree farms are treated differently from trading operations, for example. Before an accountant (or an investor) could suitably assess the financial performance of s f c, the company would have to specify the nature of its business operations.

When we looked at the financial statements of s f c, what did we see? The balance sheet (Table 3.1), showed billions of dollars invested in timber holdings (Line A), recorded as long-term investments, similar to land and buildings. ("Capital assets.") Long-term investments, as the term says, are held for a period of years. In the case of s f c, trees held for a period of years will presumably grow into more mature trees, and the company will not sell them in return for cash until it harvests them; which could take 20 years or more. This is what a tree farm does.

s f c recorded only $62 million as inventory as of December 31, 2010. (Table 3.1, Line B. For more details please see Appendix 1). As inventory, these trees would be sold quickly, in the same way as a department store sells goods on display. Inventory intended for quick sale is often called a liquid or *current* asset; when the company sells it in a few months, it will become cash derived from sales. This is how a trading company operates.

Based solely on its balance sheet, SFC appears to be a tree farm, with a large investment in long-term assets, namely trees. As a tree farm, SFC will not generate significant profits until the growing trees are cut and sold. This could take as long as 20-30 years.

In SFC's income statement on the next page (Table 3.2), the company appears less as a tree farm and more as a trading company. Its income statement resembles a department store's: billion-dollar revenues (Line C) and almost $1.3 billion in costs incurred to sell the inventory in 2010 (Line D).

How does this make sense? SFC's balance sheet (Table 3.1) shows that the company has relatively little inventory for sale. Yet its income statement (Table 3.2, Line C) shows that SFC generated $1.9 billion in revenue from the sale of its inventory.

SFC's audited financial statements included this anomaly not just once but year after year. In 2010, for example, (and this point is especially crucial) if SFC had accounted for its sold timber as inventory, which is a cash-like asset, the $746 million in so-called depletion, a non-cash figure (Table 3.3, Line E), would have disappeared.

Accountants and auditors should have recognized this discrepancy and transferred timber that was to be sold to SFC's cash-like inventory account. The inventory sold by SFC would then have appeared as a cost on the income statement (Table 3.2, Line D) and would have deeply reduced cash from operations on the Cash Flow Statement. (Table 3.3, Line G).

Instead, SFC inappropriately accounted for its sale of timber as non-cash amortization, which enabled the company to add this figure to its net income and overstate its cash earned from operations (Table 3.3, Line G). The *cash* cost of trees being sold became minor dollars of expense, which made little or no sense.

By removing Line E ("Depletion of timber holdings included in cost of sales"), SFC would have reduced its cash flow from operating activities by $746 million. Instead of showing $840 million, this figure would now become $94 million ($840 − $746). Applying a 10-times multiple to $94 million, an analyst would conclude that SFC was worth much less than it claimed in these audited financial statements.

Yet sfc's external financial statement auditors approved the company's statements year after year without blinking an eye at this astounding distortion.

sfc might have argued that it acts as a broker, buying and selling timber products quickly and carrying little inventory. If this is the case, and sfc sells enough trees to generate $1.9 billion (Table 3.2, Line C), who then are the buyers and sellers? And why does sfc's balance sheet show billions of dollars in *long-term* timber holdings? (Table 3.1, Line A.)

Presented with this puzzling situation, financial analysts should have deeply questioned sfc's financial statements. (Purchased timber required a cash cost.) Unfortunately for investors, they did no such thing.

SFC & FINANCIAL ANALYSTS

Between 2008 and 2011, most financial analysts told investors to buy shares in sfc.

Observe that the number of analysts who were following sfc increased over the years (Table 3.4), as more new stock underwriting opportunities arose. Also, from January 1, 2009, onward, no analyst recommended to investors to sell sfc's shares. Until sfc's collapse in 2011, all of them recommended buying or holding.

As late as May 2011, two financial analysts continued to push sfc stock, quoting a 12-month target price of up to $34 per share. Here's what they said in their well-distributed research reports:

"Concerns on Sino-Forest Represent a Significant Buying Opportunity."
    "Outperform. Above Average Risk."
    "Recent Share Price Weakness Represents Buying Opportunity."
    "Action Buy List."
    "We have no concerns regarding company-specific issues at Sino-Forest."

In our experience, a "Buying Opportunity" for individual investors sometimes occurs at the same time that people with better knowledge

Table 3.4 Analyst recommendations

As of January 1, 2008:	(All sources = Bloomberg)
Stock price (Canadian dollars)	$21.44
Recommendations by analysts; (written reports):	
Buy, or thereabouts	2 Analysts
Sell SFC's shares	1 Analyst
As of July 1, 2008:	
Stock price	$17.86
Recommendations:	
Buy	5 Analysts
Sell	1 Analyst
As of January 1, 2009:	
Stock price	$9.87
Recommendations:	
Buy	3 Analysts
Hold onto your shares	2 Analysts
As of July 1, 2009:	
Stock price	$12.40
Recommendations:	
Buy	3 Analysts
Hold or equivalent	4 Analysts
As of January 1, 2010:	
Stock price	$19.38
Recommendations:	
Buy	5 Analysts
Hold	2 Analysts
As of July 1, 2010:	
Stock price	$15.13
Recommendations:	
Buy	8 Analysts
Hold	2 Analysts

of the company are selling their shares. We advise investors to stay away from such "Buying Opportunities," or equivalent terms, unless considerable research has been completed.

By July 1, 2011, allegations had been raised about possible fraud at SFC. The stock price had dropped to $3.20. Yet two analysts recommended that investors hold onto their shares.

FINANCIAL STATEMENTS

Investors who looked closely at SFC's financial statements prior to January 1, 2011, would have ignored such far-fetched recommendations. From SFC's Cash Flow Statement (Table 3.3) they would have seen that the company generated $840 million of cash flows from its ongoing operations (Table 3.3, Line G). SFC arrived at this figure by attributing $746 million in faked cash flow in 2010 to non-cash depletion of timber holdings (Table 3.3, Line E) and not to the sale of inventory, (which would be a cash-type expense). Instead of recording the cash cost of inventory for which it had paid cash, it recorded non-cash amortization. Observe (Table 3.3, Line T) that purchases of timber holdings were being falsely labelled as investing activities instead of being a component of "operating activities." [This type of problem is common in Canada: use tricks to bloat cash flow from operations (Table 3.3, Line G).]

Canada's accounting rules at the time did *not* allow this far-fetched reasoning. SFC had to spend cash to buy the timber that it allegedly sold. Pretending otherwise had no basis in fact. Yet, the contorted SFC financial statements were alleged to have been, and were stated to investors to have been, audited.

At the risk of taxing your patience, we'll explain in more detail the tactics used by SFC and their implications for investors. (You might also take a look at Appendix 1 for a more general discussion.) As we've stated, SFC described the vast majority of its timber holdings as a non-current asset, along with long-term investments in land and buildings ("capital assets"). But there's a critical difference. As a building gets used and wears out, a company can record a *non-cash* expense called amortization or depreciation as a cost of earning sales revenue. The company initially purchased the building for cash; as it wears out, the company incurs an expense. But unlike the cost of inventory or the cost of wages, which are cash-based expenses incurred in the current year, depreciation becomes a non-cash expense, after the year in which the cash purchase occurred.

Should a company that generates income from the sale of trees account for timber stands in the same way as it accounts for buildings? We obviously say no. When SFC sold its timber, it should have accounted for it as inventory, which is an asset somewhat equivalent to cash and which is recorded as a cash expense when it's sold. (Table 3.3, Line D, "cost of sales".) Instead, SFC recorded its sale of timber as non-cash depletion of timber holdings included in cost of sales (Table 3.3, Line E).

In simple terms, SFC recorded a long-term investment in timber land, then allegedly sold the timber in the short term, but recorded the process as non-cash amortization rather than the sale of cash-equivalent inventory. Instead of operating as a long-term tree farm with sales projected to occur years into the future, SFC's Cash Flow Statement reflected a much different type of daily trading operation, which bloated "cash flow from operations."

Since *many analysts* use "cash flow from sales operations" to help to arrive at company and share valuations, SFC magically became a massive generator of faked *cash* profits. Through its creative accounting, SFC generated large cash sales revenue but seemingly incurred few cash expenses, thereby recording a large and mostly fictitious *cash* profit. As we've mentioned, SFC convinced analysts of its enormous cash-generating potential, and it satisfied its external financial statement auditors that its statements described reality.

Unfortunately, it's not hard to deceive financial analysts in Canada. Most have little training in detecting cooked books. As we'll discuss in more detail in later chapters, they tend to accept the audited numbers even though they're not really suitable for drawing analytical conclusions. Why? One reason is that Canadian legislation and Court decisions ignore the needs of prospective investors. Available published financial statements too frequently are misleading. Elaboration will occur shortly.

SFC also bamboozled several teams of financial statement auditors from two of the world's Big Six auditing firms over a period of less than 10 years, as well as a Board of Directors, which included former financial statement auditors, and provincial Securities Commissions, which approved the issuing and sale of further s f c shares in Canada. Unfortunately, such blindness is not uncommon in Canada, which was one of the motivations for writing this book.

s f c is just one example of the manipulation that prevails in Canada's investment environment. We'll describe more in later chapters. In most of these cases, alleged audited financial statements contained detectable warnings, years in advance of the companies' ultimate failures. But few people bothered to review and catch the major inconsistencies, not only in s f c's financial reports but in most others, as well.

CANADIAN INDUSTRY

A word about Canadian resources companies may help at this point.

Being a resource-based country, in need of risk capital for start-up companies, Canada bends over backwards to help companies to attract capital. In the case of s f c, some analysts tried to equate the company's operations with a mining company's. This does not make sense.

In mining operations, there are three main costs associated with extracting ore from the ground:

1 Cash costs of the extraction, such as wages;
2 Non-cash amortization expense for mining equipment used directly for extraction; and
3 Non-cash depletion for recovering the costs of developing the mine, such as building shafts, ventilation systems, and similar items.

The difficulties with the attempted mining analogy for Sino were:

1 Ore volumes are relatively finite. A mine has a definable ore life, and depletion costs per ton of ore can be approximated. Trees may grow indefinitely on company-owned land. There is no read-ily definable limit on their life.
2 Ore cannot be purchased at a local market for subsequent trading or processing. But logs can be bought and sold, which explains why they're classified as inventory, ready for sale. Inventory gets turned into accounts receivable, which then become cash. Hence, inventory is a cash-equivalent type of asset.

3   The costs of discovering ore and developing a mine involve cash outlays years before a mine generates revenue. Non-cash depletion represents one of the expenses of earning revenue from sales of refined ore. Depletion expense is recorded strictly for the purposes of *measuring income* on the income statement. For the purposes of the Cash Flow Statement, non-cash depletion is *not* relevant. It gets eliminated when calculating cash generated from sales and service operations.

Comparing SFC to a mining operation does not make sense. SFC allegedly bought and sold timber frequently and should *not* have labelled these transactions as non-cash depletion or depreciation. The to-be-sold timber was inventory, a current asset, and was a cash-like expense when the timber was sold. The cost of acquiring the inventory that was sold should have reduced cash income/profit.

Trees that were to be sold in the next year should have been transferred out of "timber holdings" (Table 3.1, (A)) to "inventories" (Table 3.1, (B)). Inventory, as a current asset, is thereby a cash-like expense item when sold, and not a non-cash.

THE FINANCIAL CALAMITY

The last annual audited financial statements for SFC were for the year ended December 31, 2010. On that date, roughly 246 million common shares in SFC had been issued, "valued" at $1.26 billion in share capital, an average price above $4.50 per share.

SFC's share capital base (Table 3.1, Line Y) increased as follows:

December 31:	
2003	$67 million
2004	139
2005	143
2006	144
2007	537
2008	539
2009	1,214
2010	1,261

Shares were offered in blocks of public offerings through an offering Prospectus, as follows:

May 7, 2004	$2.65 per share
June 1, 2007	$11.00
June 5, 2007	$12.65
December 10, 2009	$16.80

Overall, SFC raised more than $1 billion in common share capital in Canada in less than six years. It allegedly raised another $200 million in Hong Kong in April 2007, by way of a private sale, at $9.15 per share. The only stock exchange that was listed for trading SFC's shares was the Toronto Stock Exchange. Thus, Canada was chosen (from the many countries of the world) to provide cash for SFC's alleged operations, even though virtually all of these operations were *not located* in Canada.

Interestingly, several financial analysts were recommending SFC to Canadian investors in 2009–2010, suggesting that the company's share price would shortly rise to $24 or more. The slide in SFC's share value to zero began in mid-2011, amid extensive allegations of fraud.

In our opinion, many red flags appeared long before 2011, and they were evident within SFC's so-called audited financial statements. If an investment watch dog or more talented external auditors had paid attention, they should have saved investors millions of dollars. It's that basic.

Class action lawsuits have recovered some money for selected people, but mainly only pennies on the dollar, after legal costs.

The Governments of Canada have not inquired in any worthwhile depth into SFC's activities to see what went wrong. Nor have financial media paid much attention to SFC's failure now that the dust has settled. Some attention was paid by regulators to auditing issues, but financial reporting was largely ignored.

Overall, business continues as usual with the public being kept in the dark. Investors are thereby being set-up to be fleeced.

SUMMARY

The case of SFC draws attention to a number of glaring inconsistencies and shortcomings in Canada's accounting and auditing procedures and ultimately its lack of protection of investors:

1 SFC's absurd reporting occurred over multiple years despite warnings from us and others about this type of cash flow game.
2 Financial statement auditors from two major auditing firms in three different cities accepted SFC's distortions of revenue, and expenses incurred to earn that revenue and legitimate cash flows. Nor did they appear to check publicly available documents for other questionable practices by the company, which we'll discuss later. (Essentially Sino was alleged to be frequently selling to itself.)
3 SFC's officers and auditors must have known that analysts utilize cash flow from operating activities (Table 3.3, Line G) in their process of calculating a company's share value. Yet they accepted SFC's contrived figures, and so did Canada's securities commissions, even though such distortions play directly into the hands of Ponzi schemers.
4 The underwriters of SFC's equity issues ought to have checked the absence of consistency and logic within SFC's financial reporting.
5 SFC's board of directors, which included former auditors, ought to have scrutinized the company's financial statements and noticed the many red flags staring them in their collective faces.
6 Canadian financial analysts never questioned the credibility of SFC's financial results. SFC's alleged fraud embarrassingly had to be exposed by non-Canadians, being by US analysts.
7 Securities commissions presumably assessed SFC's prospectuses and annual report filings, but somehow never detected the glaring problems.

Investment in Canada is needed. But, Governments are making life exceedingly difficult for prospective investors. Self-regulation has collapsed in the financial reporting arena. Needed reforms do not appear on lawmakers' radar screens. This point alone should tell investors where they are positioned in Canadian society.

4

The Hercules Managements Case

When the Supreme Court of Canada (SCC) sided unanimously in 1997 with external auditors in deciding the case of Hercules Managements Ltd., it sent a message to Canadian investors that they should *not* rely on audited financial statements in making investment decisions. At the same time, the decision removed one more theoretical protection from potential investors against shady companies that cook the books. It also practically extended immunity to external auditors who fail to detect the cooking.

The SCC drew a distinction between shareholders who owned the stock in a particular year of an audit from those who might become shareholders at a later date. The latter were abandoned by the SCC, while the former received impractical, only indirect, coverage. Greater elaboration is provided later. The distinction becomes vital, because many savers are not aware of the consequences 20 years later.

Hercules Managements was a mortgage company based in Winnipeg owned by two small families. Hercules constituted a public company because it sold debt to investors. The families sued the company's auditors for negligence in auditing the company's financial statements, which had been prepared by managers employed by the owners.

The case wound its way through the courts until it reached the Supreme Court of Canada and has been used ever since to defend financial statement auditors against claims from corporations' investors. Here's a brief summary of the decision, as written by a judge in another case:

In Hercules Management (sic) Ltd. *v. Ernst & Young*, [1997] 2
S.C.R. 165, the Supreme Court of Canada held that a company's
auditor does not owe a duty of care to the shareholders of its corporate client. The purpose of audit reports is to allow shareholders, as a class, to supervise management – not to assist them in
making individual investment decisions. Therefore, shareholders
do not have individual causes of action against an auditor. If the
corporation suffers losses attributable to its auditor's negligence,
then the corporation itself has the cause of action, which may if
necessary be pursued by way of a derivative action.

In reaching its decision, the court accepted an argument from the
Canadian Institute of Chartered Accountants (CICA) that external
auditors would be exposed to legal action from an indeterminate
number of investors unless the court placed limits on auditors' liability. This seems to contradict extensive reassuring phrases then published in the CICA's Handbook and other texts. (See Appendix 2.)

A course syllabus prepared by the CICA in 2010, for example, states
that external auditors "prepare reports that often have a wide reader-
ship (for example, the thousands of shareholders of Air Canada or
BCE Inc.)." The CICA's Handbook for March 1996, stated that "the
objective of financial statements for profit-oriented enterprises focuses
primarily on information needs of investors and creditors." The CICA
in its latest form continues to this day to publish such reassurances.
(See Appendix 2.) Investors believe them at their peril.

In the summary of the court's decision, two phrases are especially
noteworthy:

1 "to allow shareholders, as a class, to supervise management"; and
2 "may if necessary be pursued by way of a derivative action."

In accepting the CICA's argument of providing protection against
"indeterminate liability," the court said shareholders, as a class, could
use audit reports to supervise management. But they should not rely
upon these reports to make investment decisions. This raises several
concerns. How could shareholders "as a class" ever meet to discuss
their concerns? The means are not practical.

As we will continue to demonstrate, fraudulently inclined managers can find all sorts of ways to cook their books and still obtain the approval of a company's external auditors. If investors rely on a company's audited financial statements to evaluate management performance, and if auditors have no legal responsibility to investors for the competence of their audits, how can investors feel confident that the statements appropriately portray the company's financial condition? Couldn't management simply have cooked the books to make themselves look good? The Supreme Court bypassed the issue of management's reporting choices.

Under the terms of the Hercules decision, investors occupy a role similar to parents whose children prepare their own school report cards. These student-prepared report cards are taken home for parents to sign and are then returned to the school by each student for filing. Teachers have no input into the assigned grades and do not see the report cards until months later. Some parents understand the faulty process, but others do not.

Is it possible that some students will give themselves unwarranted high grades in each subject? How many? Will there be consequences to having misled their parents? Would early detection of honestly assigned, low grades have allowed for extra tutoring of weaker students and other remedies?

Under the terms of the Hercules decision, management is preparing its own report cards, based on Canada's loose reporting rules, with access to many reporting options or choices. External auditors have largely been granted legal immunity. Auditors can also protect themselves in other ways, such as by restricting their liability limits in private companies to the amount of the fees that the company paid, which we will delve into later.

As well, prospective investors (as opposed to current shareholders) have been completely ignored by Hercules. They have been left with no independent alternative sources of information for investment decisions. This is not a trivial point. Analysts have to use management-biased financial statements, because little else exists for them to see, under Canadian financial reporting laws. Such a deficiency should have been addressed by passing corrective corporations and securities legislation, many years ago.

POST 1997

Since 1997, Canada's lawmakers, securities commissions, external auditors, and other affected parties have done little to address the contradiction between the restrictions of the Hercules decision and what auditors assert to the public that they do. One legal exception may be that some judges allow restricted class actions on behalf of investors. Otherwise, in every province except Quebec, whose civil law code draws from different concepts and precedents than other Canadian jurisdictions, the Hercules decision continues to leave investors extensively exposed to financial manipulation. (In Quebec, external auditors are not granted overall immunity, but have to comply with broad standards determined by the Quebec courts, and legislation.)

The Supreme Court also said that a corporation may take "derivative action" if it alleges losses were caused by the auditors' actions. But while such a procedure may ultimately assist some of the corporation's creditors, who get first call on any money awarded in a settlement, it provides little comfort to equity investors. That's why equity investors rarely pursue costly derivative actions in such cases.

The Hercules decision clearly shielded external auditors against charges from investors for deficient auditing. Understandably, to those who are aware of the Hercules decision, the credibility of audited financial statements in Canada has diminished since then. Nor, after nearly 20 years, do auditors feel any urgency to correct this situation. Public companies in Canada are required by law to open their books to external auditors every year, and they pay substantial fees to auditors to do their legally required job. However, external auditors have no legal liability to investors to ensure that a company's statements are appropriate, nor do they earn any money from investors by ensuring that a company's financial statements are not materially misleading. So why should they jeopardize their fees by supporting investors while antagonizing the managers who pay them?

If investors can't rely on the so-called gatekeepers of corporate financial information, where else can investors turn to obtain credible information about Canadian public companies?

Canada's lawmakers have avoided addressing this hugely-significant concern.

External auditors in Canada continue to regulate themselves, with little governance or oversight from Ottawa or the provinces. Such self-regulation is not permitted in countries such as the US. With extensive and unsupervised power over financial reporting in Canada, audit firms charge an annual fee to public companies to perform a legally required function. Despite a continuing series of corporate disasters with million-dollar losses attributable to management deception in preparing financial reports, auditors continue to be permitted by our lawmakers to regulate themselves. If cars drove off the road as often as companies in Canada go out of business and squander billions of investment dollars because of undetected defects sanctioned by self-regulated "third" parties, the law would change in the blink of an eye.

While the Hercules decision practically warns Canadian investors not to rely upon audited financial statements for investment purposes, the decision's consequences extend far beyond individual investors. Financial analysts routinely consult these financial statements when they prepare advice for pension and mutual fund managers. That leaves Canadian savings, especially pension plans, highly vulnerable to financial thievery.

Yet the law in Canada surprisingly continues to allow external auditors to keep telling the public that they are gatekeepers for investors. More discouraging for investors is that the external auditors are permitted to choose the level of a required Canadian reporting standard. For many public companies in Canada, weak IFRS can be utilized. But IFRS gives substantial power to management to distort results. Hence, in essence, Canada's financial reporting system has collapsed.

Not only do they allow auditors to regulate themselves, lawmakers frequently consult these self-regulated external auditors when they make major policy decisions, such as the adoption in Canada of IFRS, on which external auditors have clear conflicts of interest. In such situations, lawmakers confuse self-regulation with independence.

Some lawmakers claim that, gradually, Canada is moving towards adoption of a National Securities Commission, but it is highly unlikely that investors will benefit. If the staffs of provincial securities commissions are hired to operate a national body, the same unacceptable attitudes will be brought into the new commission. It is vital to recall that none of the provincial securities commissions opposed Hercules, IFRS and other inappropriate recent deregulation. Such should never be forgotten.

In the meantime, where should investors look to find credible financial information about public companies in Canada? If they currently cannot put their faith in audited numbers, where else can they turn? Canada has always refrained from providing independent alternative financial information to investors. IFRS has made the deficiency that much worse. More frauds are thus inevitable. In contrast, the US requires much supplemental data for cross-checking reported figures.

We believe that Canada needs a publicly financed body to regulate and supervise the activities and standards of external auditors. We think that lawmakers are far too influenced by lobby groups that put the best interests of investors behind the self-concerns of auditors. But we don't see change on the horizon. As we explain in more detail in Appendix 2, and have stated in the Preface and Chapter 1, when it comes to protecting investors, lawmakers in Canada have a history of passing the buck. And the buck never seems to end up in the pocket of the investor.

5

Evolution of Canadian Financial Trickery

As we've shown with Sino-Forest Corporation, financial trickery can lead to serious losses for investors in Canadian companies. While corporate skulduggery in the US may get more attention, Canada attracts a disproportionate share of financial cheats. Why does this happen? Why do investors face such serious scams in Canada? How frequently does it occur? What risks do investors face in Canada? We'll try to address these questions initially in this chapter, and then develop the themes throughout the book.

It's no exaggeration to say that financial manipulators are attracted to Canada because its government does so little to protect investors. As you can see in more detail in later chapters and Appendix 2, Canada's government has done little in this regard for more than 80 years. Instead, lawmakers have relied upon self-regulated, yet seriously conflicted, financial groups to try to provide the protection that the law ignores. While Canadians need to invest in public companies to build their savings and create jobs, lawmakers do little or nothing to protect them when these companies turn out to be fraudulent. At one time, up to about 1987–1988, governments held judicial inquiries into collapsed company situations. Reasons for losses were investigated and identified. Since the late 1980s these unexpected collapses have been ignored. Learning has thus not occurred.

For about 50 years after World War II, small groups of external auditors and accountants tried to semi-regulate financial reporting in Canada. These groups provided guidance for corporate accountants and auditors and attempted to build confidence in the reliability of published Canadian financial statements. Their efforts have led to variable results. Volunteer regulators cannot possibly compensate for the unethical behaviour of determined, uncontrolled con artists. Without the support of legislators, informed by hard data about the number and frequency of fraud-related financial failures that have evaded early detection, self-regulation will remain an inferior and ineffective way to protect investors and the economy against questionable corporate behaviour. Too many conflicts-of-interest arise from self-regulation; deficiencies lead to huge investor and creditor losses.

To see how far the government falls short in delivering effective protection to investors, we simply have to compare the regulatory regimes that govern investing and taxation in this country. The contrast is startling.

Canada's *tax*-collection system extends from laws like the Income Tax Act to a blizzard of regulations, interpretation bulletins, tax forms and advisory papers prepared with the help of bureaucrats, think-tanks, conferences and consultants. The governments take every possible measure to collect taxes from corporations and individuals and issue dire warnings about the consequences if they fail to pay them. The government hires thousands of public servants to work in dedicated tax offices. An entire multiple-level court system has been created to adjudicate tax-related issues. Specialized tax lawyers, tax auditors, tax assessors, fraud investigators, tax collectors and accountants ply their trade, using documents and publications housed in vast libraries of tax materials and cases, to keep themselves informed. All of this apparatus helps to ensure that individuals, corporations, corporate officers, boards of directors and managers of public and private tax-paying enterprises in Canada pay their legislated share of taxes.

The government depends too much on tax revenues to allow individual taxpayers and taxable entities to regulate themselves. Tax-related regulations are backed up by the strong arm of the law. When it comes to paying taxes, no one can excuse his or her negligence or worse by claiming ignorance.

Observe the vast differences to how investors are treated by Canadian governments. Just try to find anywhere close for investor protection as exists for the tax empire. These same corporate officers who file personal and corporate tax returns under the watchful eye of the government typically are the *very same people* who also prepare suspect financial statements that are used by investors and creditors.

But the government pays little attention to these investor-based activities. Instead, the government tells investors and creditors to trust these corporate officers and their financial statement auditors, even though the government itself doesn't trust them to pay their taxes without close supervision, scrutiny and prosecution.

The government audits corporations in case they evade their taxes, and imposes stiff penalties if they do. Yet it allows these same managers and corporations to issue statements to investors under the complacent gaze of self-regulated auditors who are not accountable to anyone but themselves. And when one of these corporations collapses in a heap of fraudulent debris, who pays a penalty? The investor.

If Canada claims that it has a regulatory system to protect investors, it's fragmentary and undefined at best. While a few people have tried over the years to assist investors and creditors, particularly authors of books (e.g., Ross M. Skinner and Rodney Anderson) and analysts of ongoing financial games, the time and expense involved have become prohibitive for these individuals. Simply, Canada permits too much evasive financial reporting, and the financial consequences are being ignored. Too cozy?

Summed up, since the introduction of income taxation in 1917, Canadian lawmakers have focussed on collecting taxes, while they virtually ignore investors' and creditors' needs. Yet, the same people in the corporations are involved in both filing income tax returns and preparing financial statements for shareholders. Strange indeed.

HEADING BACKWARD

Although the heading of this chapter uses the word "evolution," the direction in Canada has not been "forward," for investors and creditors. Such will become obvious as we provide examples in later chapters.

Over the years, external auditors have attempted to apply risk-based auditing procedures, which identify the risks involved in various corporate activities. However, external auditors then usually place responsibility on management and the board of directors to identify and manage those risks. But, financial statement auditors have allowed so much room for judgment and interpretation in their self-regulation reporting requirements that the approach doesn't achieve its intended results: to hold management and boards accountable. Auditors may monitor management's financial decisions, for example, to determine whether they have a material impact on investors. But too many external auditors then base their definition of a "material financial impact" on a percentage of sales or other dubious figures that management can easily manipulate. And, they allow so much room for error that investors receive little protection at all.

"Materiality" is an important concept in financial reporting. Whatever is deemed to be "material" has to be quantified and reported. The definition of "material" is directly tied to whether knowledge of the transaction and dollar amounts involved would "influence or change" an investor's decision. Guesswork, such as percentages of sales, miss the point about impacts on investors' decisions.

Since the Supreme Court's 1997 decision in the Hercules Managements case, auditors and securities personnel have received even less training in detecting fraud and deception in financial statements. Today, their education programs are overly narrow and inadequate for detecting seriously perfumed financial statements. Clichés such as earnings per share have not been replaced with solid financial analysis, and with increasing cautions about their validity, thereby playing directly into the hands of financial cheats.

After 1997, as many auditors balked at the costs involved in improving financial reporting in Canada and governments continued to pass the buck, fraudsters descended on the Canadian investment scene. For example, between 2000 and 2010, investors lost billions of dollars to questionable business income trust swindles, and Nortel-like collapses. As we'll see in later chapters, IFRS's weaknesses from 2011–2012 onward have made it even easier for these frauds to succeed. While the US generally continues to reject IFRS for its domestic public companies, Canada has allowed even more freedom to corporate management to cook the books, while reducing auditors' liability for negligence even further. It is not unfair to label what has happened in Canada since the late 1990s as extreme anti-investor behaviour.

This is just the beginning of a disturbing trend that inevitably will lead to further investor losses in Canada, arising from faked financial statements that are detected only when the companies involved can no longer borrow money or sell shares. Use of reporting games can become a last resort for companies that are destine to fail. Hence, cover-up techniques are widely employed in Canada in declining companies.

Under these circumstances, we advise you to primarily invest in companies in jurisdictions that extend greater protection to investors than does Canada. You should look for Canadian companies that utilize US GAAP reporting rules, with US-based external auditors, and that file their financial statements with the US Securities and Exchange Commission (SEC). Although the SEC is not perfect, they are decades ahead of Canada in preventing large amounts of financial deceptions, and pursuing scams.

Lawmakers have to change their attitudes about the credibility of Canada's self-regulation system, and the reliability of alleged white-collar crime data. Pretending that investor protection is adequate is just not supported by readily available facts. The current self-regulation system is both dismal, and is not self-correcting. Exactly why lawmakers choose to ignore fundamental realities is disappointing. Non-independent, conflicted sources of data are just not worthy of belief. Listening to what lawmakers may prefer to hear is not helping investors to protect their savings. Nor, are jobs being created in Canada when extreme protection of self-regulators is a top agenda item for lawmakers.

6

The Basics of Scam Detection

We now focus on some financial scams that investors encounter in Canada and how they work. Here's a list of some of the most common:

1 Revenue inflation; fake revenue or sales.
2 Related-party transactions arranged at prices other than fair market value.
3 Placing operating expenses on the balance sheet and calling them assets.
4 Manipulating the cash flow statement, especially "cash flow from operating activities."
5 Inventing an alternate financial report that excludes certain expenses or might include additional revenue.
6 Manipulating interest and discount rates to reduce the present value of liabilities and increase the "value" of certain assets, such as real estate.
7 Accelerating or delaying the date of signing or finalizing important contracts to acquire another company, for example, or to sell a division so that these transactions become effective at an opportune time to inappropriately enhance the company's financial condition.
8 Netting operating expenses against gains on sales of assets to show a lower gain, but also to report lower recurring operating expenses.
9 Grouping assets and liabilities together as an operating unit to avoid writing down intangible assets, especially goodwill. This is

used extensively during economic downturns, or when commodity prices collapse.

10 Allocating the overall purchase price paid for another company to speed up the inflation of income and to defer the recording of losses. This is seen frequently in companies that repeatedly acquire other companies.

11 Cookie jar adjustments such as increasing current assets and decreasing current liabilities in order to increase pre-tax income in periods of otherwise low profits.

12 Capitalization and quick amortization on a balance sheet to convert cash expenses into non-cash amortization. This frequently occurs when companies place leased assets on a balance sheet.

13 Utilizing phrases such as "more likely than not" and other vague wording that can result in an asset (such as a tax asset) today turning into a write-down expense tomorrow.

14 Categorizing an unusual arrangement as a capital lease to inflate the balance sheet and convert cash expenses to non-cash. (Creates problems for analysts who apply valuation multiples to operating cash flows; becomes a greater problem under IFRS.)

15 Use of first-time adopters exceptions under IFRS that allow companies to define assets, liabilities and revenues differently for reporting purposes than they may have done in previous financial statements. (This results in dollar figures that are not comparable when investors examine a company's historical performance.)

16 Understatement of land restoration liabilities. (Used by some oil sands and other resource companies.)

17 Overstating receivables, especially in financial institutions, by overvaluing pledged collateral and recording fake revenue.

18 Spreading executive compensation over several companies, especially those that are only partially owned.

19 Treating gains on sales of longer-term production facilities and equipment as a revenue item, thereby inflating gross profits and operating cash flows.

20 Switching long-term debt that will soon come due into a current liability to inflate cash flow from operations.

21 Lowering operating expenses by manufacturing machinery in-house, which is then used to make products for sale. (Such a

procedure adds to the cost of the machinery a large amount of what should otherwise be basic operating expenses. Profits are thus faked.)

22 Recording proceeds from a windfall gain such as a settlement from a lawsuit as a reduction of operating expenses or an increase in revenue.

23 Providing money to friends, who then kick back money to management, by settling a fake lawsuit for a large amount.

24 Driving down a stock's price by issuing gloomy press releases and expensing assets, then issuing stock options to executives at the reduced price.

25 Treating funds received from a highly unusual transaction, such as an insurance claim, as a separate multiple-year cookie jar faked liability. The liability is then reduced in the future to offset excessive executive expenses, for example, for lavish entertainment. (Each time an excessive expense occurs, the cookie jar liability can be reduced. Reductions occur only on the liability balance sheet account, leaving expenses untouched on the income statement. Profit or income is thereby overstated.)

26 Overstating on-hand inventory by "renting" items from friends for the days of the annual physical inventory count by external auditors, and then returning the items after the auditors have gone. (Popular in scrap yards and industries with fluctuating inventory.)

27 Granting a loan to executives, often at low interest rates, then offsetting the loan on the income statement, in return for services rendered, thereby cancelling the loan.

28 Treating interest expense on the Cash Flow Statement as a reduction of financing borrowings instead of a reduction of "cash flow from cash operating activities."

29 Self-dealing with executive-owned companies.

30 Providing portions of an explanation across several notes in the financial statements, which then can be misinterpreted.

We'll discuss these and other schemes in more detail over several chapters; but this list gives you an idea of the extent of the possible deceptions, and emphasizes how easily a cheat can mislead investors, especially when external auditors are permitted to overlook several of the tricks.

Unfortunately, many investors still continue to believe that financial statement auditors check everything in a company's financial statements and that these schemes will be uncovered before the statements are released to the public. This is definitely not the case. Auditors use small samples from a company's accounting records to conduct their audits, and they rely on management to confirm the rest. This explains why, according to surveys, financial statement auditors detect only about one in 20 frauds.

Rather than looking for deceptive practices that might cost investors money, financial statement auditors focus on the "reasonableness" of corporate financial statements, to try to confirm that they are not materially misleading. They do this, primarily, by seeking reassurances, believe it or not, from corporate managers, the same people who might cook the books in the first place. Obviously, there's a problem here.

If corporate management benefits from cooking the books – receiving a bonus based on the magnitude of net income, for example – how likely are they to *lower* net income, if loose accounting rules also permit them to increase income? Same for management's stock options; and for various plans such as bonuses for percentage net income increases above last year's amounts.

Financial statement auditors may talk about their duty to lend credibility to financial statements, but as we've discussed, they have no legal obligation to help investors make investment decisions. They theoretically merely help shareholders as a group to evaluate management, who may or may not be cooking the books. Since accounting rules such as IFRS give management wide leeway in recording a particular financial transaction, such as the purchase of another company or the bulk sale of inventory, investors simply have to find ways to determine for themselves whether a company's financial statements are credible.

They can start by assessing a company's situation and the way that its management operates the business from one reporting period to another. Based on news releases, articles in newspapers and magazines and statements and press releases from the company itself, investors can look for situations that sometimes lead a company to cook its books. They can look, for example, at whether a company is stagnating, declining or blossoming and why this is happening? Here are a few situations to look for:

1 A company may be borrowing more money from a bank or private lender after encountering mediocre financial results, and likely has obtained the loan by disguising its weaknesses.
2 A company's Board of Directors may have put pressure on corporate management to improve profitability or return on investment.
3 Lending covenants such as debt to equity ratios imposed by bankers may be close to their limit, thereby requiring management to make an "improvement."
4 When a company has to raise more equity by issuing shares, the underwriter may ask for "more attractive" financial statements, leading management to apply accounting cosmetics to its financial face.
5 Management wants to grant large quantities of stock options and consequently takes suspect measures to boost the company's stagnant stock price.
6 Management is greedy and wants higher bonuses.
7 Management wants to record continuing and substantial growth to stroke its massive collective ego.
8 To build a huge company from humble beginnings, management buys other companies at excessive prices, recording much of the cost as goodwill and intangibles and thus hiding future expenses, which would otherwise tend to reduce profit.
9 Management wants to cover up its previous financial manipulation until the company reaps its largely imaginary fortune in the future.
10 The Board of Directors and management want to attract an offer to sell to or merge with another company and receive personal termination bonuses in the process.

Investors may have to re-think their previous views and now realistically assume that Canada's accounting and auditing rules will not discourage such deception and dishonesty. They have to assume, as well, that most financial writers do not have the time or expertise to detect these deceptions and that the law, as it stands, is often too vague or badly constructed to support prosecutors in laying charges against financial cheats.

And so the tricks continue.

The two most common financial scams of the past 50 years have involved padding sales revenues, a favourite game of financial institutions, and recording expenses on the Balance Sheet, as fake assets. In both cases, the deceptions increase net income and inflate cash flow from operations, which makes a weak company look more attractive to investors.

It is vital to always know how cash received from selling bonds or equity is to be used. Is the company expanding their profit-earning assets? or paying Ponzi-like dividends? or buying other companies at excessive prices in order to cover-up declining results? or more? Always check the Cash Flow Statements for periods subsequent to the equity/debt sales. What actually happened to the cash?

Companies resort to some or many of the foregoing techniques in certain critical situations, such as when:

1 Income/profits are trending downwards;
2 The company is in danger of violating a borrowing covenant imposed by a banker or other lender;
3 Profits have to be increased to pay bonuses for key employees; (e.g., Nortel's allegations.)
4 The company needs more cash to stay afloat, and has no choice but to borrow.

In these situations, investors should look for:

1 Increases in accounts receivable on the Balance Sheet over a few previous quarters, thereby possibly reflecting faked last-minute sales;
2 Suspicious increases in sales over the same quarter in the previous year, such as huge sales discounts being offered to boost sales;
3 A change in wording in accounting policies, typically published in the Notes to the Financial Statements, that affects the income and

cash flow statements; (Be especially alert for changes that do not affect the current year, but are likely to affect future years.)

4 An increase or irregularity in the company's gross profits arising, for example, from faked revenue accompanied by no increase in costs to produce the higher asserted gross profit;

5 Management comments about a new contract or other develop-ment, in the quarterly and annual report's "Management Discussion & Analysis" section. Is this reality, or another optimis-tic promise?

Fake revenue becomes difficult to detect when a company records no change from the prior year, to give the impression that all is steady. In such a case, investors should look at levels of inventory such as finished goods. Increased inventory might indicate that sales have been poor, although some companies are affected by seasonal ups and downs. This would be apparent in prior years' results; comparisons are thus necessary.

In a company involved in merchandising or manufacturing, inves-tors should look specifically at current and previous quarterly results to compare sales revenue to:

- Accounts receivable;
- Inventory;
- Costs of goods sold;
- Gross profit;
- Bad debts, if specified;
- Accounts payable for inventory purchases and related accounts for sales commission liabilities, if reported.

Financial manipulation may not reveal itself for a few quarters, but if you suspect it's happening, you can at least sell your shares before the bottom falls out.

SELF-DEALING

One of the nastiest financial manipulations involves self-dealing. We've encountered corporate officers who have lent money to relatives, which the relatives use to buy the company's stock, inflating its stock price. More commonly, self-dealing involves financial transactions between the corporation and its managers or board members and works like this:

1 Corporate officers and board members and sometimes their spouses form their own individual corporations. (Initially, such may occur for legitimate income tax reasons.)
2 The individual management-owned companies acquire inventory, land or other assets.
3 The individual companies then sell the asset to the publicly traded company at a substantial profit.
4 The public company obtains two friendly valuations to support the price that it pays for the asset.
5 Such dealings seldom lead to further investigation, and shareholders usually remain in the dark.
6 Management walks away with the cash "profits."

To add insult to injury, Canada's financial reporting rules allow companies to report the inflated price of the asset as its so-called "transaction value," simply being based upon two friendly appraisals. Often there is no specific requirement to confirm the original price of the asset or to validate the friendly appraisals.

So how could investors detect such cozy arrangements? Theoretically, reporting rules require companies to identify related parties involved in such transactions in the notes to their financial statements. In practice, a few problems arise:

1 Responsibility for identifying and reporting related parties lies with management. And a company's officers and directors have wide leeway in defining relatives for this purpose. Management sometimes interprets this responsibility through a narrow lens. Is a wife a related party? (Should be yes.) A step-sister? A nephew? Let management be the judge?
2 The rules do not require external auditors to search for the names of undisclosed related parties. They may be found by accident, when their names appear on unrelated documents, for example,

and their relationship would then be added to the notes, but only if a transaction occurs. But this seldom happens.

3 Companies sometimes include different aspects of related-party information in a number of notes. They may use words like, "Except as described elsewhere, the related parties are ..." One note may say that the company has lent money to a corporate officer. Another note may say that the loan is interest-free. Still other notes will mention that the loan carries no specified repayment date and that the borrower provided no collateral to secure the loan. The notes will often not make clear why the loan was granted in the first place. They will usually not explain the benefit to shareholders or specify whether the loan is part of a salary or bonus arrangement. An investor has to put all the pieces together to get the full story. Mistakes by investors occur from their assuming that the exchange occurred at a legitimate fair market value.

Given such games, we can only advise investors to read every word in the notes to a company's financial statements if they suspect self-dealing or are otherwise not comfortable.

BLATANT REPEATED TRICKERY

Companies often describe their performance by referring to the following type of ratio:

$$\frac{\text{Cash Dividends Paid}}{\text{Cash Flow from Operations}}$$

Underlying this calculation is the belief that companies should pay a cash dividend from money they earn by operating the sales or service business. But if a company pays a dividend from money that had to be borrowed for the purpose, investors should suspect that the company is operating a Ponzi scheme, borrowing from Peter to pay Paul. One common variation occurs when companies record an expense on the balance sheet and call it a non-current asset, in order to inflate cash flow from operations.

As we discussed earlier, Sino-Forest Corporation used this alleged scam, but it's far from the only culprit. We often see companies record a marketing expense as an asset and then they (non-cash) amortize the asset over a short period. In fact, these companies should record the marketing expense, or so-called prepaid commission, on their income statement as a deduction from sales revenue, to arrive at income/profit.

Here's an example, based on a company listed on the TSX:

Table 6.1 Expenses recorded and amortized as assets (in $millions)

Year	Marketing dollars spent	Amortization recorded in year	Year end Balance Sheet (non-current asset) (cumulative)
1	$40	$12	$28 ($40 – $12)
2	35	19	44
3	30	26	48
4	28	28	48

For Years 1, 2, and 3 the marketing asset accumulates because amortization (a non-cash item) is less than the money spent each year. By the end of Year 3, though, the company has $48 million of a fake asset on its Balance Sheet. This means that it overstated its profit in years 1, 2, and 3 by $48 million. But, in Year 4 amortization equalled dollars spent; hence, no overstatement of *profit* arose in Year 4. Overall, management has considerable freedom in determining the amount of amortization each year, and how many dollars to report as an asset.

There's much more to this story. In Year 4, for example, the company added a non-current *investment* of $28 million, representing marketing dollars spent, to its balance sheet. In fact, the marketing dollars represent cash expenses, not assets. (We saw that Sino-Forest Corporation pulled a similar deception, recording timber instead of inventory, as a long-term asset, to be amortized.) By adding non-cash amortization of $28 million to reported net income, the company falsely increases its cash flow from operations by $28 million.

Here's how this affects the company's recorded financial performance:

1 Profit/income is *not* affected in Year 4 because amortization expense equals the marketing dollars spent, (but not expensed): $28 million.
2 However, cash flow from operations is falsely increased by $28 million in Years 1, 2, and 3 because (a) $28 million of spent cash has been added to the balance sheet as a non-current cash investment (and is *not* recorded as an expense), and (b) non-cash amortization has been added to cash flow from operations instead of being recorded as an expense, which would have reduced cash flow from operations.

For Years 1, 2, and 3, *both* income and cash flow from operations have been overstated, but by different management-estimated dollar amounts. What was added to the Balance Sheet each year and recorded as non-cash amortization, thereby increasing the company's cash flow from operations, should have been expensed.

When a company pulls this common trick, it also has to account for the $12 million that it doesn't record as current assets. (In this case, $12 million in Year 1 became a non-cash expense.) The company's capitalized (but incorrectly) current assets have a false impact on its profit, because only $12 million and not $40 million was recorded in Year 1 as a non-cash expense. $28 million was called a dubious asset.

The lessons from this story are:

1 Financial cheats can inflate profit/income by falsely recording expenses as assets, and by playing other games.
2 Expenses recorded as *non-current* assets falsely increase cash flow from operations because cash was spent but was not recorded as such in the cash flow statement. (See the Sino-Forest example.)
3 Analysts who fall for such games use these inflated numbers as the basis for their evaluation of the company. When the company's stock market price eventually erodes, investors lose.

Here, in simple terms, is the way a company can run a Ponzi scheme by manipulating the ratio of dividends to cash flow from operations by recording expenses as non-current assets:

Faked Record: Expenses Called Non-Current Assets:

Dividend paid	$100 million
Faked cash flow from operations	$125 million*
Dividend pay-out	80%

*See the Sino-Forest example of how this figure was bloated. Many more examples are provided in subsequent chapters, especially faking revenue and decreasing expenses.

Real Picture: Expenses Recorded truthfully:

Dividend paid	$100 million
Cash flow from operations	$60 million
Dividend pay-out	167 %

Conclusion: Ponzi Scheme in Progress. To pay a dividend of $100 million, this company had to borrow $40 million. It did not generate the money from its cash flow from operations. The next step is to ascertain the source of the cash ($100 million – $60 million). Then, ask yourself for how long this type of scheme is likely to be successful.

WINNING ATTITUDE

As we'll explain later, IFRS has significantly, and some times outrageously, expanded the opportunities for management to redefine items in a company's financial statements to their advantage. As we mentioned earlier, they may have any number of reasons for doing it, and investors should try to understand management's motivations (such as increased bonuses) when they look for these manipulations.

Investors should be aware of the following:

1 The ease of carrying out financial games using unspecified or vague accounting rules that allow creativity.
2 Attitude of the company's financial statement auditors. Do they have a reputation for lax application of the rules? (Keeping track of the names of auditors who were alleged to have aided, or

simply audited, companies that failed under suspicious or Court-held situations is useful.)

3 Ease of covering up deceptions from one year to the next by adjusting non-current intangible assets, for example. Unwarranted management optimism may hide actual losses, while IFRS may not require detailed disclosure of a company's current situation.

4 Past successes with a certain scam. Management may have pulled the same scam before, without detection or knowledge of external auditors or Securities Commissions. (Again, keeping a record of the nature of the games, and who was involved, is vital in Canada. Perhaps, at some future time, a national prosecutor system in Canada will provide library sources for investors. Meanwhile, this book lists several common schemes.)

5 The capacity to hide overstated assets with subsequent transactions. The acquisition of another company with positive operating cash flows can cover up cash flow manipulations prior to the acquisition, confuse trend lines and make it difficult to follow the continuity of the company's financial performance.

6 Other companies in the industry may be using similar financial manipulation techniques.

7 Imminent changes to reporting rules that may limit the time in which a company can continue its financial deception; or, may open up to a new set of tricks.

If you have suspicions based on any of these conditions, you should further assess a company to confirm them. You can conduct Google searches on the backgrounds of directors and officers, for example. You can determine whether board members are friends of the company's majority shareholders and see whether individuals at the company have been involved in the past with other suspect companies. You can check to see whether individuals have employed the same lawyers, external auditors and advisers at previous companies.

DIFFERENT FRAUDS, DIFFERENT CLUES

Some cover-up techniques are easier to detect than others. A one-time fraud covered up by a one-time reduction of revenue can be difficult to catch, even by inside managers. Unless the decline in revenue is huge, and revenue falls significantly from prior periods, it's almost impossible for an investor to detect a fraud from a company's publicly disclosed records. In fact, many one-time frauds come to light only after a company enters bankruptcy proceedings, or the company is sold to third parties.

By comparison, a one-time cash fraud covered up with fake receivables will become apparent if investors ask questions about the uncollected receivables. Eventually, the company has to turn the uncollected receivables into a bad debt expense. Meanwhile, the uncollected receivables stand out as evidence of a suspicious one-time transaction. In smaller companies, investors should always analyse bad-debt expenses.

From time-to-time, an uncollectible receivable will be converted by management into a long-term loan or investment in the declining company. Such a tactic avoids having to record a bad debt, or to reverse revenue. Descriptions such as "other assets" should be analyzed. Years later, the faked investment will have to be expensed, or netted against some windfall gain.

Sometimes, a one-time scam merely hides a single mistake by management such as negotiating a money-losing contract. Management may try to hide its mistake or incompetence in its financial reporting, a cover-up that investors can usually detect through close analysis.

In most cases, companies execute scams over a period of years and apply a combination of cover-up techniques. These are the easiest scams to detect, because they require more techniques to cover them up as such thefts continue. For example, in a current year, a cheat must cover-up:

Last year's and the previous years' scams
Plus the current year's scams $20 Million
    (such as accrued interest on undisclosed borrowings) $7 Million
Total cover-up schemes needed this year $27 Million

To unravel the thread of ongoing deception, investors must find a critical piece of information. For example, they should look carefully at balance sheets to see where actual *expenses* have been stored. They should look for increases in the dollar value of inventory, income tax assets and current assets that have the same or a similar title as non-current assets. Vague balance sheet phrases such as "other current assets" or "contract initiation costs" can disguise expenses as a fake asset.

Investors should also study balance-sheet goodwill and intangibles to detect significant upward or downward changes. Financial cheats assume that no one cares about such intangible non-cash accounts and they use them as convenient locations for a cover-up.

180 DEGREES

So far we have initially looked at scams executed by:

1 Increasing net income;
2 Increasing cash flow from operations;
3 Reducing liabilities;
4 Bloating assets; or
5 Self-dealing and related-party transactions.

Greater elaboration is provided throughout the book.

In some cases, a management team may take the opposite approach. Instead of inflating values, they try to *drive down* values and their companies' stock prices. They may do this by inappropriately writing down asset values, thereby reducing future expenses, and by issuing scary press releases. A few months later, with lower expenses, they drive the price up again by publishing higher profits and operating cash flows. They do this to:

1 Allow friends to buy the company's shares at lower prices;
2 Grant stock purchase options to themselves at much lower prices per share;
3 Re-pricing, downward, stock conversion prices on previously sold convertible bonds, so that their friends can receive more shares for conversion into common stock. A bond that entitles a holder to six shares at $50, for example, may entitle the holder to 10 shares if the stock price can be dropped to $30.

4 Receive bonuses for "turning the company around" after its stock price has collapsed.

Investors can detect this type of manipulation by examining a company's previous financial statements, press releases and reports:

1 Are write-downs of assets, which increase expenses, supported by authentically independent valuations? Companies frequently employ friendly valuators to provide lowball figures.
2 Does the company use negative, gloomy words in its press releases to suggest declining prospects?
3 Has there been an increase in short-selling in which individuals borrow share certificates and sell shares. Later, they buy the shares back at a lower price, and return the share certificates to the lender. A rise in short selling indicates an expectation that a company's share price will drop. Stock exchanges periodically publish information on short sales of specific stocks. Manipulation can be extensive.
4 Has a lawyer required elaboration in notes to previous audited financial statements addressing whether the company will remain a going concern? The start of financial manipulations commonly coincide with a quarterly financial report, instead of a year end report.
5 Have company executives sold their shares lately? If so, they have to file this information with provincial securities commissions, and it's available to the public.
6 Who owns most of the shares? Are they reliable people?

In sum, as we proceed through the book's topics, it is necessary to place most efforts on detecting the favourite cover-up techniques that are being employed in Canada. Detecting even one scam tells you something about management's attitude concerning ethics and integrity. Follow-up becomes necessary.

By the time a fraud (which led to the cover-up) has been detected by you or your friends, the stock price could have tumbled appreciably. With this warning about focusing first on spotting peculiar reporting, being the cover-ups, it is time to examine Canada's list of the top tricks, many of which are cover-ups for previous frauds.

Sometimes we never discover the extent and full nature of frauds, because we do not know whether we have failed to detect one of the several cover-up techniques that the schemers employed. An example could be a manager who was selling more scrap metal (or perhaps finished goods inventory) to non-customers, which then did not appear as scrap sales on the company's records. The manager keeps the unrecorded cash, and tells people, such as external auditors, "we have had less scrap in recent years; our equipment is more efficient now."

Then various testing of relationships among dollar amounts can occur. For instance, given the magnitude of sales revenue, does the company have too much or too little inventory? Are the accounts payable in line with inventory levels? Results may show:

- "no; they are not manipulating these assets, or liabilities, or other"; or
- "yes; they are manipulating; hence, let's continue our analysis, to determine the degree of impact"; or
- "at this point, we are not sure; thus, let's keep an eye on what they do with the matter for the next 4–5 quarters."

SUMMING UP

We have tried to show a few patterns and the possible motivations of financial manipulators in Canada in the hope that Canadians will become aware that they have to protect themselves. We hope that, with a little effort, they will learn how to guard against these popular scams. We also hope that lawmakers may change their behaviour and stop ignoring investors and start to protect them. As we've discussed, the US has had an investor protection system for over 80 years. Canada's system can only be described as disgraceful and wide-open to thefts.

Without such protection, investors face disastrous consequences. If that seems exaggerated, we simply have to remind readers that significant failures have occurred in Canada wherein a variety of allegations were made about the validity of financial statements:

- Sino-Forest Corporation;
- Nortel Networks;
- *Many* failed business income trusts;
- Livent Entertainment;
- Poseidon Concepts;
- Hercules Managements;
- Confederation Life:
- Castor Holdings;
- Philip Services; and dozens more.

Financial failures will occur in every country. In Canada, a steady stream of these failures should have been caught at early stages. After all, US regulators detect a large percentage of failures, especially mid-sized ones, including several that originated in Canada. While Canada's lawmakers pass the buck, investors have to turn to the US for protection. It's an embarrassment as well as a recipe for disaster.

7

Interest Rate Manipulation

Readers may have to look more than once at technical chapters such as this one, about the manipulation of interest rates, to grasp essential issues. But we think it's important to explain selected complex material so that readers can protect themselves against such financial manipulation. If they don't, the consequences can be costly.

First, some basic concepts about interest rates: If you bought a $10,000 government or high quality bond that matures in 30 years, with a fixed annual interest rate of 5%, it would generate $500 in interest every year for the 30 years.

If the interest rate on a similar 30-year bond rose a few months later to 10%, you could generate $500 in annual interest with a bond costing only $5,000.

But this considers only one aspect of a bond: the interest rate. We should also consider the principal amount: At the end of the 30-year period, the owner of the $10,000 bond receives the principal amount, $10,000. In contrast, the owner of the $5,000 bond gets back only $5,000.

Even now, we don't have the full story. That's because $5,000 or $10,000 in today's money will lose its value and purchasing power over the next 30 years. So we have to consider how much you'd have to invest today to ensure that you received the same amount when the bond came due in 30 years. For example, how much would you have to invest today at an annual interest rate of 10%, to receive $10,000 after 30 years? This requires a calculation of "present value" (meaning "today's value").

Fortunately, rather than delving even more deeply into the mathematical complexities of present-value calculations, we can refer to a table that provides the figure that we're looking for. This figure is called a present-value factor. In our example of a 10% annual interest rate over a 30-year period, the present-value factor is 0.0573.

Here's how we use that factor to calculate the amount that we need to invest today at 10% interest to receive $10,000 after 30 years:

$$\$10,000 \times .0573 = \$573$$

In contrast, to receive $5,000 in 30 years, at a compounding of interest, and at an interest rate of 10%, the amount that would have to be invested today thus would be $5,000 × .0573 = $287. The combination of 10% interest per year compounded over 30 years plus the initial present value of $573 would add up to the principal amount of $10,000 at the end of the 30-year period.

Among many other considerations, this demonstrates the impact of a rise in the interest rate to 10% from 5%. As we discussed in our example, at an annual rate of 5%, a $10,000 bond generates the same amount of interest over 30 years as a $5,000 bond at an annual rate of 10%. But if you sold that $10,000 bond, with its 5% interest rate, today, after the interest rate on a similar bond had risen to 10%, you would lose considerable money. That's because the bond for which you paid $10,000 so that you could receive $500 a year in interest has quickly lost almost half its value in the eyes of a buyer. Instead of paying $10,000 to receive $500 a year in interest, a purchaser needs to pay only $5,000. It is that basic.

In the foregoing example, using 30 years, we have ignored the residual value differences at the end of 30 years, as between the present values for $10,000 and $5,000 of bond principal. For shorter periods, residual present values have to be considered.

In their financial reporting, corporations can distort the impact of interest-rate changes on the value of their assets and liabilities. As we've just demonstrated, these changes can have significant consequences. As usual, it's the investors who lose. Investors need to be aware of how companies perform these manipulations and how they can affect the risk level of an investment. Unfortunately, interest-rate effects are specified in financial reporting only in certain circumstances, leaving room for abuse.

Interest rates can change quickly, creating a legitimate impact on values. But they can also be manipulated by corporate management and analysts, and investors need to be aware of how this can be done.

IMPLICATIONS FOR LOAN LOSSES

Although Canada's top five banks remain relatively strong, the country's smaller banks, trust companies and credit unions as well as some insurance and mortgage companies often encounter financial challenges. Over the years, some of these financial companies have collapsed. Before this has happened, many of these companies have covered up large losses on their lending operations. They get away with this for a few years until, suddenly, their weakness leads to complete collapse.

In the 1980s and 1990s, the following failures or near-failures of financial institutions occurred:

- Canadian Commercial Bank
- Castor Holdings
- Confederation Life
- Confederation Trust
- Crocus Investment Fund
- Hercules Managements
- Northland Bank
- North West Trust
- Principal Group, and its Affiliates
- Standard Trust
- Teachers Investment & Housing Co-op
- Victoria Mortgage; and more.

Since the turn into the twenty-first century more failures have occurred.

The same challenges that led to these disasters remain in place today. They are of particular concern to Canada's lending institutions with large loans secured by real-estate property. Problems occur when:

1 Borrowers become unable to pay interest and principal on the mortgage or other money that was borrowed against the property; and

2 The loans provided by financial institutions plus interest exceed the cash resale value of the property.

At the root of the problem lies the issue of valuation. Valuation raises concerns about interest and discount rates. Our discussion will raise some complexities, but if you can persevere through the next few pages, you'll understand more clearly what to look for when you consider investing in a financial institution.

Property valuations are easy to do when a similar property has recently been sold and the sales terms are available. Likewise, a building under construction, where no complications have arisen and much of the space has been rented for long terms, usually presents few valuation difficulties.

Complexities arise when a property's value is determined using a method such as discounted cash flow (DCF). Here's how it works:

1 The actual operating cash flow (*not* income) must be calculated for each financial period, often for each year into the future, where possible. If the valuation involves a rental building, the valuator must estimate the percentage occupancy of the project, along with expected cash operating costs such as utilities, interest, cleaning and repairs.

2 The valuator must also determine the building's residual value. The residual value represents the building's sale price in perhaps five or 10 years.

Here's an example of a building's estimated future cash flow (ignoring land value):

	($millions) per year			
	Years 1 & 2	Years 3 & 4	Year 5	Years 6–50
Cash revenue	5	9	11	11
Cash expenses	5	6	7	7
Net cash	0	3	4	4
Cash taxes	0	1	1	1
Net Receipts	0	2	3	3

In its first two years, the building breaks even on an operating cash basis. From Year 5 onward, its cash flow stabilizes.

Still ignoring land value, we now have to calculate the building's present value for appraisal or valuation purposes. This usually consists of two cash components:

a Cash inflow, net of cash expenses, in Years 1–5.
b The residual cash value at the end of Year 5.

The resale price at the end of Year 5 is often estimated as a multiple of Year 5's cash flow. We then have to calculate the present value of this residual to the appraisal date, the beginning of Year 1. (As we've said, this sounds complicated and it is, but it's worth persevering.)

To calculate present value and residual value, we have to determine an interest rate for Years 1 to 5. As we discussed at the beginning of this chapter, a difference of even 1% can have a large impact on the estimated building value. Even in the best of circumstances, when everyone plays by the rules and no one tries to hide anything, such values involve some guesswork, especially when it comes to interest rates. In some cases, the circumstances are less than ideal. Instead of an honest guess, companies make a deliberate attempt to hide reality when calculating present values. The adoption in Canada of International Financial Reporting Standards (IFRS) in 2011–2012 allows management to engage in greater manipulation.

PRESENT VALUE

Present value calculations may appear to be mathematically precise. But enormous differences can occur depending on the interest/discount rate that management chooses in its calculations. Large companies make present-value calculations to determine their pension liabilities, for example. These companies have to determine today the amounts that they will be obligated to pay in pensions years later. For reporting purposes, they have to calculate, year by year, and month by month, their pension obligations over the next 30 to 40 or more years. The interest rate they use in making this calculation can make a huge difference to the final figure.

Here's an example, using a 10% interest rate, of a present value calculation, applied to a $1,000 amount, just five years in the future. First, we determine the amount of interest that accumulates and add it to our original amount:

10% Rate: $1,000 invested, January 1, Year 1	
January 1, Year 1	$1,000.00
Interest earned during Year 1	100.00
December 31, Year 1	1,100.00
Interest earned on $1,100 during Year 2	110.00
December 31, Year 2	1,210.00
Interest earned on $1,210 during Year 3	121.00
December 31, Year 3	1,331.00
Interest earned on $1,331 during Year 4	133.10
December 31, Year 4	1,464.10
Interest earned on $1,464.10 during Year 5	146.41
December 31, Year 5	1,610.51

Now we have to determine the present value of $1,000 plus 10% annual interest in each of the next five years. We do this by first dividing our initial $1,000 by the total of principal and interest in each year. This gives us a figure that might be called a multiplier. When we use that figure to multiply the principal and interest in each year, we always arrive at $1,000 of present value. When we use the same figure to multiply the principal alone, of $1,000, we get the present value that we need to invest now to generate $1,000 in each of the next five years. First, here's how we get the multiplier:

Present value (as of January 1, Year 1) of the December 31, Year 1 dollar amount of $1,100:

$$\frac{\$1,000}{1,100} = .9091$$

Similarly, the present value (as of January 1, Year 1) of the December 31, Year 2 dollar amount of $1,210:

$$\frac{\$1,000}{1,210} \ = \ .8264$$

The same calculation produces the following 10% interest rate multipliers for the end of Years 3, 4, and 5:

Year 3   =   .7513
Year 4   =   .6830
Year 5   =   .6209

But if we change the interest rate to 5%, we arrive at much different multipliers:

Year 1   .9524 (vs. .9091)
Year 2   .9070 (vs. .8264)
Year 3   .8638 (vs. .7513)
Year 4   .8227 (vs. .6830)
Year 5   .7835 (vs. .6209)

The difference is enormous, especially when we're calculating obligations in the thousands or millions of dollars. A company that owes an employee a lump-sum pension payment of $161,051 on December 31 of Year 5, for example, would make the following calculation to determine the present value of its obligation as of January 1 of Year 1:

At 10% interest compounded each year:
$161,051 × .6209 (as shown on our decimals table) = $100,000

But if the company changes the interest rate for its calculation to 5%, it arrives at a much different figure:

At 5% interest:
$161,051 × .7835 = $126,183

For investors, the leeway allowed in calculating such future obligations has the following implications:

1 By manipulating the interest rate that it uses in calculating a present value, a company can *reduce* its liability for a pension payment due in the future. In our example, a company with an obligation to pay $161,051 at the end of Year 5 can reduce the present value of its liability obligation, which appears on iits Balance Sheet, to $100,000 from $125,183, a difference of more than 25%, simply by using an interest rate of 10% instead of 5%.
2 The company's reduced liability obviously increases owners' equity. It also reduces the company's pension expense, allowing it to overstate its profits, each year.
3 If a company calculates a $161,051 pension liability using a 10% interest rate, when in fact the assets set aside to pay this future obligation earn only 5%, it will have to come up with the difference of $36,868 on December 31, Year 5. Needed cash will have to arise from another source, perhaps by cutting its dividend or by borrowing the amount. Either way, the value of the company is affected, and the investor is misled by the financial games.

The managers of companies that pull such tricks seldom lose. On the contrary, they receive bonuses and stock options based on falsely calculated profits and income over the five years, until their deception becomes apparent. By then, they've safely stashed their money where it won't be affected by their own shenanigans.

As investors, you have to watch for understated liabilities on financial statements. You have to determine the interest rates that companies use in their calculations and see whether they make sense. You cannot count on Securities Commissions or external auditors to do it for you.

REAL ESTATE VALUATION

By allowing this type of freedom and guesswork, IFRS makes interest-rate games even easier. In the case of real estate enterprises, IFRS enables management to pass increased values, calculated using estimated interest rates, and other deceptive techniques, directly through the income statement, thereby bloating income. As investors, you have to look carefully to see if a company's reported income arises primarily from changes in interest rates that affect the value of assets and generate unfounded profits.

Earlier in this chapter, we calculated the future cash flow generated by a rental building. We calculated the building's annual net receipts as:

	Net Receipts ($millions)
Year 1	0
Year 2	0
Year 3	2
Year 4	2
Year 5	3
Thereafter, per year	3

In the previous section on present value, we also calculated the multipliers that we can use to determine the present value of a future amount, using an annual interest rate of 10%. Assuming that Year 1 begins on January 1 and that each year ends on December 31, those multipliers, to be applied to year end cash receipts, were:

Year 1	0.9091
Year 2	0.8264
Year 3	0.7513
Year 4	0.6830
Year 5	0.6209

Using those multipliers with our building's annual net receipts, based on an interest rate of 10% and assuming the cash appears at each year end, we can calculate the net receipts' *present* value:

Year 1				$0 millions
Year 2				$0 millions
Year 3	$2 million	×	.7513 =	$1,502,600

Year 4 $2 million × .6830 = $1,366,000
Year 5 $3 million × .6209 = $1,862,700
                                                    $4,731,300

Our net receipts of $7 million
for Years 3, 4 and 5 have a net
present value of $4,731,300

For the years after Year 5, we assign a residual of $30 million of thereafter cash receipts. This figure doesn't come out of thin air. It's based on a residual capitalization rate, or cap rate. Instead of determining a present value for net receipts in each of Years 6 to 50 at a predetermined interest rate, real estate valuators tend to apply what they call a residual cap rate, based on the asset's net operating income, using the same applicable interest rate:

Applicable Interest Rate	×	Therefore Cap Rate	=	100%
10%	×	10 times	=	100
5%	×	20 times	=	100
20%	×	5 times	=	100
25%	×	4 times	=	100

In our example, net receipts are assumed after Year 5 to equal $3 million a year, every year into infinity. Multiplying this figure by the cap rate of 10, based on 10% interest, we arrive at $30 million. (There are far more complex calculations involved in the cap rate, but for our purposes, we don't need to go into further detail.)

To calculate the present value of the assumed residual of $30 million as of the valuation date, January 1, Year 1, we use the same multiplier as we used in Year 5: 0.6209:

$30,000,000 × .6209 = $18,627,000

To calculate the total present value of the building's anticipated annual net cash income, at an interest rate of 10%, we take the present value of the residual, $18,627,000, and add it to $4,731,300, which is the present value of net receipts for Years 1 to 5, to arrive at a grand total of $23,358,300.

If we change the interest rate to 5%, we arrive at a much different figure. The "multipliers" at 5% are much higher, as we discussed:

Year 1   .9524 (vs. .9091)
Year 2   .9070 (vs. .8264)
Year 3   .8638 (vs. .7513)
Year 4   .8227 (vs. .6830)
Year 5   .7835 (vs. .6209)

Based on a 5% interest rate, the present value of our building's net receipts would be:

Year 1		$0 millions
Year 2		$0 millions
Year 3 $2 million × .8638	=	$1,727,600
Year 4 $2 million × .8227	=	$1,645,400
Year 5 $3 million × .7835	=	$2,350,500
		$5,723,500

The residual of $3 million a year now has a cap multiple of 20 times rather than 10. This gives us a residual of $60 million. To discount the residual to present value as of January 1, Year 1, we multiply $60 million by 0.7835 $47,010,000

Our grand total now becomes: $52,733,500

By reducing the present value interest rate to 5% from 10%, we've increased the present value of the building's net receipts over its lifetime to almost $53 million from about $23 million. Nothing else has changed except the interest rate.

This means that buyers who feel satisfied with a 5% annual return on their investment will pay *more* for the building than buyers who want 10% a year. Depending upon the creditworthiness of the tenants, the building provides a guaranteed annual cash flow. In this respect it resembles a bond that pays 5% per annum for many years.

For our purposes as investors we also need to be aware of the impact of interest rates on the present value of real estate. The higher the risk that net receipts will diminish or disappear, the higher the interest rate demanded by investors. Economic conditions can seriously affect required interest rates. Investors should consider carefully the interest rate that a company uses to calculate the present value of real-estate income, and "asset values."

Investors should also be aware that, under IFRS, a real estate company can increase a building's value by choosing a lower interest rate and then attribute the increase to income on its income statement. In this respect, IFRS practically invites companies to engage in Ponzi frauds.

LOAN RISKS

Interest rates utilized in business obviously deeply affect real estate valuations. Mortgage lenders are at risk when the economy turns downward. In the case of the building just analyzed, a buyer that pays over $50 million for the building might need to sign a mortgage of over $35 million. If the corporate buyer then can't collect rents as anticipated, it would have difficulty meeting its required mortgage payments. Analysts and investors thus need to know how much a company is paying for its borrowings.

If we take a closer look at the real estate valuator's calculation of $52,733,500 as the present value of our example, assuming 5% interest, we can see how imprecise this figure really is. Some items worth noticing are:

1 The chosen interest/discount rate. Considerable judgment is
   involved, especially if the building is somewhat unique, making
   comparisons to other buildings problematic, and its cash flows

being somewhat difficult to predict. Investors have to be on guard
for too much management optimism. Write-downs of recorded
values may be being postponed, especially by mortgage lenders
who are not receiving their full loan principal and interest.

More commonly seen in Canada, the mortgage lender merely
asks for another higher valuation or appraisal from a friendly valuator to leave the impression that the mortgage is secure. As we
have observed throughout this chapter, lowering the interest rate
can increase a building's so-called value. Pretending that a building's value still exists has led to several failures of financial institutions in Canada (e.g., Confederation Life, Standard Trust, and
many more).

2 Calculated annual cash flows. We have seen some ways in which
companies manipulate cash flow from operations, and we'll see
more. In the case of real estate, too many real estate appraisers
accept management's calculation of annual cash flows. As we
mentioned, cash flow estimates beyond Year 5 of a building
require considerable guesswork unless many long-term rental
contracts have been signed.

Over the years, we have seen cash flow exaggerations ranging
from questionable to outrageous. Investors looking at mortgage
company financial statements have to be on guard for such items
as:

a annual increases in loan amounts on the balance sheet that do
not correspond to new loans being shown in the Cash Flow
Statement. Instead, they could simply be capitalized non-cash
interest. In the financial statements, the company's loan assets
and interest revenue both are being increased, but the company
receives minimal actual cash to cover interest and principal.

b bad debt expense is gradually increasing, but not explained;

c declines in the economy that cause an erosion of values. As an
example, property values declined precipitously in Alberta in
the 1980s and will likely decline again as a result of declining
and fluctuating oil prices.

Investors have to watch for mortgage companies that do not
have a credible current asset category. Separating non-cash
interest revenue from cash revenue is a complicated procedure,

but it can raise a red flag if it reveals that little cash is actually being received. Special close analysis may be needed to ascertain when cash is due from large borrowers, but has not been paid in cash. As an alternative, companies may increase the loan receivable on their balance sheet by the amount of the uncollected interest on the loan.

d   Sources of cash. Cash from operations ought to be growing enough to pay dividends. But if more borrowing is occurring than what existed previously, a form of Ponzi scheme may be commencing, which should be of great concern to lenders.

With respect to an investment in the real estate company itself, such deception may signal that the time has come to sell your shares. Under IFRS, companies may reduce interest rates each year to manipulate property valuations upward. As we've discussed, a reduced interest rate increases the property value. The real estate company can then record the dollar difference between this year and last year as *income* under IFRS rules for real estate entities, giving investors the impression that they own shares in a sound, growing company. (In other industries, IFRS does not allow a company to use this trick when valuing a single building.) Investors must determine the exact reporting concepts that a company has chosen when preparing its financial statements.

Companies may extend their deception to expenses for repairs to their buildings, burying the repair costs within the increased asset value obtained from selecting an inappropriate lower interest rate.

As always, you do not have to detect all of a company's deceits to know that now is the time to sell your shares. Ethics become the issue. Scepticism levels must be raised. Take your investments elsewhere.

8

Yield Scams

When Canadian investors buy dividend-yielding stocks, far too few of them address these essential questions:

- Will this current dividend/distribution rate per share apply only for the next six months, a year or much longer?
- What evidence confirms this?

The price of some stocks closely reflects their dividend yield. This makes sense if the company has paid the same yield for years. But when a company's dividend rates and cash flows from operating activities are erratic or the company has reduced its dividend rate a few times, then pricing its stock on the basis of the current dividend yield is simply absurd. If the company cuts its dividend rate in half tomorrow, the stock price could theoretically drop in half, too. That means you'll lose one-half of what you paid for the stock, and dividends cannot replace lost principal. You'll also face income-tax implications. Yet questionable companies continue to lure Canadian investors by appealing to their appetite for dividend yield. It doesn't make sense, but it is readily seen in Canada.

Even when management promises not to cut a stock's dividend, you should thoroughly analyze the company's financial reports to look for potential problems. Usually yield gimmickry will involve bloated income, manipulated cash flow from operations, and bogus assets that should be recorded as expenses. By detecting the shenanigans of unethical managers, you can protect your investment portfolio from losses when the price of the stock of a dubious company collapses. The wording of management's dividend promises typically is evasive.

INCOME TRUST INSANITY

Around the beginning of the twenty-first century, Canadians looked for investments that would deliver a higher return than the low interest rates that prevailed at the time. When business income trusts (BITs) dangled higher yields in front of them, many Canadian investors bit the hook.

The details of the income trust debacle are lengthy and complex. They'd been around for years on the sidelines of the financial world, when investment banks began promoting them heavily in the early 2000s to compensate for the loss of business they'd suffered after the dot-com crash. Basically, tax regulations enabled Canadian companies that converted themselves into BITs to deliver a dividend yield to investors higher than the prevailing interest rate at the time and much higher than the yield on stocks held in conventional companies. Investors saw the words income and trust and were mesmerized, forgetting that BITs were equities that came with the same risks as any other stock.

That didn't stop the financial press from touting BITs as the best thing that ever happened to investors. Companies in almost every industry, from oil and gas to yellow pages directories, converted themselves into BITs. Some of Canada's biggest banks said they would do the same. Simply by converting to a BIT, a company could reduce its taxes and raise the value of its stock by 20% or more. Investors thought they'd died and gone to financial heaven. Pension funds, mutual funds and individual investors poured money into BITs. Regulators sat back and watched it happen. Politicians dithered, worried about the lost tax revenue, but also concerned about alienating millions of voting-age investors who had put money into BITs. Meanwhile, financial manipulators swarmed around BITs like sharks around a cut of Grade-A beef.

While some BITs paid investors a yield based on their legitimate operating activities, many others operated as glorified Ponzi schemes, making bloated distributions to investors that included return of some of their initial capital. As long as they could attract more investors, these Ponzi-like BITS could continue paying bloated yields in their game of financial musical chairs. Only when the music stopped did investors discover that they had nowhere to sit down.

The whole emotional fiasco came to an abrupt end when the federal government changed the tax rules that had supposedly made BITS so attractive in the first place. Within days, the market for BITS lost more than 13% of its value, and Canadian investors lost an estimated $30 billion. Nevertheless, some of the BIT con games have continued to today.

Canada had shown once again to be a paradise for financial scam artists. Throughout the rise and fall of BITS, mainly between 2000 and 2006, provincial Securities Commissions stood on the sidelines, acting against blatant scams only when it was too late. The business press fed the frenzy with hype about BIT yields. Politicians did nothing until they recognized the consequences of losing billions in tax revenues. Securities lawyers and external auditors remained silent while seniors lost their savings and some pension funds poured more of their money into BIT Ponzi schemes. Hungry for fees, underwriters and financial analysts turned pathetic companies, some of which had previously gone bankrupt, into BITS with the reassurance that "this time it would be different." When the final tally was made, some investors had lost their life savings. A few of them committed suicide.

How did our lawmakers react? Did they authorize a judicial inquiry to find out how BITS were allowed to do so much damage? Did they tighten legislation to make sure it never happened again? Not really. They just passed the buck back to the self-regulators, who had stood on the sidelines.

What did the self-regulating external auditors do? They brought International Financial Reporting Standards (IFRS) to Canada, loosening reporting requirements and making another BIT-like fiasco possible.

No fresh thinking was applied to Canada's investment environment. No light was cast on the financial games that challenge the savings of Canadian investors. Instead, the stage was set for even more deceptions to occur.

Weak companies in Canada continue to use the same sets of tricks to attract investors while they pay salary and bonuses to executives. We've already explained those games. They include:

- Inflating income by faking revenue and placing expenses on the balance sheet as bogus assets;
- Inflating cash flow from operations by including amounts that belong in the financing or investing sections of the Cash Flow Statement, thereby artificially inflating the value of their stock;
- Using alternative measures of income and cash flow, as we'll see later in this chapter when we mention Nortel Networks.
- Labelling capital obtained from investors as income by sending money to a partially owned company, for example, which then sends portions of the money back to the parent as a dividend distribution from its phony income.

To avoid falling for schemes that rely on high dividend yields based on manipulated cash flow from operations investors need to search for the real sources of cash. Does the operating cash flow come legitimately from operations through valid sales and service revenue? Or has the company used IFRS to disguise its deceit and thereby convert owners' capital into income?

NORTEL

An insatiable appetite for capital gains led Canadians into another money-losing company when they lined up at the trough to buy shares of Nortel Networks, one of Canada's most venerable companies, with a history in the communications industry that stretched back more than a century. A manufacturer of optical networking gear, Nortel used its bloated share price to purchase more than a dozen companies between 1998 and 2001. Its workforce ballooned beyond 90,000 people, many of whom pursued research and development initiatives that would not produce revenue, never mind profits, for years to come.

Facing the costs of its acquisitions, and with a large part of the company generating no revenue, Nortel did not produce net profits. But the company managed to convince investors to ignore the large losses and focus instead on what was called "pro forma earnings from operations," a figure that the company basically invented and which helped to distract investors. In 2000, for instance, Nortel reported revenue of $30.3 billion and pro forma "net earnings from operations" of

$2.3 billion. In subsequent press releases, Nortel continually trumpeted revenue and earnings from operations, noting in particular the seemingly impressive percentage increases from quarter to quarter.

In fact, Nortel was not actually making any money. In 2000, for instance, the company lost $3.5 billion. To account for the $5.8-billion difference between its net loss and its so-called pro forma earnings from operations, Nortel referred to "Acquisition Related Costs." It defined these costs as "in-process research and development expenses and the amortization of acquired technology and goodwill from all acquisitions subsequent to July 1998, stock option compensation, and certain one-time gains and charges."

Depending on the industry, a company might exclude certain one-off charges in calculating normal operating earnings. Nortel excluded far more, and then referred to its calculation as pro forma earnings from operations, similar enough in name to the normal measure to leave investors hopelessly confused. Technically, the word "pro forma" is used when actual results have been modified somewhat by including or excluding items, such as specific revenues or expenses.

To add insult to injury, Nortel's management argued that "acquisition-related costs" were non-cash items and could therefore be ignored. Then they calculated their bonuses to a significant degree on the creative performance metric of pro forma "earnings from operations" or "pro forma earnings." Yet the acquisition-related costs were incurred in acquiring assets that would eventually produce revenue for the company. If the company had developed the acquired products internally, how could it have justifiably ignored the cost of the acquisition?

Few questioned the figure, and even fewer drew attention to the CEO's performance bonuses and stock option grants, which were largely based on Nortel's fanciful pro forma "earnings from operations."

Nortel's CEO also criticized Canada's tax treatment of stock options. Because the US treated them less harshly, he said, Nortel executives were alleged to be leaving in droves to work at US companies. Without favourable changes to Canada's tax system, he said, Nortel's Canadian workforce would continue to shrink.

Again, few seemed even slightly bothered that management were the largest holders of Nortel stock options, and had much to gain from a change in tax treatment. Instead, management received accolades as a catalyst for change. *Time Magazine* called the CEO "the most successful businessman in modern Canadian history." *National Post Business* magazine featured him on the cover twice in 2000, first in caricature as a flying superhero over a caption giving him credit for making investors more than $250 billion and again, just three months later, crowning him as CEO of the year.

Sadly, the media jumped all over Nortel and reinforced the notion among individual investors that they would profit if they stuck with the company. When we saw what was happening, we urged investors to sell, and sell quickly. Many months later, Nortel collapsed from $120 plus per share to essentially zero, and it was seeking bankruptcy protection.

The story of Nortel Networks presents many lessons to investors. One of the most important is, watch out when a company claims that "Canada's reporting rules are unfair to our company," and then invents a way to get around them. What the company invents usually has little credibility, as will be described later in this book.

Rather than promote losses that existed in its audited financial statements, Nortel devised its own form of financial reporting. By transforming expenses into something else, Nortel magically turned its losses into profits. And since Nortel had invented this profit, it had to find a name for it and came up with the term "net earnings from operations."

Not only did Canadian investors, as well as the financial media, believe Nortel's manufactured numbers, they also didn't learn their lesson when Nortel collapsed. Within a few months they were buying into another alleged scheme devised by Sino-Forest, and similar offshore companies.

WARNING SIGNS

Since the media, the regulators and the government seem reluctant to upset the corporations that invent such tricks, and since IFRS practically encourages companies to manipulate their accounts in a way that defies reality, how can investors protect themselves against these situations? Pretending that Canada has investor protections amounts to deluding yourself.

When it comes to yield scams, here are some considerations that investors should make in assessing a company:

1   Why is a particular company in a position to pay such a high dividend? What is its secret? Is the company exceptionally profitable because it holds valuable patents or has discovered a particularly lucrative ore body? Many business income trusts claimed that their high dividends arose from a high level of tax savings. But these savings were far lower than the bloated dividend could justify. The cash was coming from bond and equity investments in the company. The BITS were operating a Pyramid scheme. Investors could have discovered this for themselves by asking a simple question about the source of cash, and then discovering that the funds were flowing in a circle. Dividends were not from earnings.

2   Does the company operate a dividend reinvestment plan (DRIP)? Instead of sending a dividend cheque to investors, some companies keep cash within their own treasury and issue the equivalent amount in company stock to investors. The more cash a company keeps to itself in this way, the less it has to borrow to pay a dividend at a rate higher than warranted.

3   Does the company borrow cash? From whom and on what terms? You can answer these questions by checking the balance sheet and cash flow statements to see if a company's short-, mid- or long-term debt is increasing. Has the interest rate increased over time, perhaps because the company has borrowed beyond a justifiable level? You should distinguish short-term loans that a company might use to finance a temporary build-up of receivables or inventory from two- to five-year loans that a company might use to keep a Pyramid scheme in operation.

4   Has the company sold more shares or units (other than DRIP) every year to the public? How much has it made from these sales? Can you detect a trend in the company's share price? Has it fallen with each new issue, indicating a decline in investor enthusiasm for the stock? If so, probably it is time to sell.

5 Using the company's cash flow statement (and keeping in mind that companies such as Sino-Forest can manipulate these statements) determine the percentage of net income represented by the cash dividend. If it's a high number, say 75% or more, this could indicate that the company is more interested in attracting investors than sustaining its operations. You should analyse the company's financial reports from previous years to detect trends in its distribution rate. Has cash flow from operations been manipulated?

6 Check the company's cash from operating activities on its cash flow statement thoroughly, to track down all potential manipulation, such as expenses shifted to the balance sheet. A temporary increase in income might appear after a windfall, one-time gain from a successful lawsuit, for example. You should regard surprises in cash flow from operating activities from one year to the next as a red flag. Remember, companies fool people with inflated dividends by moving or mislabelling items as cash and shifting them around the cash flow financial statement. Watch for borrowing among related companies, for example, including executive-owned entities.

7 The foregoing points ought to have provided some initial clues as to whether the high dividend rate (or yield) is unwarranted, and is only temporary.

Now it's time to determine whether the income statement has been manipulated so that it shows a higher net profit than is warranted. Companies inflate their net profit to justify paying a high dividend. For example:

	Honest Profit	Faked Profit
Dollar Amount	$100	$200
Dividend Paid	150	150
Dividend Percentage	150%	75%

You should determine whether the dividend equals or exceeds cash generated by legitimate operating activities. If it's increasing each year, or if the company has to borrow money to pay the dividend, be on guard. You should also check the company's reports over several years to see whether it has increased its borrowing significantly and whether its loans carry an increasingly high rate of interest, which will affect its ability to pay a high dividend in the future.

As you look at a company's patterns of borrowing, you should check whether the company has any remaining tangible assets available to pledge as collateral security for additional loans. If not, it will likely cut its dividend in the near future.

AN EXAMPLE

In the following example, we'll explore a dividend yield scheme in action. First, we'll provide the basic facts about the company:

1	Common shares issued, as of year-end:	120 million
2	Dividend rate per share the past year (Assume the dividend was declared and paid at year end)	$0.80 per share
3	Reinvested dividends (DRIP)	$10 million
4	Amount borrowed late in the year	$12 million
5	$ raised from late-year share sales (not including DRIP)	$18 million
6	Net income (corrected for tricks) for the recent year and expected for next year	$19 million
7	Non-cash expenses included in arriving at net income (e.g., amortization)	$13 million
8	Capital expenditures that are essential to maintain the company in operation for next year (often called "maintenance or sustaining CAPEX")	$8 million

From this data we can make the following calculations:

Cash needed to pay dividends:

120 million shares at $0.80 per share	$96,000,000
Less non-cash DRIP reinvestment	10,000,000
Cash dividend requirement	$86,000,000

Cash Sources:

(1) Borrowings, at high interest rate $12,000,000
(2) Additional dollars of common shares sold
    (in addition to DRIP)   18,000,000
                                                         $30,000,000

Cash required from operating activities
to maintain the dividend rate
($86 million – $30 million) $56,000,000

Next, we have to determine the amount of cash available from activities listed on the income statement, after necessary adjustments (such as those previously explained in the book).

Net income $19,000,000
Non-cash expenses (e.g., amortization)   13,000,000
Cash available before necessary capital expenditures   32,000,000
Essential capital expenditures needed to maintain
    the company's sales and services business assets   (8,000,000)
Net cash available from operating activities $24,000,000
Cash *shortfall* if next year's dividend remains at
    $0.80 per share and $30 million of equity and cash
    debt is obtained: $56 million – $24 million $32,000,000

But, if the company reduced its dividend from $0.80 per share to $0.50 per share, it could reduce the cash needed to pay to $60 million from $96 million (ignoring minor adjustments for the DRIP, increases in interest expenses, etc.).

If the company continues to pay the higher level of dividend, it may reach its borrowing limit within a year. It may not be able to raise more money through further borrowing or by selling more shares. At that point, where does it find necessary cash? The company could sell its productive assets. But that amounts to a desperate decision. More likely, it will cut its dividend again, and again (which occurs in Canada).

What is the moral of the story? With so many variables to juggle in order to keep such a yield scheme working for any length of time, a company will eventually run out of options. When that happens, investors will likely lose part of their principal investment as the company's stock price falls. The decline in stock price will exceed the net amount, after tax, that investors have received as a dividend. Perhaps, income tax was paid on the fake dividend. How much?

To make these pyramid schemes work, companies need the following conditions in place:

1. Ability to borrow and/or sell shares, including DRIP re-investment, each year.
2. Unsuspecting investors who believe a company can maintain its high dividend rate over many years.
3. Financial deception to inflate net income and bloat cash flows from operating activities.
4. An external auditor who will turn a blind eye to financial shenanigans, such as recording operating expenses on the balance sheet.
5. Artificially reducing the amount of money needed for capital expenditures ($8 million in our example) to replace worn out equipment, etc., and earn future revenue. As this trick reaches crisis proportions in Canada, investors should be wary of the many companies that record trivial CAPEX deductions.
6. Persuading ill-trained financial analysts to support the company and its apparent financial performance.
7. Eluding detection by financial analysts who recognize manipulation when they see it. There are a few around; but, not enough to quickly correct stock prices, as we saw with Sino-Forest, and others.

SUMMARY

As long as management is allowed to exaggerate the prospect of future dividends, investors should be very wary of high dividend yielding companies. Somewhere behind the dividend you'll find a statement from management that "circumstances may change." When they do, those changes could easily lead to investor losses.

With a few exceptions, the financial press has paid far too much attention to annual yields, or cash returns on investment and has not done enough to warn investors that a higher yield usually indicates a higher risk of losing their investment.

Dividend yield scams gain credibility by their association with so-called wise investors, identified in the media as financial gurus whose word should be taken seriously. More than one of them has recently been caught by dividend decreases in suspect companies, thereby incurring significant losses.

Yields rise and fall depending on the rates paid on government bonds. If a company's dividend exceeds the rate paid on a 10-year government bond by maybe 3 % or more, investors and lenders should ask questions. Even today, such schemes are not uncommon.

9

Cash Flow Games

Investors may not trust IFRS, but many of them believe that they can circumvent the major limitations of IFRS by referring to a company's Cash Flow Statements. This usually doesn't work unless they make several adjustments to elements of the Cash Flow Statement. This chapter will show them what to look for. All too often unfortunately, needed information for adjustments is not provided by IFRS in Canada.

A company's income statement, prepared without manipulation, measures its latest period's profitability. By contrast, its cash flow statement focuses on liquidity which measures its ability to settle bills coming due in cash.

As we've discussed, two of the most common types of tricks in Canada involve exaggerating annual and quarterly income/profit and bloating cash flow from operations. We've also mentioned other games, such as inflating the balance sheet, asset levels and equity, and self-dealing or hidden related-party transactions.

In this chapter, we'll look more closely at the way companies bloat cash flow from operations, to the detriment of investors who may follow the advice of duped financial analysts and buy the company's stock.

Two factors in particular affect cash flow from operations:

1 Changes during the period in *non-cash* current assets less current liabilities (such as increases or decreases in accounts receivable, accounts payable, inventory, and other current accounts), and

2 Net income plus or minus non-cash items (e.g., non-cash amortization).

Some people look at a company's earnings before interest, taxes, depreciation, and amortization (EBITDA). They should know that EBITDA and cash flow from operations are both subject to the same kinds of manipulation. In either case, by not counting valid expenses such as interest and taxes and thereby inflating income, financial cheats in Canada can take advantage of simplified analysts' models of corporate valuation to repeatedly dupe investors. If investors can grasp the concepts in this chapter, they can avoid paying a premium for a company's fictional profits and bloated operating cash flow.

CASH FLOW STATEMENTS

A typical Cash Flow Statement includes these categories:

1 Cash flow from operations:
  a Net income, plus a listing of items that increased or decreased net income but were *not* cash-based. Net income is a combination of cash and non-cash revenues and expenses. To refine net income into its *cash* flow components alone, we have to work backwards on the Cash Flow Statement. (Such as by adding non-cash amortization to income.)
  b Changes in current assets less current liabilities, except for the cash balance itself. These typically offset income statement accounts. For example, a company that shows an increase in accounts receivable over a period (reflected in sales revenue on the income statement) has received less revenue-based *cash* during the period. To determine cash flow from operations on the Cash Flow Statement, we have to show the dollar impact on the cash asset that has occurred as a result, for example, of cash not collected but recorded as outstanding receivables.
    Cash flow from operations is intended to show the cash that a company generates over a period from activities *other than* financing and investing or disinvesting. To remove the temporary impact of a day or two delay in collecting or paying

receivables or payables, companies record these non-cash current assets and non-cash current liabilities in a *separate* category within their cash flow from operations.

Financial schemers try to distort cash flow from operations by playing, among other dubious activities, with the recording of a company's financing and investing activities.

2 Financing:

By blurring the distinction between financing transactions and cash flow from operations, Ponzi schemes get away with borrowing from Peter to pay Paul. Ideally, cash flow from operations indicates the amount that a company earns in cash over a specified period. Financing indicates the amount that a company has borrowed and theoretically, at least, has to repay.

Within a company's Cash Flow Statement, the *financing* category typically includes the following transactions:
- Sales of the company's bonds or debentures;
- Sales of the company's newly issued common shares;
- Redemptions / repayments of previously issued bonds or debentures; and
- Long-term (not current) bank borrowings or repayments.

In general, the financing section in the Cash Flow Statement focuses on changes in long-term debt and equity. A growing company usually shows an inflow of cash from borrowing and from issuing shares, which it uses to acquire long-term assets.

Ponzi schemers often move cash received in the form of loans, which they should record under financing activities, into cash flow from operations. This manoeuver raises a company's cash profit (from operations) and gives the false impression that the company has earned this cash profit from regular sales and services operations. (Since the arrival of IFRS in Canada, in some companies, interest expense has become deleted as a reduction of cash from operations, and has become a reduction of cash from financing. The effect is the same, which is to fake an increased cash from operations.) The result is a faked higher stock valuation:

	Honest portrayal summary	Ponzi manipulation summary
Cash flow from operations	$1,000	$1,000
Devious switch from financing to cash from operations	–	800
Rough "cash profit"	1,000	1,800
Reported valuation multiple applied by analysts to approximate stock price (illustration only)	× 8	× 8
Shareholders' stock value	$8,000	$14,400

Some of this deceit is sanctioned by current accounting rules. For example, IFRS allows companies not to count legitimate expenses, such as cash payments of bond interest, as a reduction of cash flow from operations. Instead, they can bury the reduction of cash that results from this expense in the Financing category. Thus, a company transforms $1,000 of cash profit into $1,800 by not including $800 of bond interest expense in its cash flow from operations. Unfortunately, it takes careful analysis to ascertain how a company treats interest expense.

Unaware, financial analysts issue inflated stock values in their reports and unsuspecting investors lose money when the share price eventually drops.

3 Investing/Disinvesting:

Some companies increase their cash flow from operations from one year to the next by including cash received from selling or disinvesting in long-term assets. They may record the sale of old equipment as ordinary revenue, for example, even though the company does not operate a revenue-generating business based on selling old equipment, buildings or even land.

Or they may re-structure a long-term asset into a capital lease by arranging the lease with a friend and attributing a gain in cash flow from operations to revenue earned from the disposal of the asset. This manoeuver may take time to detect, but if the company tries to pull it year after year to maintain an upward trend line, it will soon run into difficulty arranging for these faked leases.

If investors notice an increase in cash flow from operations without a solid explanation from management, they should avoid or sell the company's stock.

SOME BASICS

As we've discussed, to get away with their shenanigans, cheats have to coordinate the three basic components of a financial statement: balance sheet, income statement and cash flow statement.

In the example of Sino-Forest Corporation (SFC), which we discussed in Chapter 3, these three components seemed to reflect the activities of three different companies.

SFC's financial statements	Probable industry
Balance sheet	Long-term *tree farm* (with huge non-current assets, of trees)
Income statement	A large *department store* chain or a broker involved in frequent trading (with high sales and cost of sales)
Cash flow statement	A large *manufacturing* organization with major assets that are subject to wear and tear; hence, very large non-cash amortization or depreciation.

The structure of SFC's Cash Flow Statement was an impossibility and had been for several years. The most revealing clue was the huge non-cash amortization recorded under cash flow from operations.

Since similar situations arise often in Canada, investors have to pay close attention to *every* component of cash flow from operations, in each of its two categories:

a Net income plus or minus non-cash items; and
b Changes during the period in current assets less current liabilities, except for cash itself. (Cash itself is our cross-check or balancing figure, and cannot be counted twice in our tabulations. Hence, we state "except for cash" when "current assets less current liabilities" have to comprise category B.)

Net income

With net income, investors have to remind themselves that a company can cook the books for *each* revenue and expense account that netted to net income. Most cheats focus on revenue manipulation. But they may also suppress a few expense items. They may, for example, record an expense as an asset on the Balance Sheet and include an expense amount as an investment (instead of in operations) on the Cash Flow Statement. Then, as sfc did, they amortize the so-called investment as a non-cash item over the next few years. The result is that a non-cash expense by-passes the Cash Flow Statement.

Alternatively, a company might accept ownership shares in a shaky business in exchange for selling its older-style goods. In the process, the company increases its revenue, and records its investment in the shaky business as a long-term or non-current asset, until the shaky business goes bankrupt. The result in this case is that revenue may be recorded in Year 1, but the bad debt expense or asset write-down does not occur until Year 3, or 4, or more.

Non-Cash Current Items

The second category, changes in current assets less current liabilities (except for cash), is also open to serious manipulation, and investors should look closely at these changes when they assess a company. In Table 9.1, we refer to net income (Category A) and changes in current assets and liabilities except for cash (Category B) to show potential deception:

Table 9.1

	What the Company reported last year	Choices for this year	
	($ thousands)	Option X (honest portrayal)	Option Y (scam)
Net income	$ 2,150	$ 3,000	$ 3,000
Amortization	200	250	250
Category A. (from previous illustration)	$ 2,350	$ 3,250	$ 3,250
Category B:			
Current assets (except cash)	$ 1,000	1,500	1,225
Current liabilities (unchanged in the year)	820	820	1,165
Net	180	680	60

Comparing the Honest Portrayal in Option X to the Scam in Option Y, we see two deceptions:

1 With Deception 1, the company reduces its current assets by $275,000, to $1,225,000, (such as by prematurely accepting and falsely recording a post-dated cheque), from a friendly customer. Alternatively, $275,000 may have been transferred to a non-current receivable, by manipulation (because the amount will never be able to be collected).
2 With Deception 2, the company withholds paying $345,000 of accounts payable recorded under Current liabilities until a few weeks into the *next* financial year, increasing its liabilities to $1,165,000 at the current year end.

In total, the company, by its deceit, has decreased its net *current* assets by $620,000. Instead of $680,000, the company records a net change of just $60,000. Hence, the change from last year end is:

Deceit: Addition that would have to be made to Category A figures, to arrive at cash flow from operations:

         Category B: last year $180

                     this year   60

                     Net during the year,

                     Option Y (Scam) $120

Honest Portrayal: Subtraction that would have to be made from
                   Category A figures:
                   Category B: last year $180
                                this year   680
                                Net during the year,
                                Option X (Honesty) $500

The net manipulation adds up to $120 and $500 = $620 (Addition plus subtraction.)

Overall, the current asset less liability deceit has bloated "cash flow from operations" by $620,000. That is, instead of a subtraction in Category B of $500,000 from Category A, the manipulation adds $120,000, for a difference or swing of $620,000.

In Table 9.2, we subtract the current year's net change, under each option, from the previous year's final net change ($180,000) to show the impact of the company's manipulation of its cash flow from operations.

Table 9.2 Cash Flow From Operations ($thousands)

	Option X (hon-est)	Option Y (scam)
A. Net income plus non-cash amortization	$3,250	$3,250
B. Current items, except cash; change from beginning of year ($180):		
Honest	(500)	
Scam		120
Cash Flow From Operations	$2,750	$3,370

By manipulating the calculation to eliminate this $500,000 deduction and record a $120,000 addition under current items, the company increases its total cash flow from operations to $3,370,000. Unfortunately, this scam is commonly seen in Canada, but only by those who do the searches. Hence, those who utilize the Cash Flow Statement to compensate for deficiencies in IFRS have to be careful to not fall into a trap.

In other words, by falsely increasing the collection of receivables or recategorizing the receivable as non-current, and delaying a payment of accounts payable, the company increased its cash flow from operations during the year by $620,000.

Table 9.3 shows the possible impact of this manipulation on the company's valuation.

Table 9.3

	Option X	Option Y
	($thousands)	
Cash Flow From Operations	$ 2,750	$ 3,370
Valuation Multiple	× 8	× 8
Company Value	$22,000	$26,960

In this example, we focused solely on a company's manipulation of current items. The company did not manipulate its net income plus non-cash amortization. That Category A figure of $3,250,000 remained constant under both options. In our experience, cheats who manipulate current balance sheet items usually manipulate net income, as well, often by fiddling with revenue and expense figures. This makes the company appear even more attractive than it really is. In many of these cases, IFRS easily allows these and other cons to occur. For example, write-ups of inventory dollar amounts were prohibited for decades. IFRS permits certain write-ups, which lead to premature recording of income.

THE IMPACT OF INVENTORY

In the last example, the company manipulated its current assets by reducing its accounts receivable by $275,000. Companies can do this in various ways, such as by shifting them to a long-term category.

If the company decreased its inventory by $275,000 instead of reducing its accounts receivable by that amount, we would see a much *different* impact on its cash flow from operations. Because of the $275,000 reduction of inventory, the company would have to increase its cost of products sold by the same amount on the income statement.

As a result of this increase in expenses (i.e., the cost of goods sold), the company's net income would drop by $275,000.

Thus, we have two *offsetting* effects:

	Increase	Decrease
Category A (Net income plus non-cash amortization)		$275
Category B (Current items except for cash)	$275	

Net effect on cash from operations is nil.

Unlike the reduction in accounts receivable, the reduction in inventory has no impact on overall cash flow from operations. The decrease in net income offsets the increase in current items. Among other matters, this offset illustrates the close relationship in the cash flow statement between net income and current items. When investors look for schemes, they should consider the impact on both categories.

SUMMARY

For growth and survival, companies have to manage both their profitability and their liquidity. But as the example in this chapter shows, including changes during the period in current assets less current liabilities (except for cash itself) in cash flow from operations leaves room for manipulation. In our example, an honest company may subtract $500,000 from its current items (Option X) while a cheat can add $120,000 to the same company's current items (Option Y) while the income statement, adjusted for non-cash items, remains the same in both cases. Instead of believing the all-powerful (but vulnerable) cash flow statement, investors have to monitor these cash flow figures closely to avoid falling victim to another Ponzi or other scheme.

Companies don't play around with their cash flow statements unless they want to cover up financial weaknesses. In some cases, incompetent management has made costly errors over several years and then cooks the books to cover them up. In other cases, such as Sino-Forest Corporation, management could have something else in mind.

Investors should also remember that they're on their own. No one else has their best interests at heart. In the case of Sino-Forest Corporation, as we've stated, none of the following alleged gatekeepers noticed anything amiss:

- Board of Directors
- Provincial Securities Commissions
- External Auditors
- Stock and Debt Underwriters
- Financial Analysts
- Lawmakers

Investors should remember this when the next major Canadian financial failure occurs.

10

Nortel and Its Clones

In Chapter 8, we referred to an approach used by Nortel Networks to circumvent one set of accounting rules by creating another means altogether (pro forma earnings).

By no means is this all that we can learn about tricks from Nortel. By the time the company failed, costing investors billions of dollars, the company had inserted a number of subtle warnings in its financial reports that it wasn't as healthy as investors had been led to believe. For the most part, these warnings were not adequately analyzed, and were ignored.

Nortel might have come and gone, but those warnings continue to appear in the financial reports of other companies. Here's an example from another company:

These ... financial statements have been prepared on the basis of the going concern assumption, meaning the company will be able to realize its assets and discharge its liabilities in the normal course of operations. However, certain adverse conditions and events cast significant doubt upon the validity of this assumption. [The note then expands upon the doubt.]

The problem for investors is that this material appears in the *notes* to the financial statements. To find such gems, as well as information on revenue recording methodology and related-party activity, investors have to look beyond the auditor's report and the other financial statements.

To correct alleged misstatements of revenue and expenses, Nortel had to restate its *audited* financial statements multiple times. But the restatements came long after a prolonged and significant decline in the company's stock price. It did not prevent investors from losing billions, primarily because they believed the company's promotional hype and did not analyze its financial statements thoroughly.

After criminal charges were filed against Nortel's senior executives in 2008, a judge concluded that they had not deliberately cooked the company's books. Several civil lawsuits were also filed against Nortel and its management, including actions by former Nortel employees trying to recover their pension savings. Some settlements have been announced. But regardless of the outcome of these legal proceedings, investors will never recover the vast majority of millions of dollars that they lost.

In an important sense, Nortel invented its own method and basis of financial reporting. Nortel then managed to convince the media to evaluate the company based on its invented method. Between 2000 and 2010, the media largely abided by Nortel's wishes.

Basically, Nortel issued two different sets of financial results to analysts and investors. One set of financial results was prepared in accordance with securities legislation and showed significant losses. The other set of financial results, called the "pro formas," showed a profit. Technically, pro forma financial statements include modifications to a company's financial results and are not audited. But guess which set was chosen for the purposes of paying management bonuses?

The reason that Nortel's pro formas showed profits is simple. They did not include certain types of expenses. When expenses disappear, it becomes easy to produce a profit. Similarly, inappropriate revenue was alleged to have been recorded by Nortel. For example:

($million)	
Actual results (loss)	$(40)
Expenses not counted	75
Pro forma profit	$35

Nortel justified its use of pro formas by claiming that certain expenses were unfair and deprived executives of much-deserved

bonuses. Without bonuses, Nortel said, executives would not be sufficiently motivated to work on behalf of shareholders.

Newspapers and TV business news stories routinely quoted only
the pro forma profit figures as a sign of Nortel's success and hyped the
company as the new corporate Golden Goose.

If Nortel had patented its financial reporting inventions, it could
have stayed afloat on royalties from the many Canadian companies
that have since adopted variations of the company's pro forma
reporting techniques for themselves. Like Nortel, these companies
have already cost investors significant amounts of losses, and there is
no end in sight.

Not only do financial analysts accept these pro forma and similar
inventions, encouraging investors to "buy," but provincial securities
regulators have stood by as these tricks have become more popular.
As long as these Nortel clones include in their financial reports some
boilerplate phrases to the effect that the figures do not meet the standards of Canada, then investors are on their own to try to find the
manipulations.

THE EBITDA TRICK

Financial analysts have long become enamoured of a figure based on
Earnings Before Interest, Income Taxes, Depreciation and Amortization, pronounced by the cognoscenti as EBITDA. To arrive at this
figure, analysts look at a company's income statement and then perform the following computation:

	$millions
Earnings before income taxes	50
Add:	
Interest expense	16
Non-cash amortization	14
EBITDA	80

EBITDA then becomes a form of revised earnings, along with its
companions, EBIT, EBITA, and similar.

Analysts explain the logic underlying EBITDA as follows:

1 They are not valuing the shareholders' equity portion of the company, for which interest on debt would be a legitimate expense.
   They are valuing the entire company, which could be financed
   with long-term debt as well as shareholders' equity. In this context, interest is not an operating expense but a financing expense
   and should be excluded from earnings. (To be consistent, proponents of EBITDA argue that dividends on common share equity
   should not be deducted either.)
      The same rationale was used by companies that did not want to
   deduct interest on long-term bonds as an expense when computing cash flow from operations. Financial analysts who accept this
   explanation perform no service for investors.
2 Amortization is a non-cash estimate of the wear and tear on long-
   term assets that a company uses to earn sales revenues and generate a profit. To measure the current cost of replacing assets that
   have suffered wear and tear, analysts who worship at the altar of
   EBITDA prefer to calculate maintenance capital expenditures, or
   maintenance capex. They deduct this expense later in the process,
   referring to the outcome as "EBITDA less CAPEX." This revised
   figure acknowledges that the company cannot tap into its entire
   EBITDA to pay interest and dividends. It must first deduct maintenance capex from EBITDA to allow for the cash necessary to
   replace assets worn out in generating the current period's
   earnings.

   Unfortunately, the following considerations make it easy for cheats
to manipulate EBITDA:

1 All of the individual tricks such as faked revenues and lowered
   expenses that can be applied to the income statement can seriously alter the "earnings before" (EB) portion of the EBITDA
   formula.
2 The income statement may show misleading figures for amortization, depending on management's choice (under IFRS) to value
   depreciable assets at cost or at their current value. If management

chooses the lower value in calculating maintenance capex, then it often leaves insufficient cash available to replace out-dated or worn-out equipment. Whether the company replaces the equipment or stumbles along using its dilapidated assets, future earnings will decline.

3 In calculating EBITDA, a company does not have to include cash income taxes (as opposed to deferred, non-cash taxes). Yet they obviously have an impact on earnings. Investors should examine a company's financial reports for references to income taxes and their impact.

ADJUSTED EBITDA

The usage of "adjusted EBITDA" and similar alternatives has to be analyzed carefully. The actual companies cited in this chapter have experienced significant stock price collapses, such as up to 50%. Not all users of these alternative measures are troubled companies. But enough are, to call for special attention to their computations.

Because many analyst training courses do not teach elementary financial-reporting scams, too many analysts do *not* confirm the integrity of a company's numbers when compiling their reports for investors. They simply believe the financial statement figures on which a company bases its EBITDA. When this doesn't give cheats enough room to manoeuver, some of them opt for more flexibility. These companies resort to "adjusted EBITDA" to manipulate revenue and income and eliminate pesky expenses from their so-called profit calculations. Often, the amounts are far from trivial.

Despite the significant dollar differences between a company's reported net income and its "adjusted EBITDA," analysts and the media often accept the adjusted figure (as they did with Nortel). Many seldom ask whether management is using this figure to calculate bonuses or to make the company look good before issuing new stock.

Nor as matters now stand in Canada is there anything illegal about hyping a company's adjusted EBITDA. But investors should still regard the term as a warning about a company's possible manipulations, as the following examples show:

1 *Aimia*: Listed on the Toronto Stock Exchange, Aimia was previously known as Aeroplan. The company offers airplane flights and other rewards to its loyalty customers. In a recent year Aimia made two questionable decisions in calculating its adjusted EBITDA:

(a) bringing forward estimated future revenue to include it in a current year's profit, and

(b) counting distributions from a Mexican affiliate as income rather than as a reduction on the balance sheet of the cost of acquiring the affiliate.

In return for a fee, loyalty companies like Aimia issue points to sponsors such as credit card companies. The credit card company then awards the points to individuals who use its credit cards. The individuals can redeem the points for rewards such as airline flights. They may wait to redeem their points for 30 months or more after receiving them from the credit card company.

The recording of revenue by a loyalty company like Aimia depends on whether it uses conventional accounting methods or adjusted EBITDA. Under the rules of conventional accounting, the company records revenue only after the ultimate customer – the credit-card user – redeems the points and uses them to purchase an airline ticket or other reward and the credit-card company issues a cheque to pay for the reward. In other words, companies like Aimia record revenue only after they know with reasonable certainty what is will cost them to provide the reward (such as the cost of an airline ticket).

In calculating adjusted EBITDA, Aimia recorded revenue on the date when it issued the points to the credit card company. As we've mentioned, another 30 months or more could pass before Aimia would be able to calculate income (being revenue minus expenses). The expense or cost of delivering the service would be known when the service was actually purchased. Under adjusted EBITDA, the company has to estimate the future cost of providing the reward and also estimate the number of people who will not redeem their points at all. (This latter estimate is recorded as "breakage").

In effect, with adjusted EBITDA, Aimia records revenue before it can determine its costs. Conventional accounting rules did not allow companies to do this. (As we'll discuss in more detail later in the book, IFRS often seems to take a different approach.) In any case, a company can inflate its profits substantially by using adjusted EBITDA, versus what is shown in its audited financial statements.

In its approach to its Mexican affiliate, Aimia's accounting choices should not even be debatable. When one company buys another company's shares, it can count as income only the profits earned *after* the date of acquisition. If the other company earns zero profit, it cannot pass along a legitimate earned dividend to the purchaser. In Aimia's situation, its Mexican affiliate made profits before Aimia arrived on the scene, but in the year after Aimia bought its shares, the company earned little or no profit. Any money that it distributed to Aimia should have been regarded as a rebate, similar to the rebates given by car companies to reduce the cost of a new car. Rather than defining this rebate as income, Aimia should have defined it as a return of its own capital. But for the purposes of adjusted EBITDA, Aimia chose to record distributions from the Mexican company in 2010, 2011, and 2012 as income. To add insult to injury, some financial analysts accepted Aimia's contrived income when they calculated the company's value, helping to drive up the stock's price.

2 *Mainstreet Equity*: Another company listed on the Toronto Stock Exchange, Mainstreet did not call their approach "adjusted EBITDA," but legally built it into their regular audited income statement. (A lengthier explanation will be provided when we delve into IFRS and its extreme biases that have been granted to corporate management to make valuation guesses and thereby alter income.) Mainstreet, like Aimia, looked ahead to future or hoped-for values for its real estate properties and in essence included the increase in values for a future year into their *current* year's income. Such manipulation, reminiscent of the 1920s build-up to the 1929 stock market crash, is permitted by loose IFRS.

As always, investors must ask why such tactics are being chosen. For example, has management received greater compensation as a result? Does management hold significant stock options? As an investor, do we know management's motivations?

3 *Just Energy*: This Toronto Stock Exchange company has sequentially employed more than one of the Nortel pro forma ideas described earlier, including adjusted EBITDA, embedded margin, which we'll describe in a moment, and various combinations. In Canada, they comply with our weak reporting rules, and all have been offered by Just Energy as alternative financial reporting mechanisms, in addition to what is required by our Securities Acts.

The alternatives were advocated by the company as being "better methods of measuring the company's success." They were also the basis for significant management bonuses for attaining financial targets. As stated, investors must determine the basis for management compensation to discover which choices, or perhaps games, may have been selected for the company's financial reporting purposes. Sometimes, ratios and restrictions required by lenders cause companies to use adjusted EBITDA or similar measures.

Just Energy's adjusted EBITDA calculation essentially was based on *not* immediately counting in its calculations certain selling, general and administrative expenses. Hence, adjusted EBITDA was a much larger figure than audited income. Excluding expenses obviously had the effect of increasing earnings.

In order to sign up customers for its energy distribution business, Just Energy had to pay considerable marketing costs. Significant amounts were curiously permitted by the Board of Directors, Securities Commissions and external auditors, among others, to be recorded as assets on the company's balance sheet. The marketing assets on the balance sheet then had to be amortized/expensed over the life of any revenue contracts that were signed as a result of the marketing efforts. So cash marketing expenses became non-cash amortizations, which are an add-back to EB in the EBITDA calculation, and thereby creatively increase cash flow from operations.

Just Energy's thoughts apparently were that some of the marketing costs would be beneficial for several years in the future and therefore should not be called expenses. Given the absence of proof, many people would likely disagree. What would happen, for example, if large numbers of clients did not renew their initial contracts or simply stopped paying the company?

As with other Nortel clones, eventually the earnings mountain becomes too steep to climb. In Just Energy's case, if renewal of contracts was not occurring at profitable prices, more money had to be spent to maintain an aura of profitability. Where should the money that was spent be recorded? More in assets? Or more in expenses?

Just Energy often marketed their contracts door-to-door in residential neighbourhoods. Some US states and Canadian provinces were passing laws to prohibit such marketing.

If too much had already been dumped on the balance sheet as dubious assets, the excess spent had to become an expense. Next problem: How does a person hide the increasing amount of expenses? At first, adjusted EBITDA was chosen by Just Energy to exclude many expenses. But, when necessary marketing expenses continued to increase, something new had to be arranged. Adjusted EBITDA would have to ignore just too many expenses and would lack credibility.

Along came "embedded margin" and a new basis for calculating executive bonuses in Just Energy. Whereas adjusted EBITDA did not count large amounts of expenses, embedded margin ignored *all* selling, general and administrative expenses.

Embedded margin was just a different name for gross profit. (See Appendix 1 and the Sino-Forest financial statements.) Apparently, the chosen term was confusing enough to deceive several analysts, who did not comprehend that gross profit did not come close to net profit/income. When selling, general and administrative expenses eventually were deducted from embedded margin, along with other expenses that had usually not been included on the company's income statement, very little profit, if any, remained.

Lacking strong, fully independent oversight, self-regulated auditors stepped aside and allowed these alternative measures of profit and operating cash flow to occur. Investors' money often went into the pockets of financial manipulators instead of creating new jobs and strengthening Canada's economy.

DIVIDEND YIELDS

In addition to misleading investors with various financial manipulations, public companies also pull off yield scams, comparing dividends to adjusted EBITDA, for example.

In the era of low interest rates that began in the early part of this century, it was inevitable that financial cheats would rush to cook the books and pretend they had enough profit to pay a high, enticing dividend per share. Canadians have been repeatedly duped into paying high prices for a company's shares, based solely upon the dividend yield.

Just Energy's share price was closely tied to the dividend rate that it was paying. While several analysts did not anticipate dividend cuts that should have been obvious, based on the company's pro forma shenanigans, Just Energy announced two dividend cuts that resulted in dramatic drops in the company's share price between 2012 and 2016.

Just Energy's year-end financial statements for 2013, 2014, and 2015 are worthy of study for investors curious about the company's permissible accounting creativity.

CONCLUSION

As companies have switched from EBITDA to their own, special creation with names such as "adjusted EBITDA" or "free cash flow," investors and lenders should realize that a financial manipulator will choose whichever creation most flatters the company and attracts the most money from investors. Too often, management's bonuses are also tied to the most flattering set of numbers. Two birds with one stone results: conned investors and fat bonuses for executives. Virtually no worthwhile regulations are in place in Canada to prevent such behaviour.

Some companies switch the basis on which bonuses are calculated from year to year. The basis chosen, unfortunately for investors, will be whatever produces the highest executive bonuses.

Summed up, investors must watch for companies that assert that pro forma profit, or adjusted EBITDA or some similar choice is the "best way to evaluate the company." When you see such words, check the company's annual securities filings such as proxy circulars to ascertain how management bonuses are being determined. Such information can prove to be a good clue that the time has come to sell your shares or to not buy in the first place.

In our view, Nortel clones are out of control in Canada. They have been given full freedom, through lack of regulation, to invent whatever figures they choose to report. Eventually, the balloon bursts, at each investor's expense. Yet reporting laws in Canada remain unchanged. Nortel clone companies continue to invent their own alternate, but legal in Canada, financial reporting rules. IFRS not only makes it more difficult to conduct financial investigations, it also gives excessive power to corporate management to cover-up.

Sometimes, though not always, a company presents two sets of reports, one of which complies with Securities Act requirements. Each set of financial statements requires analysis to determine which is more worthy of belief. Watch for the basis on which management's bonuses are being paid, and whether dividend yield games are being practiced.

In the meantime, for investors, Canada remains the old wild west. Lawmakers, by their inactions, apparently think that no change is needed. Trusting the self-regulators is beyond dangerous. Investors are definitely on their own.

Why the differences? Our horse racing tracks in Canada with wagering facilities are required to test horses, especially race winners, for any evidence of doping or drug variations. Such has been the case in Canada for over 60 years. Yet, the equivalent of testing for financial statement doping of the numbers is largely unregulated. Try to explain these types of differences to your friends. Who administers the drugs? Who should be tested?

11

Related Party Nastiness

Financial reporting by public corporations has several inherent limitations. These limitations are rarely explained to readers of financial statements. As a consequence, bad investment decisions are made because faulty assumptions have been made.

For example, as a generalization, financial statements are comprised of:

1 *Quantified* dollar amounts that are shown on balance sheets, income statements, cash flow statements, and other supporting financial statements or schedules. These amounts are interlinked to form a financial statement package.
2 Notes to the financial statements, which are commonly used:
   a To provide additional descriptions of how the dollar quantifications were assembled and some of the implications. A company may set forth its policy of recording revenue/sales and the conditions that must be met in qualifying revenue for recording purposes.
   b By financial manipulators to meet some legal requirement, but they avoid providing enough information to tell the full story.

Journalists and many analysts focus almost entirely upon the dollar financial statement quantifications and not on the notes. Phrases appear such as "the company's recent results exceeded the earnings per share estimates of analysts." Such comments are misleading in the following types of situations:

- The analysts were previously told by a company to expect a lower number per share than it eventually reports, so that the company appears to have done better and merits praise.
- The books have been cooked more successfully than was previously expected to be possible.
- An unusual transaction occurred, such as a gain was realized on the sale of long-term assets.

A quantified dollar obsession is akin to quoting a person's IQ to explain his behaviour. (He had a heart attack because he had a low IQ.)

In some situations dollar financial statement quantification has to be relied upon, primarily for administrative reasons. Income taxes, for example, are based on a percentage of quantified taxable income. Similarly, for convenience, an annual bonus may be based on a quantification, such as 5% of income for bonus purposes.

In these types of dollar-quantified situations, note disclosure becomes irrelevant. Your family cannot eat 5% of a note showing how income for bonus purposes has been calculated. You obviously need the actual bonus money to be able to buy food.

In short, we have to know when oneness dollar quantifications make sense, and when note disclosure applies. All too often, accountants do not address such important distinctions: the result is published nonsense.

The subject of related-party transactions, or self dealings, brings us face-to-face with dollar quantification versus mere note disclosure and how at times they become incompatible. Similar situations arise elsewhere in financial reporting, such as for long-term estimated liabilities such as the costs of restoring the land and surroundings for an eventual exhausted mine or oil and gas operation. Such estimates may involve wide variances between low and high estimates.

Financial manipulators can smell out such loopholes in financial reporting requirements. Then they take advantage of vagueness and loose rules.

Indeed, vagueness, loose rules, silence, contradictions and too much freedom of choice for corporate management are good descriptions of the components of IFRS. As we will see, many IFRS note disclosures are useless to investors, as well.

Given that IFRS's treatment of related-party transactions is extensively note-disclosure-based, we will return to this topic later in the book. In this chapter we will primarily concentrate on the way self-dealing cheats have functioned in Canada.

Our main focus is upon public companies, but private companies can be seriously manipulated, as well, using IFRS processes. Shareholders who own 5%, 10% or so of a private company have to be aware of financial games and self-dealing. The deceptions in private companies usually involve large dollar amounts related to outrageous expense accounts, for example, that are unfairly obtained by the majority shareholder.

With most self-dealing situations, *one* party is *both* the buyer and the seller. An example would be when the chief executive officer of a public company is permitted to choose her/his salary and bonus amounts. (Such tends to occur when the Board of Directors is made up of "friends" of the chief executive officer.) Clearly, the chief executive officer cannot bargain on behalf of the company and also on behalf of herself/himself. All too often, personal dollar benefits to the executive will be the winner in such an arrangement.

What should happen in such situations is that truly *independent* (and perhaps multiple) sources of market value data for wages and bonus should be obtained to support the utilized dollar figures. However, Canada's financial reporting rules (essentially having been worded by external auditors) have not sufficiently required that independent market values be obtained for financial reporting purposes. Perhaps an exception would be when sufficient scepticism exists about the quantum of money involved, and the dollars at stake are too large to ignore.

Instead of absolutely requiring adequate proof about market value prices being used in self-dealing transactions, the reporting rules have required only, often vague, note disclosure. The measurement dollars that would be utilized for self-dealings therefore would be whatever the self-dealer chose. Hence, the "door was left wide-open" to possible problems.

In Canada, the requirements to report self-dealing can only be described as pathetic. Extensive thefts occur frequently because weak reporting rules have consequently been written to aid the cheats, and ignore investors.

Canada's external auditors promoted IFRS and other inferior reporting and made unsupportable claims about their alleged merits. But the introduction of IFRS to Canada greatly opened the doors to more related-party financial games.

IFRS claims that it is conceptually founded upon the use of current values. But it is not, because permitted exceptions are extensive, including the use of vague notes. Related-party transactions are but one huge example. In fact, IFRS was a step backward from the unsatisfactory state that existed previously in Canada.

SELF-DEALING BASICS

Without a strong, independent Board of Directors in a public company applying appropriate governance, corporate management retains considerable freedom to benefit itself at the expense of shareholders and others. Self-dealing or related-party transactions remain ill-defined. Regulators and external auditors have avoided dealing with the subject, and over many years. In broad terms, the following types of financial activities involve self-dealing and related-party transactions, structured to benefit corporate officers and board members:

1 Salaries are increased beyond market values for individual officers;
2 Bonuses, and bonus plans, are enhanced for executives, and are based on management-set bases or rules;
3 Expense account entitlements become bloated, including what constitutes a reimbursable expense;
4 Promotion expenses are increased (and could strangely extend to the weddings of daughters and sons of corporate officers);
5 Terms of loans granted to executives become enhanced, providing minimal interest rates, extended repayment terms and loan forgiveness, allowing them to acquire a larger home, allegedly to entertain possible customers, for example;
6 Meetings held in vacation resorts become typical corporate expenses;
7 Share or stock options are granted, on generous terms. At one point in Canada, back-dating was utilized so executives could

exercise options to buy company stock at a previous price that
was lower than its current price;

8 Executives and their relatives are permitted to be on the payroll
   of related companies;

9 Loosening of rules are permitted for receiving gifts from suppliers, clients, and others, for personal purposes;

10 Similar benefits are devised that would otherwise not be received
   if the recipient were not an officer or director of the public
   company.

In addition to murky ground rules addressing these situations, the
definition of family members regarded as being related parties is
unclear. Full disclosure to shareholders should be provided, but is
quite spotty in many Canadian companies. Spouses and children of
executives thus share in the deceit.

Non-disclosure or trivial reporting of self-dealing has always been
a major shortcoming of financial reporting, but IFRS made matters
worse. Given that IFRS was supposed to be designed to report current
instead of historical costs, promoters of IFRS sharply *backed-away*
from requiring full reporting of departures from the usage of fair
market values. Flimsy note disclosure replaced previous Canadian
requirements. Thus, shareholders are even less aware that corporate
executives and their friends are fleecing them.

As self-dealing becomes more prevalent in Canada, our Criminal
Code needs re-writing. Our courts also need to re-think some of their
decisions in which shareholders were abandoned to predatory corporate cheats.

At a minimum, financial statement notes have to be analyzed carefully as related-party manipulation reaches crisis proportions in Canada.

THE ISSUES

Traditional Canadian financial reporting (prior to IFRS) was largely
confined to recording when third-party bargained transactions
occurred between customers, suppliers and others. The prices involved
were mainly (but not always) known, because they resulted from an
independent bargaining process for each product or service provided.

That is, third-party terms and other specifics were generally needed before a transaction could become recorded. Deceptions still occurred, but it was more limited than it is today.

What has made matters more troublesome for investors is that the growth of corporate acquisitions and international activities has significantly increased the volume of self-dealing transactions.

Previous to IFRS, investors had to interpret note disclosures provided by a company to ascertain such matters as:

1 which entities or people were involved in the suspected transaction and who might have benefitted if fair market values had not been utilized? (Avoidance of providing adequate information would be relatively easy.);
2 how frequently such transactions have occurred, and is a worrisome trend developing?;
3 why market value information was *not* obtained, assuming the disclosure note is vague. Was the transaction too complex?;
4 were crucial terms clearly defined, such as the definitions of related parties such as brothers and sisters of the chief executive officer;
5 the dollar difference between fair market value and the agreed upon price.

As self-dealing becomes more prevalent in Canada, the following are some of the favourite tricks. Board members or executives:

· own buildings that they rent to the public company;
· own aircraft that they rent to the public company;
· own companies that supply goods and services to the public company;
· receive discount prices that are excessive.

AN EXAMPLE

Canada has seen many situations where companies owned by a director or officer buy from or sell to the publicly traded company that they manage. For instance, a director may purchase land from an unrelated party for $5 million through his private company. One month later, the director's private company sells the land to the publicly traded company for $12.5 million.

Where did the $12.5 million figure arise from? Are similar pieces of land being sold for similar amounts? Did some friendly appraiser decide that the price was reasonable? Or were the publicly-traded company's shareholders being swindled? The absence of third-party, unrelated, independent bargaining can cast a cloud of doubt over what occurred. Nevertheless, self-dealing has become commonplace in Canada because the financial reporting requirements do not mandate the use of sufficient independent evidence.

Financial reporting of these related-party transactions has always been generally weak in Canada. Partly this is the result of lawmakers' acceptance of inept self-regulation in place of a serious oversight body to monitor selected activities. (To be fair, other countries have been slow to improve their auditing and reporting of related-party transactions. The US has tightened its rules over the years, and did so again in 2014.)

To return to our example, if the public company should have paid the fair value of $8.5 million rather than $12.5 million for the land, the $4 million difference should appear on the public company's balance sheet as a receivable due from the director's company in the form of a refund obligation for the excessive price. That's not likely to happen. No company in Canada, to our knowledge, has ever included on its balance sheet an amount labelled "Due from swindler." This means that either all related-party transactions are being conducted in Canada at fair market value, as our courts seem to think in their recent decisions, or the financial schemes are being ignored.

Yet we know, beyond any doubt, and especially from evidence tied to the many failures of financial institutions in Canada over the past 30 years, that real estate and similar appraisals used in company financial reports are often materially different from fair market values. (We'll discuss these failures in later chapters.) We've seen, for example, property falsely mortgaged for over $300 million that has later been sold to independent third parties for $100 million, even though environmental and economic conditions have not materially changed. Clearly, the mortgages were based on falsified figures in a maze of self-dealings.

PROTECTION STEPS

In brief:

1 Canadian governments have pretended for several years that the country does not have many white-collar scammers.
2 Blatant conflicts-of-interest are being ignored.
3 Inept self-regulation is tolerated by lawmakers.
4 Lawmakers take advice from seriously conflicted persons.
5 Deceptive transactions are thus being tolerated.
6 Investors have to be alert to self-dealing.

For the most part, auditing rules permit external auditors to merely ask management for the names of the related parties. Unless the auditors stumble over evidence of deception, self-dealing does not require special audit attention and companies do not have to provide market values from clearly independent sources for property, goods and services involved in self-dealing.

Accordingly, investors must:

1 Read notes to financial statements very carefully, especially for large dollar transactions, such as purchases of other corporations. Who was the seller? Are they related? How was the purchase price determined? Was the business valuator (or valuators) clearly independent? Was a merger and acquisition firm engaged, and if so, were they related to board members and corporate executives?
2 Check whether the related-party and other financial statement notes use words like "transacted at verified fair market value." Or do they use vague words that leave the impression that arbitrary dollar figures were chosen? If so, who benefitted from the vagueness and dollars spent? Do you know?

Be suspicious of words such as "the price was approved by the independent members of the board of directors." Does this particular company have truly independent board members?

3 Watch for related-party transactions described in two or more
  financial statement notes. For example, look for wording such as
  "unless as described elsewhere", or "as mentioned elsewhere".
  This may be an attempt to make difficult the task of putting all
  the facts together. Terms such as financing details and interest
  rates could be separated from important matters such as who was
  the seller and who controls the seller. All important details are
  necessary to judge what occurred and whether overall matters
  make sense.

4 Check whether the public company has partially owned subsidiaries? If so, how are the prices of sales made from the subsidiaries
  to the publicly-owned parent company determined? A below-
  market-value price means that the minority shareholders of a subsidiary have been deprived of cash profits. They might later sue
  the parent for minority shareholder price oppression, and incur
  a liability for the public company.

5 Analyze the wording in any note referring to related party transactions. Exactly what are you being told and not told in these
  notes? Which words are being chosen in place of clear phrases
  such as "transacted at fair market value, as established by independent consultants."

    Is there any hint that the company is not really interested in
  specifying market value? Words such as "in the normal course" or
  "typical" may be used to dismiss the significance of self-dealing.
  The actual transaction could be quite unusual, but is being passed
  off as "typical" to avoid attention.

Perhaps the worst offenders are those entities that do not even display related party notes.

We'll return to the topic of self-dealing later in the context of IFRS.
IFRS claims to use current values as its measurement foundation. But
with respect to self-dealing, IFRS simply requires note disclosure,
instead of directly addressing fair-market dollar *measurements*. The
principal issue of shareholders having to pay too much for self-dealing
activity is ignored too much in Canadian financial reporting. Yet, the
frequency of self-dealing is growing quickly.

12

The Saga of Castor Holdings

Castor Holdings Ltd. was a private real estate lender with its principal office in Montreal. From the late 1970s until it went bankrupt in early 1992, it attracted money in Canada from pension funds and in Europe from supposedly sophisticated lenders and investors by promising annual returns of 16% to 18%. Large dollars were then loaned to a small number of borrowers, such as the York-Hannover Group, which owned hotel and revenue-producing properties in cities like Ottawa, Toronto, and Niagara Falls. Other lending was made for development projects in the US. Montreal's Eaton Centre, for example, was built using significant amounts of Castor money, and became one of its larger multi-million-dollar losses.

At some point in the 1980s, increasing numbers of Castor's borrowers became unable to make interest, and some principal, payments on mortgages that became due, and also on other borrowings. Castor's response was to lend them more money to make payments, so that they would pay interest to Castor, but with a twist. Castor operated related companies in Europe and elsewhere. A Castor loan customer that became overdue in Canada could receive a loan from Castor's European division. This deception was a form of Ponzi scheme.

By this same multi-country process, Castor also recorded multi-million dollar increases in its borrowings by buying its own debt, under a disguised name. Overall, none of these schemes were adding more cash to Castor because the cash was merely circular, within Castor in total. Yet, Castor's loan assets and borrowing liabilities appeared to be increasing, thereby giving the impression that Castor was a growing, successful entity.

Probably the most glaring example of circularity occurred in 1990 when $5 million was cycled over a few days in order to produce a total of nine new loans averaging about $5 million each. The same money went in and out of a law firm's trust account nine times in a matter of a few days to create the impression that roughly $40 million had been borrowed by Castor and then loaned on nine supposedly worthy projects. All loans were imaginary, and yet were alleged to have been audited for purposes of the year-end 1990 financial statements.

Meanwhile, Castor continued to record revenue on overdue loans using the bogus mechanism of increasing its loan receivable asset. Castor's Cash Flow Statement did not describe that Castor was paying itself by using circular cash flows. Readers of the financial statements were often left confused by Castor's creative Cash Flow Statement. Reality was that no cash was being received from many borrowers, other than what Castor had sent in circles to itself.

The same lead audit partner (at one of the large Canadian audit firms at the time) signed the audit report on Castor's financial statements year after year, for over a decade. Effective internal checking and follow-up within the audit firm apparently was close to negligible. Worse, the head scammer in Castor held joint investments with the wife of the lead audit partner. So much for independence.

Castor's audit was performed by two separate audit teams: one in Europe; one in Canada. People who worked as auditors in Canada were not permitted to be on the European team (of Canadian-based auditors) at any date. Staff turnover within the separate teams was encouraged, which complicated auditors' abilities to put all the pieces together, over multiple years. Planned auditor turnover of staff was clearly a concern, but investors/lenders did not know that such was occurring.

Friendly appraisals were being obtained by Castor to show that the value of a property on which Castor had loaned money was much higher than Castor's mortgages. Some properties had first, second, third and perhaps fourth mortgages, as a result of money being loaned by Castor to pay itself. As an example, a Castor fourth mortgage would be used to pay interest on the first, second and third mortgages on the same property.

Adding insult to injury, Castor would charge a fee for arranging to provide the fourth (or similar) mortgage. The fee amount was then immediately recorded as revenue each year to give the appearance that Castor's profits were growing.

Meanwhile as each audit year passed, apparently none of the foregoing arrangements was found to be troubling to Castor's external auditors. Independent appraisals were generally not obtained by the external auditors to determine why property and mortgage values were increasing. Sufficient tracing of cash did not occur in order to ascertain that it was circular, and was not increasing as a total.

A large portion of Castor's loans were to a theoretically related party, the York-Hannover Group, which was facing liquidity problems. Audit follow-up appeared to be minimal, at best.

Valuation letters prepared by Castor's external auditors were sent to investors and lenders roughly twice per year. Per share values of Castor magically were increasing at a steady pace, thereby conveying that Castor was financially healthy. Combined with the signed external audit reports on Castor's financial statements, investors were being deeply misled.

In 1992 and 1993, all of Castor's equity and much of its debt was wiped out, because it was heavily artificial. Assets of over $1 billion before interest (according to Castor's financial statements) generated trivial amounts on liquidation of the loans. Fees of liquidators and initial fees of specialists left essentially nothing for those who had lent to or invested in Castor. An extensive number of lawsuits were commenced in 1992 because Castor's wealth in actuality had long been a myth.

COURT JUDGMENTS

To minimize the complexity of Castor's case, the Superior Court of the District of Montreal, Province of Quebec, heard a representative case. [*The Estate of the late Peter N. Widdrington (Plaintiff) v. Elliot C. Wightman et al (Defendants)*.] The court's ultimate decisions were slated to become binding for the other cases. By the time the case made its way through the court, one judge had excused himself because of illness. His successor did not render a judgment until April 14, 2011 (nearly 20 years after Castor's collapse). The English-language decision runs to 781 pages. Here's the opening sentence: "Time has come to put an end to the longest running judicial saga in the legal history of Quebec and Canada."

Evidence in court about financial reporting, accounting and auditing focused on the years 1988, 1989, and 1990, the last three years for which audited financial statements of Castor had been released to shareholders and lenders. A separate, auditor-based share valuation for Castor was dated in 1991.

The Court's main conclusions were:

- the audited consolidated financial statements of Castor for 1988 (1989 and 1990) are materially misstated and misleading;
- Coopers & Lybrand (C & L) failed to perform their professional services as auditors for 1988 (1989 and 1990) in accordance with generally accepted auditing standards ("GAAS");
- C & L issued various other faulty opinions related to Castor's financial position during 1988 (1989, 1990, and 1991), (valuation letters and certificate for legal for life opinion);
- the governing law is Quebec civil law;
- [the plaintiff's] reliance on [C & L's] professional opinion was reasonable;
- as a direct result of C & L's negligence, [the plaintiff] did suffer some damages and shall be indemnified by C & L accordingly.

These decisions were upheld in 2013 by the Quebec Court of Appeal. An out-of-court settlement was eventually reached after the Supreme Court of Canada declined to hear the appeal of Castor's external auditors. Payments to investors were pennies on the dollar. Several minor plaintiffs had settled with the defendants early in the litigation process, for undisclosed amounts. Needless to say, litigation costs were in the multi-millions.

In all, more than $2 billion was lost in the Castor failure, yet most Canadian investors have never heard about Castor.

In essence, Castor was merely repeating the same financial games we saw in a series of failed financial enterprises involving Hercules Managements, Victoria Mortgage, Standard Trust, Confederation Life, Northland Bank, Canadian Commercial Bank, and several credit unions.

The trick is simple. Get a friendly appraiser to provide an inflated value for a piece of real estate property, such as Montreal Eaton Centre. Then, use the bloated appraisal number to record an inflated mortgage loan receivable on the balance sheet. Then, to offset the inflated asset, *increase* the revenue figure on the income statement. This will improve profits but, above all, will not indicate any additional expense for a bad debt or an uncollectible mortgage loan on a hotel or shopping centre property.

For example, suppose that a $75-million mortgage had been placed on a rental building at an annual rate of interest of 15%. If the annual interest account was *not* paid in cash to the mortgage company, the mortgage with its accumulated interest over the first five years would be as follows:

	($millions)		
	Current Year's Interest	Cumulative Uncollected Interest	Principal Plus Interest
Beginning of First Year			75.00
First Year at 15%	11.25	11.25	86.25
Second Year (15% on $86.25)	12.94	24.19	99.19
Third Year	14.88	39.07	114.07
Fourth Year	17.11	56.18	131.18
Fifth Year	19.68	75.86	150.86

This accumulation of principal plus interest may have happened for a number of reasons, such as:

1 A large tenant in the rental building could have gone bankrupt, causing a cash shortage.
2 The general economy could have soured, leading to unpaid rents.

3 A fire or similar unfortunate event could have taken place, delaying occupancy initially, or re-occupancy.
4 The rental rates were unrealistic and space rentals were slow,
   while expenses remained high.

Suppose further that the building had been appraised at the beginning of the first year at $100 million. The $75 million first mortgage
would therefore be for 75% of the building's supposed value at that
time. Dependent upon which problems arose, the building's value
could have declined, or not have increased by very much.

Now the swindlers come along. Here's what they did in Canada
prior to the mid-1990s, when financial reporting rules changed, and
what they're beginning to be able to do again under IFRS:

1 They obtained a friendly appraisal report stating that the value of
   the building was not $100 million but $250 million.
2 They increased the mortgage receivable asset on the balance sheet
   in our example above each year from $75 million at the beginning
   of Year 1 to $150.86 million at the end of Year 5.
3 They recorded the uncollected interest each year as interest *revenue* on the income statement.
4 They did not recognize that the uncollected interest and principal
   may not be collectible and therefore did not record them as a bad
   debt expense.
5 Instead, they gave the impression in their financial statements that
   all was rosy and wonderful until the mortgage company collapsed.

So, prior to the mid-1990s, how could financial institutions:

1 Increase the mortgage receivable asset on their balance sheet
   by the amount of uncollected interest?
2 Increase interest revenue on the income statement even though
   no cash had been collected and no additional collateral security,
   beyond the real estate itself, had been pledged?

The quick answer is that vague rules of financial accounting and
reporting in place at the time allowed them to do it. Specifically, there

was no reporting-based rule that prohibited such an increase in the mortgage receivable asset, as long as some form of a fake appraisal existed.

After the collapse in Canada in September 1985 of Northland Bank and Canadian Commercial Bank, the rules in Canada were eventually tightened to make it more difficult to record interest revenue on loans. An arbitrary 90-day or so cut-off period was introduced, over time. That is, since the mid-1990s:

1 If interest receipts remained overdue for 90 days, a company was typically not supposed to record further uncollected interest as revenue; and
2 Uncollected interest accrued over the 90-day period would have to be reversed where possible to reduce the current year's interest revenue; and
3 The company would have to record a bad debt expense for the uncollectible principal amount (up to $75 million in our example); and
4 Any restructuring of the mortgage terms, such as lowering the interest rate or permitting delays in payments to the lender, that would reduce the value of the mortgage, would require a bad debt provision or expense.

These revised rules remained in place in the CICA Handbook until 2011–2012, when IFRS came into effect and they were largely no longer applicable.

Prior to the mid-1990s, (except for specific financial institutions) financial cheats could increase the balance of the mortgage receivable asset if they had obtained a real-estate appraisal that suggested that the receivable could be collected. In our example, the scammer could raise the value of the $100-million property to $250 million based on a friendly appraisal that assumed:

1 Perfect conditions, such as 100% occupancy at top rates.
2 Unrealistically low operating expenses.
3 An unrealistic interest/discount rate. (We've discussed the impact of interest-rate manipulation in earlier chapters.)

With the introduction of IFRS into Canada in 2011–2012, rules that had disallowed such games for more than 15 years were eventually abandoned. Once again, cash receipts became less important because vague phrases such as receiving "economic benefits" (which means what?) became acceptable in place of ensuring cash receipts. Unreliable appraisals became acceptable again, as they had been before the mid-1990s.

IFRS allows variations of the same games as Castor Holdings performed. Once again, investors have to read accounting policy notes carefully to determine how loans and mortgages receivable are being valued and to determine how and when interest revenue is being counted.

Given Canada's history of financial institution losses for investors and taxpayers, reverting to pre-mid-1990s reporting can only be described as embarrassing. Who the decision makers are in these types of financial collapse situations cannot be ignored. Research is essential; prosecutions are vital.

MESSAGES

The Castor case exposed a number of weaknesses in the Canadian financial reporting and securities administration arenas, even though Castor was not listed on a supposedly regulated stock exchange. Castor obtained its cash mainly by selling units of shares and debt in Canada and in Europe, in what are often described as private placements.

Investors/creditors alleged that share valuations prepared by Castor's external auditors, as well as the audited financial statements, were materially misleading. Ultimately, the Courts agreed that the auditors and valuators were negligent.

Investor losses from the Castor Holdings collapse could have been prevented by moderate early action. As with Sino-Forest, basic oversight of alleged audited financial statements would have caught the deception.

Despite the mounting losses incurred by investors, our lawmakers have continued to ignore the financial collapses of the past 30 plus years. What is worse, they continue to believe that self-regulatory bodies have matters under control. They need only to talk to investors to learn otherwise.

As the case of Castor Holdings wound its laborious way through the courts for more than 20 years, it gave Canada a bad name in Europe. Canada acquired a reputation for complacent regulation, particularly of large private companies, and for deficient auditing practices. Criminal proceedings took so long to contemplate that the main participants in Castor left the country, largely untouched, with all their ill-gotten money, while police and prosecutors were still mulling over the situation.

One specific issue in the Castor case is especially noteworthy:

· At some point, investors and lenders should have become suspicious about a company like Castor. Castor had promised returns of 16% to 18%. Was this too good to be true? If so, and the lenders decide to cease providing money, a Castor-like company quickly collapses.

Why the external auditors did not pursue the 16% to 18% promotion rate is yet another matter; but, it is worth contemplating.

FINANCIAL REPORTING AND AUDITING

The court concluded that Castor's financial statements for 1988, 1989, and 1990 were materially misleading and that the auditing fell below accepted standards. The tactic of inflating its loan receivable assets and its interest revenue was easily traceable to the fact that cash for interest on the loans was not being received by Castor from its borrowers. The auditors failed to notice, but investors could have if the right questions had been probed.

Investors could also have seen whether Castor could generate adequate cash flow from operating activities (as opposed to financing activities or investing activities). To do this, they have to:

1 Focus on the operating activities section of the Cash Flow Statement to ascertain from where the needed cash is being received. Accounting games can distort totals, as we discussed

when we described Sino-Forest's amortization techniques, and other manipulations. Nevertheless, questions should have been asked of management and others.

2 Determine whether the operating activities cash flow figures have been manipulated, faked, contrived or cooked. In Castor's case, the important dollar figures were being hidden in a misleading way. Better disclosure should have been requested.

3 Evaluate whether the operating cash flow can support the quoted (by the external auditors) market price of the entity's common shares.

To raise its needed survival cash, Castor was borrowing money and selling shares. This is *not* a favourable sign, unless the new money is mainly being used to acquire additional revenue-generating products or services. The basic business (before adding any new money) has to be evaluated for its ability to generate operating cash flow. Borrowed cash that is being diverted to keep alive a disguised operating cash flow that is negative is more than worrisome.

Yet, we see this basic *failure* to reconcile cash flow from operations to reported profits year-after-year in analysts' reports to investors. Such a red flag could not be larger.

Castor's revenue was not cash-based. Mostly, it was derived from accounting games: increased loans receivable and increased revenue; no new cash. In the case of Sino Forest, the deception was easily detectable. In Castor, a manipulated cash flow statement made detection more difficult. Castor's revenue was *not* cash-based but was an addition to loans receivable. Financial institutions in particular are vulnerable to such manipulations. This same problem of confusing cash and non-cash unfortunately is built into IFRS, as will be explained later.

There are exceptions. New or start-up businesses are inclined to have negative cash flow from operating activities for a few years. So-called functioning companies, however, have to be watched carefully. Insufficient cash to pay dividends is but one manipulation that has repeatedly been covered up in Canada.

Castor's deficiency also involved the income statement and *noncash* revenue. Nortel Networks had a similar, very serious problem with revenue that was never received in cash. Nortel's trick was to show the receivable asset as a long-term investment. Indeed, many Canadian financial collapses (especially in financial institutions) have arisen from overstated revenues. In other industries, collapses have occurred because so-called revenue customers did not actually exist.

NON-CASH REVENUE

Some types of financial manipulation are much more devastating than others. In Canada, non-cash revenue has repeatedly been utilized to bilk money from investors, and the situation will only get worse as a result of our adoption of IFRS. It permits revenue to be recorded on flimsy grounds, such as the mere existence of a 50.0001% probability of receiving "economic benefits" (whatever that means). Recent amendments to IFRS have maintained the more likely than not, 50.0001% figure.

Previously, the revenue recognition criterion in Canada was requiring reasonable assurance instead of a probability of a legitimate sale having occurred. Reasonable assurance has been defined in the professional literature as a "high level of assurance."

In US GAAP, for example, as it is supposed to be applied in roughly 2018 and later for public companies, "high level" is being defined as greater than a 70%–80% probability of cash collection. In contrast, under IFRS, 50.0001% is sufficient. Hence, IFRS allows corporate management considerable freedom to record questionable revenue and dubious assets. Investors should watch for how practitioners eventually apply new rules.

Castor was recording revenue on its income statement by inflating loans receivable as assets on its balance sheet. But, there is more to the story.

In financial institutions, a distinction is needed between payments of interest by borrowers (an income statement transaction), and repayments of the principal amount that was originally borrowed (a balance sheet transaction). The receipt of interest theoretically produces revenue for the lender. Repayments of principal merely reduce the loan receivable asset on the lender's balance sheet. If the principal cannot be collected, it becomes an expense (such as a loan loss), at some time in the future.

Theoretically, uncollected interest should result in a *reduction of previously recorded interest revenue* on the lender's books. But a problem can arise if the non-collection of interest occurs in the year after the revenue has been recorded and reported by the lender. If this happens, the years cannot be matched up so that the interest revenue can become nil for that specific bad loan in that particular year.

Castor's recorded revenue year after year, even though little or no cash was being received from the borrower. Occasionally, years later, Castor might record a bad debt expense when the loan receivable was definitely beyond all hope of collection. Under Castor's accounting, the loan receivable consisted of two elements: uncollected interest revenue accumulated for many years and original as yet uncollected principal.

Castor's accounting methods had the effect of showing faked interest revenue in growing amounts. Interest accrued each year on previously uncollected interest, and the loan receivable asset kept increasing. As time passed, interest revenue increasingly became built into the loan receivable. Here's how it worked:

	$million
Original principal loaned	100
First year's interest at 15%	15
End of first year	115
Second year's interest at 15%	17.25
End of second year	132.25
Third year's interest at 15%	19.84
Principal & interest at end of third year	152.09 million

Interest accrued on previously accrued (non-cash-receipt) interest assured Castor of an increased amount of interest revenue year after year. The huge hole in the Castor approach, however, was that *no* cash (or minimal cash) was actually being received to operate the business. Rent, wages and taxes still had to be paid, so cash had to be borrowed to fund negative operating activities, which created an inevitably doomed pyramid scheme. In short, Castor used a fake revenue trick to cover up insufficient cash being generated from operating activities.

Unless a company accounts for uncollected interest as a reduction of interest revenue (and not as a later bad debt expense) on a timely basis, it will dupe investors with an *upward trend line in* unwarranted interest revenue. Investors and analysts adore upward trend lines (such as sales growth). Over the years, many analysts have fallen for false revenue trend lines as their basis for valuing a company. Special investor attention has to be paid to checking trend line legitimacy. In Castor's case, increasing interest revenue had been faked. In other cases, seemingly growing sales revenue could arise by buying out competitors. Revenue growth becomes a massive lie because of the absence of cash receipts. If such lies become audited and accepted, investors will surely become swindled.

With this in mind, investors have to monitor closely cash inflow from operations compared to reported income. Sadly, IFRS makes much of these comparisons difficult dependent on the industry.

SUMMARY

The Castor Holdings reporting formula has been utilized in whole or in part over the years many times by several companies in Canada. From about 1995 to 2010, tighter reporting rules curtailed much of this Castor-type games. However, irresponsible concepts such as permitting uncollected revenue to be called revenue are accidents waiting to happen. Financial cheats will clue-in and apply optimistic probabilities as opposed to a higher level of assurance concerning cash receipts.

The Castor case was pursued to its conclusion because it was largely financed by abused creditors beyond Canada's boundaries. Canadians themselves have not taken the necessary steps to protect themselves against financial deceptions. They rely upon others.

Billions were lost in the Castor fiasco. Yet we have not seen any serious progressive action being taken by Canadian lawmakers and governments to head off similar oncoming financial collapses. Instead, we see governments supporting securities *deregulation,* such as IFRS, even though our current self-regulation does not self-correct the financial scams that continue to arise.

Meanwhile, lawmakers ask self-regulators for assurances that everything is under control without having acknowledged the absurdity in their stance. That should tell Canadian investors all they need to know about their lawmakers' attitudes toward them.

13

Revenue Trickery

Overstating sales/revenue is one of the most popular tricks used by public companies to cover-up management inadequacies or other deceptions. Understating revenue to "save on" income taxes is common in private companies. Investors must check a company's ownership and the basis of its accounting "philosophy."

Inappropriate recording of sales/service revenue, which is called revenue recognition, lies at the heart of a large percentage of Canadian financial failures. With most of these failures, the reported revenue often does not really exist, or is for fewer dollars. Nortel, for example, restated its audited revenue downward several times. A company may report year after year in its audited financial statements revenue that is too high (eg, Castor Holdings), or is a fantasy. Some companies could report revenue too early, before they've calculated the direct costs of earning the revenue, for example (e.g., an "adjusted EBITDA" trick). Companies that are in trouble may try to survive by cooking the books over several years, so that directors and officers can continue to earn salary and unwarranted bonuses. Thus, the motivation to deceive investors and lenders can be especially high. Getting caught for deceit in Canadian financial reporting usually is a minimal risk.

Investors and lenders should always read the notes in a company's reports to determine its accounting policies that are being employed for revenue recognition. The wording of the notes will reveal clues about management's ethics. Boilerplate words such "recorded when earned" can be meaningless.

Some companies publish statements that revenue is recorded when ownership is transferred to buyers. Such can also be meaningless.

Vague statements indicate that the company wants to be secretive and doesn't really care about investors. As a result, you may decide that you have to invest elsewhere.

Some companies provide clear explanations of their policies on cash collections and revenue recognition. Many others are brief, and more evasive and should be watched carefully, especially if they utilize IFRS. Companies like Castor Holdings recorded revenue without collecting the offsetting loan receivable in cash. Similarly, Nortel recorded revenue that was offset not by cash but merely as a long-term investment in an alleged buyer. The alleged received asset eventually became an uncollected and dubious item in an imagined or failing company.

IFRS aggravates this problem by allowing companies to record the acquisition of an "economic benefit" rather than the receipt of cash. The company does not have to specify the exact nature of the alleged benefit, when it was or will be received, or the form in which the benefit will be received, such as cash, property or services. Executives of Castor Holdings reported revenue based on appraisal report valuations that showed potential alleged benefits. Investors must look closely at a company's IFRS-based revenue recognition financial statement notes to learn when cash will be received for recorded revenue. If the notes are vague, a clear policy may not exist, which is obviously troublesome.

Whereas amendments to revenue recognition requirements are in the process of being implemented in both the US and for IFRS, important differences exist between the two. How each will eventually be applied in practice will have to be watched closely. No doubt new games are likely to appear, especially with IFRS and its vagueness regarding "economic benefits."

Also worth closely studying in the financial statement notes is the company's policy on the purchaser's right of return of goods, for full credit. Automobile manufacturers, book publishers and department stores may incur additional costs to support a sale or permit the customer to return the product. Hints may appear in notes that revenue reductions are possible. Loyalty companies like Aimia, which we discussed in Chapter 10, issue reward points and then estimate the percentage of people who will never use them. Estimates can vary widely, and companies may record different numbers of points as revenue at different dates, over a period of years, even if the points will never be redeemed. Each industry could produce different point redemption results (e.g., food vs. air travel). Dollars involved are often not trivial.

A complex company has to have a well-designed, well-researched set of policies for when revenue is to be recorded/recognized for different products and services, and for how much dollars. Revenue is obviously vital in the process of earning income, and for receiving cash flows, especially where the cash could be received at a much later date. By understanding the ways in which revenue is legitimately earned investors can read financial statements to evaluate management's credibility, and thereby minimize losses. After all, revenue recognition is the starting point in measuring income and judging a corporation's likely future success. Ethical business behaviour should be evaluated as revenue recognition notes to financial statements are being read.

BASICS

An honest company would record revenue when the following types of information are known, or can be closely estimated in dollars:

1 The main terms of the purchase/sale contract with a customer (such as selling price) have been agreed upon, preferably in writing;
2 The selling price for various companion goods and services can be quantified, and the dates of receipt of cash (or its equivalent) are known with reasonable assurance;
3 All knowable costs of warranties, special installation costs and delivery, and similar, can be and have been reasonably estimated;
4 Costs of development and manufacturing are known or can be reasonably estimated;
5 Ownership obligations (and legal title where possible) have been assumed by the buyer;
6 Rights of return of the product/or cancellation of services have been contractually restricted, and dollar effects can be reasonably estimated;
7 Credit status of the buyer has been checked, and is satisfactory;

8 Sale and delivery are not contingent upon some future event where risks are not known. (The seller's product may be only one component of several, and financing must still be arranged.);

9 Cash receipts and cash disbursements associated with the product/service can be reasonably determined and assured.

Obviously, the industry involved, the currency being utilized, the reputation of the buyer, fluctuations in the economy, and similar can produce other risks. Where dollar estimates become too uncertain, the company should delay its recognition of revenue on its books. For automobile manufacturers, for example, product recalls for unexpected problems can cause problems wherever inadequate estimated liabilities were built into the cost of goods sold. Similarly, such issues as currency restrictions could seriously affect the actual sales dollars eventually received from a foreign nation's buyer. Estimated liabilities have to be credible. The effectiveness of hedges must be evaluated.

Thorough knowledge of the nature of the company's operations and locations are needed to evaluate the reasonableness of the company's revenue recognition policies. In Canadian financial institutions, for instance, we have seen far too much manipulation of revenue because of non-receipt of cash and from inadequate loan loss provisions. In addition, when the sale of a combination of multiple products and services occurs, allocation of revenue to each component can be tricky.

It is important to remember that large companies, such as Nortel and National Business Systems, have been required to restate revenue figures in their published audited financial statements, sometimes multiple times. But such restatements happen long after investors, lenders, and employees have suffered huge losses.

TYPES OF TRICKS

The more common revenue tricks in Canada, likely to become more prominent with loose, management-manipulated IFRS, include:

1 Non-cash-receipts (see discussion of Castor Holdings in Chapter 12);

2 Over-billing to customers based on a company's estimate of future services involving, for example, long-term construction-type contracts. Accounting control systems have to be reliable to prevent revenue overstatements. (System deficiencies led to revenue overstatements in Poseidon Concepts, which later failed.)

3 Shipping to a rented warehouse because customers do not actually exist. Invoices are sent to postal boxes rented by the financial manipulators under false names. (This game of inventing customers is too commonplace in Canada. National Business Systems is but one example.)

4 Stuffing the product distribution channels with more merchandise than the company's wholesalers and retailers will be able to sell is a favourite. Either the retailers will have to sell at drastically reduced prices or they may be able to return the unsold goods after the company's year end. (Called premature revenue recognition, this is a popular trick, used to cover-up a low sales problem in a year, or to con the purchaser of a company).

5 Selling of long-term assets purchased for manufacturing or providing goods or services, but treated for reporting purposes as inventory is troublesome. A company's main business does not involve selling its long-term assets on a regular basis. But, when economic conditions decline, for example, it may sell spare parts for machinery or equipment but call the proceeds revenue instead of a non-revenue gain or loss. Cash from operating activities becomes overstated.

6 Splitting profits on longer-term contracts such as finance leases of three to five years so that a portion can be recorded as revenue today, with the balance spread over several future years has been a favourite for over 50 years. The total revenue to be earned over the contract's life has not changed; revenue has merely been brought forward in time. This gimmick, called front-ending or front-loading of revenue, is often utilized to con bankers into thinking that revenue is growing quickly and the company deserves a larger bank loan.

The problem for the cheats is that they have to keep this type of deception going year-after-year, by signing more of these types of potential front-end contracts. One bad year of not being able to generate new three- to five-year contracts that can be front-ended for revenue purposes becomes a serious problem. The revenue trend line quickly shifts downward, thereby alarming lenders and investors, making future borrowing more difficult for the cheats. Watch for front-ending revenue when analyzing finance companies and various lending institutions.

7 Granting of rebates or credit memos after the financial period has ended. This trick arises when managers are falling short of the sales dollars needed to qualify for a bonus. Friendly customers are asked to double their volumes on their next order to qualify for a special price discount. But delivery to the customer must occur before the company's year end to help the company's managers get their unwarranted bonus. After year end, either the company gives the buyer more time to pay the larger dollar invoices, or the customer returns the excess volume to receive a credit. Many companies have minimal controls in place to ensure that sales personnel receive bonuses appropriately. In these companies, the games may continue for years.

Investors can find clues to such situations by examining the company's subsequent quarterly reports. They also have to understand the seasonality patterns of sales revenue. (A Christmas tree company will record higher sales in one quarter than in others, for example.) But in companies not subject to such seasonal patterns, sales volumes may drop because of excessive faked prior sales and the subsequent after-year-end issuance of credit reductions. Suspicious results in a subsequent quarter help to alert investors to other financial games that are in continuing operation.

8 In addition to granting rebates or credit memos, companies may offer extra discounts for deliveries made in the last month of their fiscal year. Sales volumes increase, so that managers get their bonuses. But investors may lose money because the following year's sales drop. They also suffer in the current year because of the uneconomically granted price discounts.

This same trick occurs when a company is preparing itself for sale at a price based on past period recorded profit. The buyer may later sue the seller for the deceit, but increased costs of litigation discourage some buyers of manipulated companies from proceeding with their claims.

9 Financial institutions, especially credit unions, face problems if
   control systems are not designed well to monitor lending quality.
   Unethical loan officers can make dubious loans in disguised forms
   at excessive amounts. The cash then becomes available to falsely
   pay overdue interest and principal payments on *previously made*
   but non-paying loans. (This situation arose in the case of Castor
   Holdings, and dozens of others.)

   Investors and lenders have to monitor bad-debt losses and loans
that have been restructured to reduce the borrower's cash payments. IFRS allows companies to postpone the recording of bad
debt losses, increasing risks to investors and lenders, and in many
company reports, note disclosure is minimal. Investors have to
examine the next quarter's financial reports to detect games. If
companies do not provide sufficient information to track losses
and loan restructurings and their effects on revenue, they can hide
their losses. Investors should avoid such companies.

   Here's an example of the impact of IFRS on such games. In long-
term construction contracts, IFRS requires revenue recognition
accounting based on percentage of completion. A formula may involve
multiplying the expected profit on the contract by the percentage of
expected costs incurred up to the date of the financial statement:

$$\frac{\text{Cost incurred to date}}{\text{Total expected contract cost}} \times \text{Overall expected profit}$$

$$= \text{Profit earned to date on that particular contract}$$

   The formula results are reliable only if the dollar data has been
honestly assembled. When wide ranges exist in the dollar estimates,
biases enter the picture. But despite all judgment and choice involved,
IFRS freely allows percentage-of-completion calculations.

   Over the years, for example, contracts in Northern Canada have
required the transportation of construction materials to the site during accessible seasons of the year. No actual construction would
occur until all materials became available, on site. Under the

percentage-of-completion formula, the inclusion in "cost incurred to date" of the on-site raw materials would result in a large profit being recorded just for having delivered the materials to the construction site. Similar arrangements could be devised for prematurely recording profits. Thus, the formula has its limitations, and abuse occurs.

In the past, companies used a different method, called completed contract revenue recognition, especially in situations with a high uncertainty about future events such as the building of a tunnel under a river, with all of its risks to possible cost overruns and their impact on profit. Contractors would often not record revenue and costs until the project was complete and dollar effects became known. (Called the "completed contract" method of reporting.)

Now, with IFRS, contractors have to use percentage-of-completion calculations to record revenue prematurely and can manipulate figures by changing their estimates. IFRS has not accepted "completed contract" reporting, with its cautious implications.

In reading notes to financial statements, investors should be on guard for a company that utilizes percentage-of-completion revenue recognition reporting. How is the formula being applied? Check the previous years' financial statements to determine whether later adjustments have had to be made. If so, why?

Although the usual practice in Canada has been to try to materially overstate revenue, the opposite scenario cannot be ruled out. Financial manipulators might also try to drive down stock prices on selected stocks by being excessively gloomy in their financial reporting. This allows them to grant themselves options to purchase shares at much lower prices. They can also re-price previously granted options to the lower price.

A company might also arrange financing at lower interest rates if it can drive down conversion prices on convertible debt. Debt that is convertible into common shares often carries a lower annual interest rate than conventional debt, especially if the conversion price to acquire the common shares is kept low. Investors should look for gloomy press releases that seem to correspond with a company's offerings of convertible debt, or other convertibles.

Unfortunately, financial manipulators act quickly, issuing dreadful news about a company to drive down its stock prices. If you own shares in such a company, you may ride out the rigged market period. But if you think the company is chronically distorting its finances, like Nortel or Sino-Forest, then you may have to walk away and swallow your losses.

SUMMARY

The wording choices used in accounting policy notes to financial statements often provide worthwhile hints about management's ethics. A "we don't care about you" attitude is displayed by note brevity and a failure to address basics such as the timing of "cash collection." Nonsense words such as "economic benefits" (a favourite of IFRS) and "probable" (meaning a 50.00001% chance under IFRS) are likely to be chosen by those who intend to cover-up by being as non-specific as possible. Management may claim that they are employing "principles-based" reporting, which is ill-defined, at best, by IFRS. As we will explain later, the IFRS's list of "principles" remain a mystery. It is not cynical to conclude that, in reality, an IFRS principle has to be "do what you want."

Revenue is the starting point for measuring income. Income is especially important because of the close tie-in to Ponzi schemes, executive compensation, and more. The downplaying of "income" by IFRS should be regarded by investors as being irresponsible behaviour. Unfortunately, IFRS gives priority to the balance sheet and tends to disregard the vital role played by income and operating cash flow statements.

Financial analysts who do not grasp the severe consequences of down-playing income/profit and cash flow from operations will lose your savings. Simply stated, revenue trickery is widely in use in Canadian public companies.

14

Time for a Pause

It seems appropriate at this stage of our coverage to explain what we have tried to outline so far, and where we are headed. Canadian neglect of investor needs, over an 80 plus year period, causes considerable financial interpretation problems; and, multiple variations of financial reporting deficiencies and weaknesses have blossomed in Canada, mainly to the disadvantage of serious investors.

The gap between what investors receive in financial information about US companies and what they can obtain about Canadian companies is beyond huge. Far too much rejection of proposed reforms is occurring in Canada. The deterioration has to be reversed before we reach the stage where essentially no faith can be placed in what is being reported to investors.

Our principal continuing themes are:

1 Money put into your pension plan is at risk of being drained when the pension plan manager invests in companies that employ financial games or tricks. Losses from financial manipulation lower the rate of return that is being earned on your pension money. Most people are not even aware of the dollar magnitude of such losses.

2 Similarly, money placed into mutual funds faces the same risks. Portfolio managers in Canada can also be fooled by financial deceptions. Investors should always ask what annual management fee is being charged on your mutual funds, and do comparisons, while checking annual returns on your investment. Are you winning, or losing?

3 While Canadian lawmakers are inclined to talk that they are being tough on crime, white-collar crime generally receives negligible attention. Canada has not held a serious judicial inquiry into a messy financial failure since the late 1980s. Yet many new forms of financial deceit have been developed, and are being used in Canada on an ongoing basis. Being up-to-date is essential. Educational material for investors is difficult to find, and much investment advertising is misleading in its unwarranted assurances.

4 Many new financial instruments and strategies have been developed for Canadian usage. But reporting requirements have either seriously lagged implementation or do not exist. Holes in reporting requirements are regularly being exploited by financial cheats. Too often, major self-serving estimates become incorporated into audited financial statements.

5 Lawmakers have essentially delegated the policing of financial reporting games to external auditors, based on their politically archaic self-regulation philosophies. However, external auditors have little incentive to police. In essence, the external auditors are typically hired by corporate management, and they tend to give corporate management considerable reporting freedom. Sino-Forest, Nortel, Castor Holdings and many business income trusts are just a few illustrations of ineffective policing that resulted in huge investor losses.

6 Provincial securities commissions have virtually been invisible in curtailing financial reporting games, especially with the latest methods of bloating profit/income and cash flow from sales operations. Unsustainable dividend payout rates have also been overlooked, and have gained in popularity among financial cheats.

7 False impressions about the calibre of investor protection have been provided by various self-appointed protection groups. Many of these have been organized by those who do not favour regulation and policing. Thus, who is sponsoring each alleged investor group has to be researched so that investors reach the conclusion that they have been conned.

8 Various distractions have misled investors into thinking that they are being protected. An example is the often-proposed National

Securities Commission, which has failed to articulate how it intends to monitor, investigate and prosecute financial deceptions. The main promoters of a National Commission seem more interested in simplifying the requirements for issuing suspect securities prospectuses, to draw-in the naive. Any National Commission that is heavily staffed by people who were employed by provincial commissions is too likely to continue with a "hands-off" approach.

9 Canada lives next door to the US (and competes in a proportionate way for investment dollars). The US often has to intervene in Canadian financial failures such as Nortel that affect US citizens. The US has had a securities protection agency since 1933–1934 and has managed to compile files on financial tricks. Canada maintains few records on corporate failures and therefore has little data available to train employees of securities commissions. So far, the RCMP also has had very few successes in reigning in financial cheats. Protection can be close to non-existent in Canada for a variety of financial games; yet, Canadians do not complain until they suffer a large loss.

10 Too many financial journalists repeat nonsense to the effect that Canadian investors and lenders are protected. Yet they clearly have not read court decisions thoroughly nor have they interviewed those who have lost their life savings to financial swindlers. Thus, too many articles are seriously misleading, and needlessly comforting, especially for financial swindlers.

11 Promises by securities commissions to do something about a problem remain unfulfilled. (Reports by the Ontario Securities Commission on the Sino-Forest case, for example, show that regulators are far behind the financial cheats in grasping what occurred, and how easily the deceptions were implemented.)

12 Media comments that forms of punishment do not deter financial cheats and are therefore ineffective contradict what we repeatedly see as forensic accountants and investigators. Ponzi schemes flourish in Canada, for example, because financial reporting does *not* clearly require the full separation of borrowed cash from cash actually earned from sales and service operations. Prohibitions have to be clearly specified and

monitored. Advertising dollar impacts on the objectivity of published financial articles has to be researched.

13 While the media pay attention to US financial failures, they downplay the number of suspect Canadian corporate failures. Far more effort needs to be placed upon having Canadians better understand that they are being deprived of information that is essential for investment decisions. Related party/self-dealing disclosure in Canada, for example, is typically incomplete and misleading. Millions of dollars are being diverted every month from shareholders' resources to various financial cheats. The pretence that securities matters are under control in Canada has to cease. Strong evidence suggests the opposite; deceit has to be curtailed.

14 Some court decisions involving cases such as Hercules Managements have encouraged loose reporting and inadequate auditing. A better balance has to be struck by lawmakers and the courts so that investors are not discouraged from investing in Canada. Supporting mediocrity and easily circumvented rules invites financial games. Lawmakers are simply neglecting investors' risks, while they pour more money into trying to catch tax evaders. It is too easy for lawmakers to remain uninformed when topics are not being researched and nasty scams are not being publicized.

15 Most Canadians do not understand what external auditors do and do *not* do. We hear investors say frequently that "financial statements have been audited." Such a remark misses the main point that Canada's external auditors have been permitted by our lawmakers for over 50 years to choose the wording of Canada's accounting, reporting and auditing rules. Securities commissions in Canada rarely alert investors to what actually happened in failed-company cases. Meanwhile, external auditors often require corporate management to assume responsibility for frauds, for identifying related parties, and for similar games. In recent years, external financial statement auditors have seriously restricted what they purport to examine.

The reality is that junior auditors do much of the audit work and check only small samples of a company's records. They often do not have sufficient experience or knowledge to comprehend the signs of deceit. The chances are exceedingly low that external auditors will address the concerns of a particular investor group. With protection of investors so ineffective, we need a total top-to-bottom restructuring of our Canadian securities protection system. Admissions from lawmakers that investor protection is minimal at best are needed to overhaul a long-archaic system.

16 Financial analyst training and education material is weak, at best, with respect to financial reporting and potential manipulations and deceit. Too many analysts tend to accept at face value, the numbers that are published by corporate management, with no modifications. Hence, too often, a company that is grossly cooking its books receives a "buy" recommendation. We can only shake our heads as the stock's price rises, and no contrary comments or warnings from securities commissions are published. Many examples are being provided as the book progresses.

17 IFRS should never have been adopted in Canada. It is simply "scary." It was recommended, with trivial debate, to our lawmakers by our external auditors. IFRS passes much greater power to corporate management to choose its disclosure terminology and dollar amounts. Oversight of management is minimal under IFRS unless a very strong, independent board of directors takes necessary action. In the absence of a strong board, which seems to be common in Canada, a wide variety of games are easily conducted.

IFRS is conceptually flawed, loosely worded, and silent on many important issues. It amounts to a much lower standard of reporting than what we previously had in Canada. IFRS's serious limitations will receive considerable attention in later Chapters because it aids deception.

We are headed towards showing that IFRS is more than dangerous. It was a dreadful choice for Canada because of our history of neglecting investor needs. Why waste your money investing in Canada if the chances are high that it will be stolen?

SUMMARY

Canada, with IFRS in place, now faces a long road ahead to reach a state where audited annual financial statements and other financial reports can become worthy of belief. Self-correcting mechanisms from lawmakers are not in place in Canada to correct serious deficiencies. Further procrastination and denials by our lawmakers surely will make the Canadian investment environment even more open to abuse. Large losses will continue to have to be absorbed by investors. Some investors will likely abandon Canada and extensively invest in US corporations or Canadian companies that are registered in the US and that utilize US Generally Accepted Accounting Principles.

15

Conning Financial Analysts

In broad terms, financial analysts operate on either the sell-side or the buy-side. The sell-side typically work for underwriters, including banks. That might compromise their independence, because underwriters want them to recommend that investors buy the underwritten shares or debt.

We see too many unbalanced sell-side reports. We also see too many investors who accept the views of sell-side analysts without further analysis of the numbers that analysts have used in calculating liquidity and value. Even investment advisors or mutual fund managers who work at underwriting firms would like to see more balanced reports from the analysts employed by their own institutions. Like investors themselves, they want analysts to write balanced reports that cover the risks as well as the positive issues of a stock or debt issue.

Investors always have to be on guard in Canada. The media do not adequately inform investors when the ratings on a company were written by a sell-side analyst who has a reputation for supporting the company's underwriter group. We repeatedly saw this bias during the business income trust era, and it has continued in many stock underwritings and reports since then.

Investors have to probe into the independence of financial analysts. Many portfolio managers and investment advisors subscribe to non-bank independent research to counter biased sell-side analyst reports. Given the wide consequences of relying on poorly researched reports, an entire chapter is necessary to pull together the potential problems that are frequently observed. Analysts, unfortunately, can give unwarranted credibility to corporate management estimates.

On the other side, the buy-side, analysts tend to be employed by pension funds, portfolio managers, insurance companies and others who buy the securities that are being offered. In general, buy-side analysts try to dig into a company's operations and determine the positives and negatives.

While sell-side analysts' reports are usually available to investors, most buy-side reports remain private. The media usually base their articles about a company's securities on available reports, most of which come from the sell-side. When they refer to "analysts' estimates," for example, those estimates come from sell-side reports. Caution has to be exercised because unwarranted hype can follow a stock price decline, when the initial buyers dry-up. We've seen many examples of a large underwriting firm saying "buy" when independent analysts are saying "sell." Yet the stock price rises because few Canadian investors ask about the independence of the published analyst.

CORPORATE ATTITUDES

In our experience, Canadian stock markets are too frequently being manipulated to a company's advantage. A company that needs money will try to make the best impression possible on a sell-side analyst. Its quarterly conference calls with analysts, for example, resemble a fanclub meeting. You can tell much about a company's worthiness as a possible investment by listening to the questions asked at these conference calls. Weaker companies invite innocuous questions from supportive analysts. In its answers, the company accentuates the positives without mentioning the negatives.

ANALYST FOCUS

In preparing their reports, analysts might focus on one or more of the following valuation approaches:

1 Earnings before interest, taxes, depreciation and amortization (EBITDA);

2 EBITDA less certain expenditures needed to maintain the earn-
ings/cash stream into the future;
3 Adjusted EBITDA, as defined by the company (described earlier);
4 Free cash flow (cash from operations less an amount such as capital expenditures (CAPEX), representing the dollars required to
compensate for wear and tear on capital, such as machinery used
to manufacture products); and
5 Variations of discounted cash flow (described earlier).

With this in mind, management may try to manipulate the figures
used by analysts who evaluate their company.

THE EBITDA FAMILY

EBITDA is a favourite of many financial analysts, but it is relatively
easy to distort. Management just has to focus upon the composition
of the acronym, such as:

EB = earnings before income tax (T);
I = interest expense; and
DA = depreciation and amortization.

The EB portion covers most of the items on the income statement
and, as we've discussed in previous chapters, invites many of the
income statement problems that we see, such as:

- Revenue manipulation, with premature revenue recording, and
long-delayed receipt of cash, that may never be received at all;
- Recording expenses, such as marketing outflows, as assets and
placing them on the balance sheet;
- Manipulating cookie jars up and down for inventory provisions
and similar liability accounts; Cookie jar financial accounts are
those that can be increased or decreased easily because they are
not as precise as perhaps the cash dollars accounts. Estimated liabilities and accounts such as inventory are cookie jars because
they can be increased or decreased by management under IFRS
based on their judgment or biases. For instance, to increase

income unduly, management just needs to reduce a current liability account and place the amount in revenue, or decide to reduce an expense. Cookie jar accounts have to be monitored closely.

· Delaying maintenance-related expenses until the next financial period;

· Settling lawsuits in the next financial quarter to avoid recording losses in this quarter;

· Delaying the issuance of credit notes and adjustments until the next financial period;

· Not writing down assets that have previously been fair valued and have since lost their value; and

· Deferring non-recurring gains or losses on long-term asset sales.

There are many other potential problems, but in brief, much of the deception built into a company's income statement begins with the EB starting point of EBITDA. As well, manipulation of IFRS balance sheet adjustments flowing into the income statement can result in distorted EB figures. Since analysts apply multiples to these figures to help calculate a company's stock value, such distortions will become more prevalent in Canada. The absence of regulatory oversight of corporate management manipulations and few financial penalties for abuses makes matters even worse.

EBITDA that is worthy of use for valuation purposes requires extensive adjustment for non-cash and arbitrary valuation transactions. Yet we frequently see analysts using EBITDA with very few adjustments, if any. Corrections are needed to counteract abuses and long-standing income statement games, such as cookie jars.

The absence of serious adjustments is a sign that an analyst is out-of-date, perhaps to the point of being obsolete.

It is vital to remember that EBITDA typically produces a higher number than net income and can easily be biased from the outset because it does not count interest (I) and taxes (T), among other matters.

Analysts' reports should be scrutinized for which numbers are being quoted. For example, a report from an analyst employed by a large underwriting firm on Just Energy Inc., dated May 15, 2015, repeatedly refers to positive-dollar EBITDA in the multi-millions of dollars. In contrast, IFRS-based net income for 2015 showed multi-million dollar *losses*, which were not mentioned in the company's valuation.

INTEREST EXPENSE VARIATIONS

EBITDA includes the I because it values the whole business, not just the owners' equity portion. To determine a valuation of owners' equity alone, the I owed to bond or debt holders would have to be treated like any other expense, such as wages, and subtracted in arriving at EB. The formula would then become EBTDA (no I), with only income taxes and depreciation and amortization being added to EB.

To increase dollars of interest (I) to present a beefed-up EBITDA, management may count or utilize *all* financing-related expenses as interest expense, including fees paid to financial brokers; to banks for letters of credit; and to lawyers, transfer agents and selected employees. Such tactics raise I and lower administrative expenses thereby increasing EB.

In calculating EB, management may include all interest on convertible debt, which is a hybrid of debt and equity, instead of just a portion of the interest. They may also include distorted figures for interest on a bank's revolving loans. Deposit-taking institutions such as sellers of short-term investment certificates may include some wages of administrative staff in calculating interest. Without clear definitions of each expense category, anything is possible.

If the amount of interest in a company's EBITDA looks dubious you should examine the notes to the financial statements to determine interest rates on the company's debt. Then multiply the interest rate by the principal dollars of debt outstanding. This should provide a rough figure for interest, after adjustments for debt redemptions and replacements. If you detect a significant difference between this figure and the one used in calculating EBITDA, you should question management's reasoning. Quite likely other EBITDA games are occurring and should be identified.

AMORTIZATION

As with the EB portion of EBITDA, the DA portion can also hide large dollars amounts. Capitalizing a lease on a company's balance sheet, for example, by recording it as an asset and amortizing it, and recording an offsetting liability at an estimated interest rate, enables the company to convert a cash rent expense, which would otherwise reduce earnings, into non-cash amortization, which then inflates cash flow from operations. Recent changes in requiring more capitalization of leases will compound the problems of trying to separate an honest portrayal of cash flow from operations from non-cash exaggerations of a corporation's actual success.

Without such balance sheet capitalization, the income statement would show a cash rent expense. But with capitalization, two contrived income statement items appear:

1 Non-cash amortization of the capitalized asset, and
2 Assumed interest expense on the long-term liability.

The IFRS obsession with the balance sheet lies behind lease capitalization reporting. Few analysts have paid much attention to the way management can bypass a lease/rent cash expense and replace it, using IFRS, with non-cash amortization. While the capitalized asset raises problems, the lease liability raises similar concerns. For example, when a company capitalizes a long-term lease on the balance sheet, it has to quantify the created liability by selecting an interest rate based on the rate in the lease contract. It also has to include in its calculation an estimate of the residual value of an asset such as an aircraft at the end of the lease.

When a lease is *not* capitalized, the company records a monthly or quarterly *cash* payment to reduce its unrecorded lease obligation over time. Over the course of 20 years, for example, it makes a series of cash payments and records each of them immediately as an expense. A company can still play games with cash payment amounts, but the problems are more easily detected. Capitalization lends itself to less detectable consequences that mislead investors.

A company may record an aircraft on its balance sheet as an asset worth $200 million, for example, with an offsetting lease liability of $200 million. To offset the asset on the balance sheet, the estimated liability involves interest expense effects, which becomes a non-cash estimate. This results in a significant increase in interest (I), which raises the earnings portion of EBITDA.

To illuminate this problem and unravel the actual cash expense buried in the company's report, analysts have to perform the following calculation for each period:

Increases in EBITDA in the time period:	($Millions)
Amortization	10
Non-cash interest expense	7
Decreases in EBITDA:	17
Rent expense no longer being charged	9
Net increase in EBITDA, courtesy of IFRS	8

Analysts do not routinely make such calculations, drastically altering their EBITDA figures for companies in industries in which company assets are often leased.

Companies also use the freedom of IFRS to justify capitalizing short-term assets on the balance sheet instead of recording them as basic cash operating expenses. Once again, with this capitalization gimmickry, they convert cash expenses into non-cash amortization and spread the expense over a couple of years instead of expensing in one year.

Loose IFRS rules tend to encourage such reporting. Some analysts fail to adjust their reports to address these issues when they compare companies.

IFRS was supposed to lead to more uniform reporting throughout the world. But since accountants and auditors do not apply judgment in a uniform way, IFRS has clearly failed to accomplish one of its primary objectives. IFRS also provides many alternative methods of reporting, to further impair possible comparability.

Such defects were obvious even before Canada adopted IFRS. But our lawmakers handed over decision powers to external auditors.

Investors thereby suffer, because they are unaware of the extensive downsides of IFRS.

Separating cash operating flows from non-cash transactions and keeping earned profits away from non-arm's-length management exaggerations is vital in preventing Ponzi schemes. Consequently, the matters now being discussed have widespread consequences.

To make matters worse, analysts followed the same approach in preparing their reports before and after the introduction of IFRS. In our comparisons of reports from 2012 with reports from 2009, we found few differences in their technical approach even though Canadian companies had adopted an entirely different reporting system. Multiple-year financial charts, for example, are often dangerously misleading. By comparison, when Canada changed from Fahrenheit to Celsius to measure temperatures, meteorologists had to amend their calculations accordingly. But when companies adopted IFRS, many analysts carried on with business as usual, which led to inappropriate comparisons and conclusions.

Instead of utilizing a new set of analytical and investigative techniques, analysts made some adjustments but carried over many of the same methods that they'd used under Canadian GAAP. Recognizing this discrepancy, management sometimes took full advantage of the opportunity.

It is vital to know, when reading financial statements, the basis on which the financial statements were prepared: US GAAP? IFRS? Something else used for private company reporting? We frequently see two companies in the same industry being compared even though they use two different accounting and reporting systems, without necessary adjustments being attempted. Thus, misleading evaluations are being passed along to investors.

More importantly, we are also seeing the use of old Canadian GAAP being adopted in situations where IFRS is silent. This shows a dreadful misunderstanding of the differences between the two systems. Further, GAAP is being referred to as the basis for reporting without defining which GAAP (e.g., old Canadian? US?). When it comes to defining each of the accounting systems, we're not even sure that some analysts know the difference.

As we'll discuss in more detail in later chapters, IFRS brought a different philosophy of financial reporting to Canada and weakened some of the rules that protected investors under Canadian GAAP. Most investors remain unaware of the vast differences in philosophy and practice between the two systems.

In short, when you read an analyst's report for a company that utilizes IFRS, carefully check to ascertain whether the analysts made necessary adjustments that we describe in this book.

NECESSARY CROSS-CHECKS

We have been stressing the need to cross-check the important numbers that are being used for investment purposes. In the case of Sino-Forest Corporation, for example, we showed how investors can compare reported income to cash flow from operations to detect discrepancies. Non-current assets on the balance sheet should be compared to cash flow statements. (Investing activities must not be mixed up with cash from operations.)

Here are some other cross-checks that investors should conduct:

1 Dividends should be compared to adjusted cash flow from operations to detect manipulations in income statement items and changes in current accounts except for cash. If dividends are paid from borrowings rather than from adjusted cash flow from operations, a Ponzi scheme may be in effect.

2 Amortization and depreciation expense should be compared to capital expenditures (CAPEX). CAPEX should be subtracted from cash flow from operations to arrive at a figure for free cash flow, from which the company can pay dividends.

Under IFRS, which supposedly emphasizes the current value of assets, CAPEX and current value amortization expense should be similar unless a company undergoes material expansion or contraction. That is, the CAPEX that has to be spent to maintain a company's earnings stream for the future should be close to what was worn out in fair-value terms during the most recent year.

CAPEX in many situations should therefore be just another name for "amortization expense" of current or fair values of specified assets.

When CAPEX is much lower than amortization, it indicates an issue that must be examined further. A single location mining property might have very low CAPEX because there is no point pretending that the business will continue after all of the ore has been extracted.

Minimizing CAPEX has become a common Canadian problem, to hide the extent of dividends that cannot be maintained without Ponzi borrowing.

3 EBITDA should be compared to cash flow from operations. The difference between them might indicate whether EBITDA has been manipulated or might be unrealistic. Cash income taxes and interest expenses are not counted in EBITDA. Yet, cash must be acquired from somewhere to pay these obligations. Ascertain the sources of cash and the applicable interest rate that has been chosen to pay cash taxes and interest. Watch for companies that may be approaching a cash liquidity crisis, because their reported profits are not cash-based.

4 Compare current year EBITDA to previous years to detect significant changes. You may find the company has made changes in an effort to cover up declining profitability and operating cash flow. One-time gains can complicate calculations, including cash flow from operations being overstated.

There are other problems, as well, particularly in specialized industries. Declines in profitability and cash flow from operations are often covered up by manipulating revenue. Expenses that are capitalized to the balance sheet, such as interest and marketing expenses have to be evaluated. Cross-check your suspicions to the income and cash flow statements to detect irregularities.

CAPEX GAMES EXPLAINED

Companies must incur frequent capital expenditures to maintain cash flow and earnings into the future. Inefficient assets require replacement. But while analysts use the term CAPEX, investors should determine whether the term describes maintenance CAPEX or maintenance plus expansion CAPEX.

Maintenance CAPEX represents the dollars needed to replace assets (e.g., machinery and equipment) that have become worn out in producing a current financial period's revenue and cash flow. The same figure used to describe the replacement cost might have been referred to as amortization and depreciation.

Expansion CAPEX reflects the dollars needed to expand capacity or product lines. Expansion dollars are typically not deducted from current cash flows, because the benefits of expansion (increased profit and cash flow from operations) materialize in the future.

With old Canadian GAAP, depreciation and amortization were based on historical cost. Under this formula, the amount recorded for replacing used-up equipment was often less than the current value of the equipment.

Theoretically, IFRS requires companies to report balance sheet assets at current values (ignoring exemptions permitted under IFRS). It thus logically follows for many companies, that for maintenance CAPEX purposes, that amortization expense based on recent asset values should roughly be the *same* amount as maintenance CAPEX. Some analysts thereby delete the DA and use EBIT, with no deduction for maintenance CAPEX. This can be sensible in several situations. However, the EB and I and T within EBIT have their limitations, as was mentioned earlier.

Under the EBITDA formula, management may subtract some trivial amount of CAPEX from EBITDA to keep net EBITDA, or free cash flow, as high as possible. For example:

(EBITDA − CAPEX) x Valuation Multiple = Estimated Value of the Company

Investors must compare amortization/depreciation amounts, shown on many cash flow statements and partially on some income statements, to the EBITDA calculated CAPEX amounts. Low CAPEX amounts relative to amortization requires further investigation. In effect, cash available for dividends can become overstated if little or no cost or expense has been ascribed to the wearing down of plant and equipment. Sadly, all kinds of unusual maintenance CAPEX numbers can be seen in Canada. As long as our securities regulators ignore this problem, it will continue, and expand.

Modified EBITDA, in short, was initially promoted as a way to make companies' profits look better. Financial cosmetics is a growing industry in Canada because IFRS is not being monitored and controlled. Ignoring the issues can be costly.

SUMMARY

The combination of minimal investment oversight in Canada, along with the adoption of weak, ill-founded IFRS, has drastically changed the nature of the investment game. EBITDA, adjusted EBITDA, CAPEX, and similar calculations can be easily manipulated by management. Corporate annual reports display all sorts of creativity, which is growing because of regulatory neglect.

16

Potentially Troublesome Scenarios

As investors become more comfortable with being able to detect individual financial tricks, they should expand their horizon to the monitoring of bothersome, overall business scenarios. Such scenarios enable a financial cheat to expand the time horizon of his/her deceit, thereby drawing-in more victims through the duping of bankers and financial analysts.

We have already explained a few of these common, made-in-Canada, structures that have been utilized for years:

1 Nortel clones that invent their own financial reporting system, which excludes certain expenses and includes dubious revenue;
2 Ponzi-based dividend payouts, disguised by overstating cash earned in basic operations while paying the dividend through borrowed funds, or the proceeds of selling more shares;
3 Taking advantage of loose reporting rules to engage in self-dealing transactions that skim-off excess cash flow and profits to individual executives, while paying a decent enough dividend to satisfy unsuspecting investors;
4 Delaying the recording of losses and then later burying the losses within one year under a windfall gain on disposal of an asset, at a fictitious price, perhaps to a related company.

Even more suspect situations arise frequently in Canada. In some cases, they involve honest companies conducting legitimate activities. But in other cases, they're scams. These situations include:

1 Expansion by acquisition;
2 Repeated borrowings and stock offerings, with much of the money not being utilized for corporate expansion but being diverted into cover-ups;
3 Repeated corporate restructurings and reorganizations, to disguise previous poor decisions;
4 Consolidations of private companies into one public entity;
5 Steady, too-good-to-be-true increases in profits and cash flow from operations, without the full cash actually being received;
6 Renaming and reviving resource companies, especially smaller mining concerns;
7 Companies jumping on the bandwagon of a current fad;
8 Ego-trip companies started by one or more executives trying to repeat the success of a previous firm that they had built and subsequently sold.

While some are legitimate, others can be devious scams. Some fall quickly when they can no longer cover up their financial games. Others prolong the scam by merging with another questionable company, providing their executives with a stream of salary, bonus and perks while investors lose.

EXPANSION-BY-ACQUISITION

Acquisitions may help to strengthen a company. But since 2001 we have seen many suspect situations that eventually have cost investors considerable money. Between 2001 and 2006, for example, many business income trusts with terrible financial backgrounds were bundled together and sold at overvalued prices. This was only the beginning of a trend that continues today.

The ugliest situations, in dollar terms, commenced around 2002, primarily because cheats caught onto a change in Canada's financial reporting rules, which IFRS has now made much worse. For many years, financial reports in Canada had to include goodwill arising from corporate acquisitions, systematically being amortized as expenses over a period of up to 40 years. The goodwill asset was broadly defined as the excess amount of the acquisition price above the fair value of the acquired company's tangible, identifiable assets less liabilities. Refinements after 2001 allowed categories of intangible assets to be classified as non-amortized, as well.

In 2002–2003, companies no longer had to amortize goodwill from an acquisition. Instead, goodwill was to be written down and expensed only when its value dropped. The concept of value was only vaguely defined.

Financial manipulators could now overpay for an acquisition without recording the overpayment as an expense. After that, few write-downs of goodwill were seen in Canada until the recession that began in 2008, when some companies had to expense portions of goodwill that had not really existed for years. In the meantime, companies could inflate profits through an acquisition by recording no goodwill-like expense.

More importantly, the change in the reporting rule passed more power to corporate management to manipulate numbers in their reports. Corporate management were permitted to decide when the value of intangibles had declined.

Here are some reasons why corporate executives would overpay to buy another company:

1 Prior to the new acquisition, the company's cash flow from operations had been declining. By combining its figures with the other company's, it could boost the trend lines of a tired company.

2 The new acquisition could improve a company's sales performance, impressing analysts to recommend its stock based on increases in the company's revenue.

3 By borrowing at low interest rates, after taxes, to finance the acquisition, the company could assume more long-term debt without significantly watering down the return on its equity.

4 As we've explained, thanks to weaker reporting rules, the company could hide the excess purchase cost on its balance sheet for years, without lowering profit.

5 The new acquisition might help the company meet the restrictive covenants of lenders such as the level of required cash from operations. The company can do this in accordance with IFRS by treating annual interest on its debt not as a deduction from cash flow

from operations but as a deduction from financing activities on the cash flow statement.

6 Merging two companies' accounting and reporting systems can generate several ways of manipulating profit and cash flow from operations, so that executives can increase their bonuses without raising questions among investors or lenders.

7 Extra fees on handling the merger, including its financing, keeps the company's lawyers and external auditors happy.

All this can happen without generating any economic benefit for shareholders thanks to loose accounting and reporting rules, which allow the many schemes that are listed in this book.

(We'll revisit the financial games and lax oversight of corporate acquisitions later.)

REPEATED BORROWINGS

Underwriters love company executives who repeatedly provide them with fees for selling debt and equity to the public. On behalf of these underwriters, sell-side analysts have an amazing ability to predict a positive future for a company when others are somehow too blind to see it. Eventually, reality catches up with the hype, much to the regret of unsuspecting investors.

In examining a company, investors should look at the reported purpose and use of the cash that a company borrows. Is it investing the money wisely, at a respectable rate of return on its investment? Or is it using the cash to pay corporate dividends as part of a Ponzi-like capital structure?

CORPORATE RESTRUCTURINGS

Companies try to hide their losses and previous deceit by restructuring their divisions and partially-owned companies. They may move goodwill from one corporate segment to another to avoid having to expense decreases in value. While objections usually cannot be made to the occasional corporate restructuring, concern should exist when a pattern of restructurings develops. Why were they needed so frequently?

Analysts often accept the restructured dollar figures without asking why the restructuring was necessary. Yet whenever losses can be netted against gains, management can hide details of past dubious decisions. Evaluations of management's competence and ethics become difficult when figures are jumbled together.

Some analysts also regard restructuring charges or losses as non-cash items of no special relevance. Rather than emphasizing profit, they put their faith in EBITDA, and the problems that it can produce. Unfortunately, as we've discussed, EBITDA and related free cash flow have their serious limitations, which seem to be misunderstood by too many investors.

CONSOLIDATORS

Private companies often sell at a lower valuation multiple than public companies. For example, two companies may each have annual cash flow from operations of $1 million:

	Private company	Public company
Operating cash flow	$1,000,000	$1,000,000
Valuation multiple: 5 times, or a 20% return on investment	× 5	
8 times or a 12.5% return on investment		× 8
Value	$5,000,000	$8,000,000

Theoretically, by merging the private company acquired for $5 million into the public company, a gain of $3 million in supposed value can be realized quickly. In such situations, investors have to look for several revealing tricks:

1 Self-dealing: Did the executives of the public company buy the private company through their own private company for $5 million, then sell it to the public company for a higher price? Investors not only have to read notes to the financial statements of the public company, they may also have to search public

documents to determine how many steps occurred between the initial $5-million sale of the private company and its subsequent purchase by the public company.

2 Repeated private purchases: The acquisition of private companies may not reduce costs or increase revenue unless the private companies together can be run more profitably than they were on their own. Unless this happens, the market may decide to decrease the public company's multiple, which they use to determine the value of its stock, while you, the investor, are holding the bag.

In the late 1990s, for example, a public company called Loewen Group consolidated many privately owned funeral homes. Investors eventually concluded that the increased sales and operating cash flows on the consolidated financial statements arose mainly from the latest acquisitions, not from increasing sales or efficiencies from the company's existing holdings. Because each funeral home operated as a separate entity, Loewen Group could not significantly reduce labour costs, for instance. For a variety of reasons, Loewen's stock price became volatile, then dropped appreciably for various reasons.

Consolidator-type companies like Loewen Group must be able to benefit through cost savings and revenue enhancements from their acquisitions. The artificial magic arising from an increase in valuation multiple ascribed to the public company may not last.

3 Consolidators may still have to pay a large multiple in buying the private companies, which then have to contribute material increases in goodwill and intangibles. That is, over the years, the private company may have built up its intangible asset value in the form of its status and reputation in its community. If the public company decides to replace personnel in a family-owned business that it acquires, the goodwill could be diminished, even if the expense is not recorded until many years later.

TOO GOOD TO BE TRUE

Some cheats tend to trap themselves. A common example involves making the company look increasingly successful year after year. The trendlines become too good to be true. Especially with IFRS, financial manipulators have ample opportunity to create faked upward trendlines, recording interest on uncollectible loans as revenue, for example, or playing with EBITDA adjustments and CAPEX.

Some companies make matters worse by advertising that they have had numerous consecutive quarters of increasing profits. Investors should always look closely at the financial reporting of these types of boasters.

MISSING ORE

To identify bogus mining companies, investors have to watch for reworked old mines with new names. Their promoters will claim to have discovered more high-grade ore, and they'll want your money to conduct further exploration while the executives remain on the payroll. Securities commissions clamped down on mining companies that made overly optimistic geological reports several years ago, but they haven't eliminated the problem, especially in the way that these companies manipulate their financial reports.

FADS

Investors in Canada often seem drawn to the latest fad, from dotcoms and business income trusts to new technologies all the time. Some of these companies have promise, but many are just problematic money pits. Investors need to ask many questions, and be wary of financial analysts who hype fad stocks on behalf of the underwriters.

EGO REPETITION

Successful executives don't like to remove themselves from their adoring public after they sell their businesses or move on. They believe that, if they did it once, they can create another winner. But previous success may not be repeatable. Conditions change. The talent required to thrive in yesterday's world may not work today. Investors should take extra care before putting money into these reincarnation businesses.

SIMILAR SCENARIOS

Financial manipulators are on alert for weaknesses and gaps in financial reporting requirements. IFRS has produced considerable softness that is being, and will continue to be, exploited. Giving unchecked power to corporate management can have benefits, but also carries serious potential downsides. More examples will be shown in later chapters.

SUMMARY

Too often, a Canadian stock moves up quickly on excessive hype, often because of underwriters' comments aimed at selling more shares. For instance, when one bank partially replaced another as the supporting credit-card issuer for Aimia (formerly Aeroplan), the ensuing hype left investors confused and bewildered. When the dust settled and investors came to their senses and realized that the use of credit cards would not jump dramatically just because Aimia switched banks, its over-blown stock price dropped by over 50%. We warned investors about the likely outcome. But, we were also drowned out by a half-dozen underwriters who wrote "buy" reports.

As we have stated, investors have to cast a sober eye on stocks that are being highly touted. Sadly, a major weakness of IFRS is that its balance sheet emphasis makes analysis of the cash flow statement hard work.

When the above is combined with the ongoing Canadian scenario where the buck is passed from lawmakers to self-regulators, and to ineffective securities commissions, and on to ill-equipped police forces, and corporate directors, with none of them recognizing the dangers of unchecked corporate management power, Canada is at huge risk.

17

Unproductive Audits?

Most investors inappropriately think that they can rely on the dollars and descriptions in a company's audited financial statements when they make investment decisions. But as we've discussed, external financial statement auditors claim otherwise to judges. In court testimony and legal argument, lawyers for the external financial statement auditors have repeatedly stated that auditors do not audit a company's financial statements on behalf of investors; and, as a consequence, investors should not rely on auditors' work in making investment decisions. Where then, under securities law, should potential investors be looking for financial information about a possible investment? In general, Canadian law does not require much supplementary measurement and disclosure.

So why does securities legislation in Canada still require public companies to submit their financial statements for external auditing? Is the law outdated? Is a possible pointless tradition being maintained unwisely, thereby misleading prospective investors?

In this chapter, we'll address the role of external financial statement auditors and the confusion that has arisen over the purpose of their work. In particular, we'll look at:

1 The specific *wording* that auditors use to express their intentions in their reports for public companies and especially their asserted objective to try to eliminate material misstatements in a company's financial statements so that investors and creditors can presumably rely on them. As we've seen in the case of Hercules

Managements, the Supreme Court of Canada has stated that external auditors may have an ill-defined duty to a company's shareholders, but that duty does not extend to investors, mainly being potential shareholders [Appendix 2 indicates that external auditors see their role as primarily assisting investors and creditors. In Courts, however, external auditors state otherwise about investor reliance on audited financial statements.];

2 Discrepancies about the auditors' *role* in auditor training material and in their published rules and concepts under which they practise. These significant discrepancies cause confusion among investors and other members of the public;

3 Major differences between the public's perception of an auditor's work and the actual extent of the processes and procedures that auditors follow in examining a company's financial statements;

4 Court cases that reveal a gross misunderstanding on the part of the public, including bankers, about the role and obligations of external auditors and the extent of their monitoring activities.

The confusion and misunderstanding surrounding the role of external financial statement auditors has led to significant losses for investors and lenders. Simply stated, Canadian law has essentially immunized external auditors, largely preventing successful lawsuits by most investors.

While some attempts have been made in the US and Europe to clarify the auditors' duties, lawmakers and securities officials in Canada have done little to address auditors' duties in this country. IFRS has made the problem even more serious, as deregulation (such as IFRS) and more flexible and alternate reporting standards give financial cheats even more room to manipulate financial statements.

The combination of flexibility under IFRS and vague and opaque auditing procedures means that Canadian companies now produce financial statements that:

1 often adhere to vague, easily manipulated rules that may vary from month to month, as corporate management takes advantage of IFRS to express their optimism or pessimism as they see fit;

2 are audited under procedures that remain unexplained to investors unless a challenge to the financial statements proceeds to
   litigation, and a judge issues a report;
3 are not under any strong surveillance of a regulatory watchdog
   who can assess their quality and completeness and, if necessary,
   apply sanctions to management abuse and inept auditing.

In short, investors have been abandoned in a system where even the
experts are often not able to comprehend what has occurred financially in an entity. Considerable financial losses repeatedly ensue, with
no lawmaker response. As stated in the Preface and Chapter 1, lawmakers have delegated considerable decision power to the external
auditors, who have serious conflicts of interest. Accordingly, they
should not be permitted to be the decision-makers for what constitutes Canadian reporting standards, and requirements for Canada.
Investors need a higher level of disclosure and integrity than what
currently exists.

Canadian lawmakers' continuous support for self-regulation for
financial reporting has played directly into the hands of financial
manipulators, who can point to exceedingly weak IFRS and soft auditor-written audit rules and say that they complied with Canadian procedures while attributing investor losses to bad luck. Unless Canadian
investors restrict their investments in Canadian entities to companies
that utilize US GAAP reporting, they remain vulnerable to such consequences as are described in this book.

HERCULES REVISITED

The 1997 decision of the Supreme Court of Canada in the Hercules
Managements case drew attention to the misunderstandings in
Canada about the role of external auditors. After the Hercules
decision, many investor plaintiffs simply abandoned their cases
against auditors, directors and officers, because they knew they
stood little chance of successfully recovering losses incurred as a
result of misleading audited financial statements. Almost 20 years
later, nothing has changed. In our experience, most investors show

negligible awareness of the Supreme Court's decision and its troubling consequences.

As we discussed earlier, the Supreme Court felt reluctant to expose auditors to "indeterminate liability" for mistakes or negligence that led to investor losses. Instead, the court said externally audited financial statements merely served to help existing shareholders as a group fulfill the stewardship role in assessing a company's management. Unfortunately, such a concept makes sense for shareholders only when management is honest, the reporting rules are clear and tight, and deviations have been policed and corrected. Such is certainly not close to being a description of Canada today.

Canada simply does not have the basic protection foundation in place to support unregulated stewardship. We've already shown in this book and in *Swindlers*, our previous book, published in 2010, numerous examples of corporate failures that have occurred in Canada. Most failures are heavily a result of management manipulation conducted in compliance with Canada's auditor-chosen reporting rules. As we've shown, management can make itself look good by carefully choosing the most advantageous of the available financial reporting rules for their purposes. Investors have to search through various documents and perform their own calculations to find reality.

Of equal concern, our lawmakers have done nothing since the Hercules decision to address this major flaw in the country's financial reporting environment on behalf of investors. They added no protections under securities legislation, nor did they tighten appropriate rules under the Criminal Code. They simply abandoned investors, leaving few credible sources of financial information for investment decisions.

Even if investors and lenders succeed in mounting a class action lawsuit against a financial manipulation, the law places so many restrictions on such legal actions that they only rarely benefit the plaintiffs and almost never lead to a respectful recovery of their losses. With so few successful legal challenges to financial games, the wheels of Canada's investment system may appear to be smoothly functioning, well regulated and unimpeded by dishonest or shady dealings.

But the system itself discourages legal challenges; accounting rules are applied by the very people who benefit from dishonesty; analysts promote companies based on a cursory analysis of EBITDA and other vague concepts; investors continue to fall for management shenanigans; regulators, lawmakers and politicians stand on the sidelines, and external financial statement auditors give their approval to corporate financial reports knowing that they have no one to answer to except the managers who produced the reports in the first place. Instead of asking what's wrong with this system, perhaps we should ask if anything is right?

AUDITOR RESTRICTIONS

Many external auditors build so many restrictions into their audit engagement contracts with public companies that investors should wonder what audits might actually accomplish. Audit reports typically state that the auditors provide "reasonable assurance" that the audited financial statements are "free from material misstatements." "Material" is defined as impacting decisions of "investors and creditors." Yet as we've seen, practical application of this definition can become deeply misleading.

According to external auditors, matters such as detecting fraud, unfair self-dealing, managements' estimates of bogus intangibles and suspect goodwill are not directly covered by an auditor's commitment of "reasonable assurance." Instead, auditors in Canada require management to accept responsibility for such systems and estimates. External auditors require management to sign "Representation Letters," stating that management takes responsibility for many matters.

As a result, auditors seldom expose wrongdoing but instead blame others for misleading them if the wrongdoing leads to litigation. This happens not only in Canada, but in the US as well. Of the 10 declared as the most egregious US corporate accounting scandals in recent memory, such as Waste Management, Enron, and WorldCom, none was exposed by external auditors.

This leads to some interesting, crucial questions. If corporate management is honest, do you need the type of audit that is common today? And, if management are a bunch of schemers, and external auditors are highly unlikely to detect scams, then is an audit a waste of money? In Canada, auditor training and examination requirements have been watered down in the last 20 years, and audits are commonly performed by inexperienced external auditors. What good does any of this do for investors?

Obviously, serious rethinking of the entire system of protection of investors is required for Canada. Such has to be carried out by thoroughly independent citizens. Conflicts of interest cannot be hidden. What other countries have implemented has to be studied.

Regulatory neglect combined with corporate self-interest and political indifference leaves investors exposed more than ever to financial risk. In the face of similar risk, investors gave up on equity investments in Canada in the 1950s and 1960s. They could do it again. Canada is just too wide open to financial swindles, with little follow-up.

AUDITING MISCONCEPTIONS

Years ago the external auditors attempted to address what they called the "Expectations Gap." This was the term that was given to "what the public perceived that auditors delivered" versus what external auditors actually provided. However, the subject was dropped from the external auditors' agenda, perhaps because of court decisions in the external auditors' favour. Having not dealt with the implications, lawmakers' procrastinations have worsened the financial implications, and frequency of financial games.

Misunderstandings continue even as *audited* financial statements fall short of protecting investors, for the following reasons:

1 Auditors utilize small sampling-size methods, much like political pollsters, and actually check very few individual documents. Documents of interest to most investors receive little, if any, audit attention. Even experienced commercial lawyers seem to have difficulty grasping the sampling limitation of audits. Audit sampling from one company to another is neither homogeneous nor uniform, leading to troubling sampling variations that thereby compromise credibility. Statistical interpretation from such small samples are tricky because of a lack of evidence, and uniformity within the population being sampled.

2 Lawyers for auditors have built into contractual auditor-client agreements dozens of disclaimers and passing-the-buck clauses that severely limit external auditors' responsibilities and diminish the worthiness of financial-statement audits. When the external audit is supposed to provide some checking of management's financial results, but responsibility has been turned back to management, a pointless circle has been completed. The benefit to investors has to be minimal; but, worse could be occurring in Canada, and has often happened, as has been described.

3 As we've discussed, successful legal challenges since 1997 of negligent audits are difficult for investors and creditors to win in court. With court-approved minimal external audit duties and vague responsibilities, external auditors have become motivated to look the other way when a client company manipulates its reporting. Investors remain vulnerable to the vagaries of audited, but unreliable, reported financial dollars.

4 Canadians have a baffling tendency to forgive shoddy financial statement audits. For example, on at least three separate occasions, Nortel Networks restated its audited financial statements. Yet hardly a whimper came from Canadians who had lost billions from buying Nortel's hyped, bloated stock, based on these later-withdrawn audited financial statements.

5 Some auditors tried for many years to improve financial reporting in Canada. But, by about 1980 they had received so little support from lawmakers that they apparently lost their enthusiasm for better reporting. By 1997 and the Supreme Court's decision in the Hercules Managements case, they largely had given up. Why try to improve reporting quality when you don't have to, when no one wants to pay for better information and few appreciate your efforts?

Lawmakers could learn from the changing attitudes of external auditors since the late 1970s. Sell-sell-sell has become a major motivation for external auditors seeking more business volume.

6 In the early years of the twenty-first century, external auditors saw a glorious chance to lower their operating costs and increase their revenues by adopting IFRS. At its core, IFRS drastically

loosens financial reporting requirements in Canada, allowing extensive choice with little oversight. The victims of this new scheme are the investors. We have seen countless examples of major cash-equivalent shortages hidden by bloated non-cash accounting estimates. Hiding such weaknesses in a company has been made that much easier by weak IFRS. A fixed-date balance sheet emphasis by definition downplays what occurred between balance sheet dates, such as the reliability of cash flows from operations. Examples are Castor Holdings, Nortel, and many failed business income trusts, where losses would have become much greater under IFRS reporting.

7 The caliber of the people who are performing external audits has dropped for various reasons, including specialization that impedes the view of the overall picture. If the nature of the business is not comprehended an audit is likely to be deficient. Broader training and education of auditors is needed.

8 Regulators in Canada have apparently chosen to ignore do-it-yourself, invent-your-own accounting and financial reporting schemes. In the case of Nortel Networks, for example, which labelled its second set of financial statements as "pro forma" results, a more descriptive term might have been "Hallucinatory accounting."

As we've discussed in detail, the pro forma dollars were being counted the Nortel way. Since then, Nortel clones have followed the same pattern: "If you incur operating losses under conventional reporting rules, then invent your own counting methods." Next, tell the media that your invention better describes the company's progression and success. Many companies have been able to guide our media into believing the created numbers. Many more lie in wait to trap creditors and investors.

9 Self-regulation of external auditors enables them to serve their own interests. The lawmakers of Canada have given external auditors *extreme* latitude to produce potentially, and actually, meaningless audits. If Canada needs risk capital to create jobs, basic protections are essential in order to control financial deceit. Serious auditing could become one of the controls. But as matters now stand, essential improvements in auditing are not

forthcoming. Indeed, recent changes to lease reporting are continuing in an anti-investor direction.

10 External auditors claim to have investors participating on their
financial reporting standards committees. But they can carefully
choose those investors who support the external auditors' interests in maintaining power and control. Flimsy reporting of self-
dealing between corporate directors and officers and their
individual companies is but one disturbing example. Not detecting obvious frauds is another. Investors need a powerful separate, government-funded investor protection *body* in Canada
to offset powerful corporate and external auditor lobbyists.
Otherwise, reporting rules against self-dealing and other
manoeuvres such as giving management greater choices will
continue to become weaker.

11 Lack of awareness of the extent and variety of financial games
encourages more schemes and makes investor education even
more difficult, especially when external auditors do not disclose
the frequency and magnitudes of financial frauds in Canada.
Regulators and external auditors tend to suppress details of
financial collapses, depriving educators, university professors,
and in-house trainers of authentic material to use in their class-
rooms. The ultimate losers are the investors and the country
itself.

Auditors' fees are paid by corporate management. In a dispute
between investors and management, external auditors obviously
would tend to favour the party who pays them. Likewise, instead
of remaining independent, many external auditors are engaged
by client companies to handle tax issues for directors or officers
and their related companies and to conduct juicy consulting
assignments. Lawyers who send business to external auditors
may later want to join a company's board of directors.

Auditors may lower their audit fees in the hope of landing
more lucrative consulting contracts from the client. Although
some changes have occurred in recent years to improve disclosure of fee arrangements, the cozy relations among officers/
directors of public companies and external auditors needs more
examination. Meanwhile, investors do not write the cheques for

financial statement auditors. Where's the motivation to stand up for investors and creditors, unless legislation requires such?

12 The authors of Canada's auditing rules of behaviour are the external auditors themselves. You might wonder who audits the external auditors? The answer in Canada for investors is, "Nobody."

Securities administrators seldom criticize external auditors for writing self-serving rules that exempt them from catching frauds or blowing the whistle on self-dealing or for revenue-faking executives who swindle shareholders for their own gain. The Canadian sanctions assessed by securities officials against Nortel were embarrassing for Canada, because they were trivial compared to what the US assigned. External auditor deficiencies for Nortel have been largely ignored. Self-regulation broke down once again.

13 What might be called severe in-breeding is another reason for dubious financial statement audits. For many years in Canada, the training and education of auditors was primarily left in the hands of the external auditors. Other, smaller organizations attempted to train accountants in industry. For a while these smaller bodies were successful, but, in recent years, mergers of these organizations have brought them all back together. They now toe the same narrow-minded party lines, including support, for external auditors who largely conduct misleading audits with impunity.

The inbreeding affects the attitude of securities regulators in Canada, drawn from the ranks of former external auditors. These regulators virtually never question the self-serving behaviour of the external auditor monopoly. To this day, unwarranted loyalties to external auditors by securities regulators constitute a major problem. Some regulators have even registered formal conduct complaints with accounting bodies against critics of external auditors' recommendations, including adopting IFRS. Pressures against those who are opposed to weak and misleading auditing and reporting are troublesome. A partially hidden "conform or else" to the "party line" theme has drifted across the country.

Overall, the too-cozy relationship between external auditors and securities regulators has caused a long list of hardships for investors and creditors. Very few prosecutions are pursued by regulators against those who engage in dubious auditing. Those prosecutions that are undertaken usually amount to just "going through the motions." Only rarely, such as for the auditors of Livent, do thorough investigations become promised.

DEFICIENCIES

As a consequence, minimal progress has occurred in tackling issues left unaddressed by a range of weak auditing and reporting standards, including:

- Related-party transaction reporting or self-dealing, at other than fair market values is mainly being ignored yet, such arrangements continue to grow;
- The detection of fraud (both fraudulent financial reporting, and corporate internal fraud) has been largely delegated to corporate management itself, which becomes circular, with negligible benefits to investors;
- Details of management compensation, especially the bases for stock options, loans, hidden bonuses, and special "favours" is clearly inadequate;
- Measurement of intangible assets and expensing of losses of their value has been given trivial attention;
- Deceptive techniques that allow expenses to be recorded as assets and revenue not yet earned to be labelled as revenue and similar distortions has become commonplace in Canada; recent changes to reporting rules has not seriously addressed basic schemes, and may have opened the doors to greater investor losses;
- Interest rate manipulation to enable recording of liabilities such as pensions at other than fair market value has become a Canadian favourite; pension liabilities need greater attention;
- Loose monitoring of transactions between partially owned subsidiaries and the parent company to assess whether minority

shareholders receive current fair values has been a longstanding Canadian tactic;

· Allowing corporate management the final power to decide what is "fair" constitutes a major violation of accountability.

Canadians have to rethink where financial statement auditors should fit into our society. Our courts (except Quebec) have protected external auditors on alleged negligence cases since the 1997 Hercules Managements decision of the Supreme Court of Canada. Is such protection warranted? Is it one-sided? Is the protection fair to investors and creditors? Obviously not.

Has the self-regulation protection led to unacceptable auditing in companies that are seeking money from lenders and individual investors? Clearly yes. Has the received money been squandered? From an investor's viewpoint the response is another clear yes. These are the types of questions that have to be addressed, but are being ignored by lawmakers in Canada. Self-regulation has prevented serious discussions of vital issues of how to help to protect investors. Investors are being seriously abused through lawmaker indifference.

CANADIAN SCENE

In our general financial analysis, corporate managers/directors fall into one of three categories:

Category 1: Honest, or honest-enough, producers of credible financial statements;

Category 2: Usually honest-enough, but tempted from time to time to hide bad news, or

Category 3: Those who will take advantage of most reporting loopholes to add to their personal wealth or accomplish personal goals, to the disadvantage of shareholders and others.

Companies managed by honest people in Category 1 do not really need external auditors. Technical questions may arise, but an external audit is not really needed for the public's purposes. But how do you know which Canadian companies fit into Category 1 without some serious oversight and monitoring by governments?

For Categories 2 and 3, financial statement auditors do not really help investors, because the law does not require external auditors to police, regulate, or blow the whistle on management dishonesty. Alleged investor protection provided by the audit safety net simply does not exist. Financial cheats have enormous freedom to con investors and lenders.

So where do external auditors fit into the Canadian system, given their extensive disclaimers of what they *do not do*? Without any doubt, they are not protectors for investors or lenders. Nor do they help in providing reliable, comprehensive financial statements that can be sufficient to evaluate corporate management.

Hence, why are the external auditors being protected, and savers are being sacrificed? The Hercules decision ignored the information needs of investors. Lawmakers' inactions are forcing investors to have to accept seriously tainted financial numbers. Taking away external auditors' motivations to perform worthwhile audits is hardly leadership on behalf of investors, and Canadians in general.

SUMMARY

Investors misunderstand the alleged benefits and severe limitations of external financial statement audits. So do bankers. While they demand audited financial statements to assess a company's credit-worthiness, we frequently have to explain to creditors that these statements were, and still are, misleading. We also have to tell investors and creditors that they will face a tough uphill battle if they try to sue the auditors, who will fiercely deny that they owe any duty of care to bankers or investors. And, this denial is contrary to their proclaimed written objectives (see Appendix 2). Nearly 20 years have passed since the Hercules decision largely took away investor protection. In turn, Canada's external auditors obviously did not ask for legislation to in essence reverse the Hercules decision. This major example of further conflict of interest has been ignored by Canada's lawmakers.

Meanwhile, it was the external auditors who brought weak, variable IFRS, with its deregulation agenda, to Canada. What was promised to Canadians was not what was received. IFRS allows extensive choices. Far from protecting investors, IFRS is heavily management-biased and anti-investor in its orientation.

This bringing of IFRS to Canada should constitute the last straw for lawmakers. Self interest more than trumped the public interest in the "adopt IFRS" lobbying.

If Canadians have concerns about auditing, lawmakers refer them to external auditors for resolution, claiming that external auditors have the necessary independence to investigate financial reporting concerns involving themselves. Such claims of independence make a mockery of the word independence. (See the Preface and Chapter 1.)

Based on the long list of Canadian cases involving misleading financial statements, we think Canadian investor protection deficiencies urgently need drastic attention. The US model could serve as a starting point for Canada. The alternative is a steady flow of losses to unsuspecting investors until investors finally clue-in, and avoid investing in Canada altogether.

One-by-one we are analyzing the supposed protectors or gatekeepers for investors and creditors. Each will be shown to *not* be doing what lawmakers, the media and others would prefer to believe. Investor protection in Canada is rapidly approaching zero, as we will see. Police investigations of white-collar crime in Canada are dismal. And so on. Lawmakers have to show leadership and stop blaming others. Too many Canadian IFRS-based audited financial statements are just fictional.

18

The Livent Inc. Case

When it comes to improving securities regulation and protecting investors with credible financial reporting, we should identify the people who most need such protection. They include:

1 Shareholders in a manipulated company:
   a those who owned the company's shares throughout the period leading to its collapse;
   b those who owned the company's shares for many months, but sold them just prior to the company's final collapse;
   c those who held the company's shares through mutual funds or pension funds in either of 1a or 1b above.
2 Investors (as opposed to shareholders in 1 above) who made inappropriate financial decisions because the company's financial statements had been materially misstated for many years;
3 Bondholders and other longer-term lenders;
4 Short-term creditors, bankers, and
5 Mortgage lenders.

The Livent case, which we discuss in this chapter, primarily involves longer-term lenders. The latest appeal court decision in the Livent case thus merits analysis to determine whether the courts are recognizing the mounting anti-investor biases of our financial regulatory system.

Special attention has to be given to legal differences between shareholders (Hercules) and creditors (Livent). The Livent decision in general does not necessarily translate into a re-thinking of the Hercules decision and does not seem to enhance investor protection.

The main purpose of this chapter is to re-examine whether the court position adopted in the 1997 Hercules case has since been modified by other courts to address injustices to investors. As we've seen, the Hercules case did not directly address what information prospective investors should be able to rely upon for their investment decisions. The court also failed to recognize how financial tricks could prevent a company's shareholders from receiving an honest financial picture of the company. Thus, stewardship oversight was dealt with only in vague theoretical terms.

In the Hercules case, the court virtually ignored the degrees of control exercised by corporate management over the content of a company's financial reports. Since then, IFRS has made the situation much worse. The value to shareholders of financial statements becomes negligible when management uses reporting loopholes to cover up its deficiencies or malfeasance. Indeed, some financial statements just prolong swindles.

As we'll see in this chapter, except for Quebec, equity investors in Canada remain unprotected, and the situation remains unchanged either by recent court decisions or by non-existent new legislation. Accountability to shareholders by corporate management by way of audited financial statements still borders on being a myth in Canada. Creative reporting continues to hide reality, and rarely is monitored in Canada.

BRIEF BACKGROUND

Livent Entertainment successfully produced stage shows in cities such as New York, London, and Toronto, including *Phantom of the Opera*, *Kiss of the Spider Woman*, *Show Boat*, and *Ragtime*. Before the company sold tickets to the public, it incurred significant costs for each show. To cover these costs, it borrowed money, which it repaid if the show succeeded at the box office. It was a high-risk operation.

Livent's financial drama occurred in the 1990s. In the 20 years since then, with opinions issued by civil and criminal courts in the US and Canada and by securities regulators in the two countries, Livent and its management remain a source of controversy for investors and lenders who lost money as a result of the company's deceit. Of particular interest in this chapter, an Ontario court concluded for 1997 that Livent's auditors, Deloitte & Touche LLP, failed to exercise their duty of care in auditing Livent's financial statements, which occurred between 1993 and 1998. The judgment against the auditors, of $118 million plus interest and costs, was upheld by the Ontario Court of Appeal in 2016. An appeal to the Supreme Court of Canada is scheduled for early 2017.

Livent sought creditor protection in 1998. This led to three noteworthy results:

1 Livent's management and its external auditors were sued by Livent's special receiver, financed by the company's major creditors, in civil court in Canada for producing misleading audited financial statements during the 1990s.
2 Criminal proceedings were instituted against some of Livent's senior management for fraud made possible, in part, by Livent's alleged misleading financial reports.
3 Professional misconduct charges were successfully laid by the external auditors' disciplinary body against some of Livent's external audit partners.

So far, at the time of writing:

1 In 2014, Ontario's Superior Court awarded $118 million plus interest and costs to Livent's special receiver in its suit against Livent's external auditors, Deloitte & Touche LLP ("Deloitte"). Deloitte appealed, but in 2016, the Ontario Court of Appeal upheld the lower court's ruling. Deloitte asked the Supreme Court of Canada (SCC) to review the case, and the SCC has agreed to do so.

   Livent's creditors (largely non-Canadians), who financed the suit launched by the special receiver and who will be the primary beneficiaries of the judgment, are now not common shareholders of Livent. Shareholders essentially lost all of their invested dollars.
2 The criminal proceedings against Livent's management resulted in convictions against two of the company's founders, Myron Gottlieb and Garth Drabinsky. After appeals, they served short

prison sentences, a somewhat unusual outcome for stock-related fraud in Canada.

3 After appeals, professional discipline charges against individuals associated with Deloitte & Touche were upheld. They were fined and had to pay for the cost of the proceedings.

INVESTOR NEEDS

Equity investors want to know what is actually happening, financially, in a company so that they can estimate what real, cash earnings are likely to be generated in future years. Such investors want to be able to separate, as much as possible, actually completed business transactions from hoped-for results and from unwarranted management optimism. Valuation estimation processes often commence with the completed cash transactions, employing a follow-the-money attitude. Then best estimates have to enter the picture, for new products, expansion, economic trends and much more.

For such estimation purposes, as much tamper-free dollar amounts have to be compiled as possible. The preferred type of financial statements are those that clearly separate completed and contracted transactions, from the maybe-it-will-happen groups. IFRS fails on this concept alone, but has other serious deficiencies. IFRS allows considerable management tampering, and management can include a mix of actual results and management dreams in one reported figure. Credibility becomes a huge issue.

In brief, equity investors have to know the degree of management optimism, or worse, that has been incorporated into net profit/income, for example, and cash flow from operations. What is fact, and what is something else? By how many dollars?

While IFRS was not adopted in Canada until after the Livent fiasco, in viewing the subsequent court decisions, we have to ask how far the *courts* have progressed with clamping down on overzealous bloating of profits and operating cash flows. (The courts alone cannot control everything that could harm investors, of course. Regulatory authorities should be closely watching for financial games as well.)

The Hercules decision extended generous protection to external auditors, while leaving investors to fend for themselves, using biased figures. Corporate and securities legislation has not changed this situation, while financial cheats have sharpened their skills.

Meanwhile, creditors share some interests with shareholders, but they have to focus primarily on cash flows required to cover principal and interest on debt and on assets pledged to support the debt.

Did the civil court decisions in Livent undo the Hercules decision in any way or provide protection for shareholder investments? Did the courts refer at all to the dangers of giving corporate management such power to hide reality under IFRS? Let's take a look.

IN GENERAL

It's important to keep in mind that the case against Livent's external auditors was funded by the company's creditors, not shareholders. With this in mind, we did not find much in the lower court's ruling to indicate that external auditors would be held more accountable to equity investors. It seemed to maintain the Hercules decision. The Appeal Court decision may prove to be more promising and seems to show greater awareness of investors' risks than we found in the Hercules decision by the trial division.

Based on a balance of probabilities, the trial judge rejected the plaintiff's case against Livent's auditors involving financial statements for the years prior to 1997. Yet, and this is troubling, many of the problems with the company's audited financial statements initially arose in these earlier years. The reporting choices made by management and accepted by Livent's external auditors are precisely the choices that we see to this day across Canada. In our experience, they have led to considerable investor losses, and they should have been questioned by external auditors. Since the Livent decision did little to put a stop to this manipulation, we must have legislation to protect shareholders and prospective investors.

IFRS has seriously aggravated the situation by allowing management cover-ups to continue, with negligible opposition. New games are being permitted by IFRS.

ADDITIONAL INTRODUCTION

In evaluating the reliability and credibility of audited financial statements, the courts have steadily referred to the Hercules case in accepting auditors' assertions that they provide "reasonable assurance" that the statements are free from "material misstatements." Yet, contradictions arise. When material misstatement cases that should have been detected through fundamental audit processes indicate that the auditors have failed in their obligations, the courts still accept the auditors' defence, supported by the Hercules case. Investors are thus left unprotected.

Securities legislation in Canada seems to suggest that investors can rely on audited financial statements to make their buy, or hold, or sell decisions. The CICA Handbook and other documents published since 2011 by the self-regulatory body that oversees external auditors strongly suggests that investors and creditors can rely upon audited financial statements in making investment and lending decisions. As we've discussed, the Hercules case cast serious doubt on these published indications or suggestions, creating much confusion about the nature and purpose of audited financial statements in Canada.

While this state of confusion has reigned for the last 20 years, legislators and securities commissions have done nothing to clarify the issues or alleviate the confusion. Hence, losses continue to pile up. Given the courts' restrictions on the purpose of audited financial statements, laws and regulations could define more explicitly the types of information that should appear in compulsory supplementary reports to a company's financial statements. Clarification regarding self-dealing, for example, should be made compulsory.

Sound legislation should address the confusion arising from audited financial statements by explicitly over-riding the Hercules decision. Instead, the Hercules case continues to leave investors unprotected. IFRS has only made the situation worse, giving corporate management free reign to create fanciful tales in their audited financial reports while corporate directors seem to have little legal obligation to conduct diligent oversight.

As we'll discuss in later chapters, IFRS deregulated financial reporting in Canada at a time when the *opposite* approach had become essential. The combination of court reluctance to help investors who have been deceived along with the deregulation of reporting through IFRS has devastated the investment landscape in Canada.

While the courts have awarded a judgment of $118 million plus interest and costs in the case against Livent's external auditors, we are more concerned with the courts' dismissal of external auditor liability for their acceptance of Livent's financial statements in the years before 1996–1997.

COURT PROCESS

At least four problems arise for investors when attempting to interpret the Livent case:

1 The litigated actions against Livent's external auditors occurred between 1991 and 1997. Except for 1997, all the contested actions in Livent occurred before the Supreme Court issued its decision in the Hercules case.
2 The plaintiff in the Livent case was the special receiver acting on behalf of the company itself and financed by some of Livent's mainly US creditors. The plaintiff did not represent investors who had lost money in Livent in 1996 and prior years.
3 The damages awarded by the lower court related only to the year 1997.
4 The courts in Livent paid considerable attention to auditor-written accounting and auditing standards as they were published for each particular year in the plaintiff's case. Of vital importance is to observe that these "Standards" were written by the external auditors' body. The validity of such wording for Canadian investor purposes was not addressed. For some reason, the court did not refer to the overall purpose of financial statements for investors and creditors, as published at the time in various documents by the CICA. The courts focused narrowly on damages sustained by Livent's creditors in one specific year, 1997.

COURT REMARKS

The lower court decision in Livent, including the following passages, reminds us once again why Canada needs to pay more attention to investor protection from financial deceptions:

1 The judge referred to the Hercules decision in discussing the seemingly non-existent duty of care that external auditors owe to various types of investors. We quoted the following passage in Chapter 4, but it bears repeating:

> *In Hercules Management* (sic) *Ltd. v. Ernst & Young,* [1997] 2 S.C.R. 165, the Supreme Court of Canada held that a company's auditor does not owe a duty of care to the shareholders of its corporate client. The purpose of audit reports is to allow shareholders, as a class, to supervise management – not to assist them in making individual investment decisions. Therefore, shareholders do not have individual causes of action against an auditor. If the corporation suffers losses attributable to its auditor's negligence, then the corporation itself has the cause of action, which may if necessary be pursued by way of a derivative action. [18]

As we have stated, IFRS enables corporate management to create financial statements that make it additionally difficult for "shareholders, as a class, to supervise management," making the Hercules decision impractical, at best. And when the corporation itself pursues a case against its external financial statement auditors, any financial award could typically flow entirely to creditors, leaving nothing for equity shareholders.

Canada clearly needs new legislation to override the court's reasoning in the Hercules case, and extend some protection to equity shareholders.

2 According to Livent's trial judge:

> In my opinion, [Livent's external auditors] should have remained firm in its resolve to sever its relationship with Livent at the end of August 1997 at the earliest, but no later than the end of Q3, or

September 30th, at the latest. The red flags were certainly aflutter by that time. While the Firm, even with the change of audit teams, was clearly aware that Livent's management was more than merely pushing the envelope from a GAAP perspective, it seemed to turn a blind eye to the warning signs, which I attribute to the fact that it was only too amenable to a line-up change, which it thought was the panacea. I shudder to think it was all about the $50,000 fee they received for the Review Engagement undertaken as a pre-cursor to the October Underwriting or the $95,000 fee charged in respect of the 1997 Audit. [201]

Reading between the lines of this passage, the court seems to agree with many of our earlier observations about the cozy relationship between external auditors and their corporate clients.

3 The trial judge added:

To succeed, the plaintiff has to establish that Livent was owed a duty of care, that there was a breach of the appropriate standard of care, that compensable damages resulted from this deviation from the appropriate standard of care, and that the damages complained of were factually and legally caused by the negligence or breach of contract of the defendant. At this stage of the decision, I will restrict my comments to the first two of these elements, namely whether (the external auditors) owed the plaintiff a duty of care and whether there was a breach of that duty. [48]

4 The trial judge further stated:

Livent alleges that the Original Statements were all false and misleading and did not fairly represent the financial condition of the Company. As a consequence, none of the Original Statements was prepared in accordance with GAAP. I am not satisfied on the evidence, however, that the Original Statements contained any errors, material or otherwise, caused by an *unintentional* act or omission. [26]

On the contrary, it was Livent's position throughout the trial that the Original Statements were replete with fraudulent statements and other 'irregularities' created by management and others in concert with management. The means used to perpetrate the fraud included, among other things:

(i)   the use of deception, such as manipulation, falsification or alteration of accounting records or documentation;

(ii) misrepresentation or intentional omission of events, transactions or other significant information; and

(iii) intentional misapplication of accounting principles relating to amount, classification, manner of presentation or disclosure. [27]

The decision stresses in this passage that Livent's external auditors were deceived not by management's unintentional acts or omissions but by management's deliberate efforts to dupe the auditors. This can be interpreted as placing a higher standard on a plaintiff to prove auditor negligence or misconduct. Given the expense involved in such a lawsuit, investors are unlikely to pursue such a case. Instead, we need legislation that would legally hold auditors to account and protect equity investors from auditor neglect.

5 Additionally, the trial judge stated:

the leading decisions in (Canada) contemplate a *corporation* bringing an action against its auditors for failure to detect wrongdoing by directors. [271, emphasis added]

In this passage, the court seems to be inadequately aware that external auditors require corporate officers to sign audit engagement contracts. These contracts pass responsibility for detecting corporate fraud back to the company's management and board of directors. Since IFRS enables management to exercise considerable choice in preparing financial reports, we have to wonder about the definition of "wrongdoing." Given this lack of awareness by the courts and the flexible interpretation of management wrongdoing, we find yet another reason why we need legislation to override the Hercules decision.

We'll look further in subsequent chapters at some of these issues raised in the Livent case.

SUMMARY

Despite occasional feeble gestures by self-regulators and groups that claim to act on behalf of investors, self-regulation in financial reporting remains seriously deficient. Our lawmakers need to pay attention. They can no longer ignore a situation that continues to lead to investor losses and needs their urgent attention. In basic terms, self-regulation has stopped being workable, and must be replaced soon.

As we've pointed out in previous chapters, the following groups and organizations are supposed to safeguard the interests of shareholder-investors:

- Boards of directors;
- Corporate officers;
- External auditors;
- Provincial securities commissions;
- Stock exchange officials;
- Corporation and securities legislators and regulators;
- Stock underwriters;
- Financial analysts;
- Your personal investment advisor;
- Self-regulating bodies that oversee mutual fund salespeople, investment advisors, external auditors and lawyers;
- Our court system;
- Police fraud departments;
- Our Crown attorneys, and
- Our elected politicians/lawmakers.

How is it possible that *all* of these groups could fail to notice oncoming multi-million-dollar financial collapses of companies like Nortel and Sino-Forest and dozens of others?

Our theoretical investor protection system in Canada quite clearly has either broken down or did not exist in the first place. Our negligence, as citizens, lies in not demanding change from our lawmakers. At the very least we need an equivalent type of body in Canada to the US Securities and Exchange Commission. Instead, lawmakers who could create such a body continue to pass the buck, and we allow them to do it.

19

IPO Traps

Many readers may be inclined to believe that we are merely analyzing the few bad apples in the corporate world and that Canada, overall, is a wonderful country for investment. We encounter this rosy attitude in virtually every training session and presentation that we make. After years of hearing fairy tales in advertising and from government officials, investors can hardly believe that financial thievery is out of control in Canada. But unless they wake up to reality, their savings are at continuous risk.

We have learned about this thievery through our own investigations and through court testimony that we undertake. We have seen the feeble defences put forward by perpetrators of fraudulent schemes. We have been attacked for drawing attention to these schemes, including the fiascos involving Nortel Networks and business income trusts. Yet our research continues to confirm not only that the thievery continues, but also that it's being ignored. In fact, our hardest task is to convince Canadians that they are being victimized and that the protection that they think is keeping their investments safe does not actually exist. Changes in recent years to financial-reporting procedures have only made a bad situation much worse.

INITIAL PUBLIC OFFERINGS

When a privately held company turns to public investors for money, it has to make an initial public offering (IPO) and obtain a listing on a stock exchange, which facilitates the buying and selling of the company's shares. Companies can go public in a number of ways, some of which we'll look at more closely in this chapter.

Some IPOs are certainly worth an investor's time and money. But many others should be approached with caution, for the following reasons:

1 Private companies generally sell at a lower price-to-cash-earnings multiple than publicly traded corporations. Promoters sometimes buy private companies at a low price, consolidate them and then take the consolidated company public. By selling shares at an inflated price, the consolidator makes a fat profit and usually walks away before the share price goes back down.

2 Some executives regard an IPO as a ticket to an easy life of inflated salaries, bonuses, generous expense accounts, stock options, and related perks. They give no more attention to shareholders than our loose regulations require, and many regard shareholders' money as their own. When investors are considering purchasing shares in an IPO, they should pay close attention to the background and ethical behaviour of the company's management and directors.

3 On a related note, newly public companies may promise investors far more than they ever achieve. Instead, money raised from investors too frequently goes in part toward increased salaries and bonuses of corporate executives.

4 As we've discussed in earlier chapters, the loose regulations and reporting requirements that enable established corporations to manipulate earnings and cash flow from operations figures can also be used by people involved with IPOs.

5 To sell shares to investors at the highest possible price, management and underwriters of the newly public company too often exaggerate the company's actual and potential value. The shares become overpriced, but when the hype subsides, the share price drops.

6 In switching from private to public status, IFRS accounting and reporting rules give management many opportunities to adjust or inflate asset and income dollar figures. Private companies usually try to keep their taxable income at low levels, for example. Public

companies may then inflate their income to attract more money
from lenders and equity investors.

As we've emphasized in previous chapters, the individuals and
organizations that claim to protect investors simply do not provide
much, if any, protection at all. With regard to IPOs, stock exchanges,
which presumably regulate the types of companies that sell shares to
the public, also receive fees from companies that issue shares through
their facilities. In raising doubts about a company's ethics and honesty, the burden of proof lies not with the company itself but with the
people who might have doubts about its credibility: in other words,
the investors. Exchanges are inclined to accept fees for an IPO unless
they receive especially strong evidence that the company is deceiving
investors. In short, exchanges are fee-motivated to list borderline or
worse entities.

AN EXAMPLE

An all-too-common example in Canada arises when a small group of
manipulators acquires a few private companies one by one from their
unsuspecting owners. The schemers then consolidate these private
companies into a single entity, which they take public through an IPO.
In exchange for selling the private companies to the newly formed
public entity, the manipulators receive generous quantities of shares
in the IPO. Of course, the share value is based on an extremely high
valuation multiple applied to the consolidated operations.

The transfer of ownership of the private companies to the newly
public company is called a non-arm's-length or self-dealing transaction. In essence, the buyer and the seller are the same people. We can
only imagine the hard bargains that these people make when they
negotiate with themselves.

Canada desperately needs stronger rules in place to govern the process of establishing a fair market value for these previously private
companies. Instead, we find companies documenting these IPOs with
passages such as this:

The transactions have been finalized at the exchange amount,
which is the amount of consideration established and agreed to

by the related parties. All transactions ... are approved by the
Company's independent members of the board of directors.

What is wrong with this picture?

1 How could such an obvious self-serving transaction basis for
   price-setting possibly be approved by securities commissions,
   external auditors, and all the others on the list of individuals and
   organizations that claim to protect investors? The process makes
   a mockery of regulation and leaves purchasers of the IPO's shares
   completely exposed to manipulation.
2 Surely, the "exchange amount" is nonsense because it could easily
   have been arranged by one person negotiating with herself or
   himself. Where's the negotiation? It does not exist. Self-interest
   prevails.
3 In Canada, many members of a company's board of directors are
   friends of its major shareholders. The major shareholders involved
   in an IPO have just converted the previously private companies to
   a single public one, in exchange for a large portion of its newly
   issued shares.
4 The term "independent" has become meaningless in Canada.
   "Independent" board members of Sino-Forest Corporation, for
   example, were supposed to investigate the company's financial
   dealings, but did nothing of consequence and never completed
   their overall report. Investors should regard the word "independent" when applied to board members as a warning that something may be amiss.

Investors should also pay attention to the volume of stock options
awarded to corporate executives and board members at the time of an
IPO. Quite often the prices and quantities involved enable these individuals to enrich themselves handsomely at the expense of investors.

Slack rules governing related-party transactions in Canada enable
cheats to fleece investors with impunity. While we don't like to blame
the victims in these cases, we have to emphasize that Canadians merely
encourage the manipulators when they allow these thefts to happen
repeatedly without raising a clamour of protest to lawmakers against
the system that allows this to happen.

With regard to IPOs, after their initial public offering, newly-public companies often issue an increasing number of shares with the help of compliant underwriters who receive a handsome fee for each new issue. To keep the stock price high, management resorts to the tricks that we've described in previous chapters, as well as more to be illustrated shortly.

In brief, read all of the available documents carefully before buying into IPOs.

MORE BASIC DECEPTIONS

We'll refer to IPOs again in later chapters, but for now it seems useful to summarize a few principal concerns about IPOs that investors should keep in mind:

1 Many business income trusts (BITs) were formed by consolidating
   a number of private companies into a single entity, which then
   sold shares to the public through an IPO. From the money they
   raised, they paid large fees to underwriters, lawyers, external auditors and others who sold their businesses to the BIT. Assisted by
   Canada's weak accounting and financial reporting rules, financial
   manipulators who owned shares in these BITs disguised their own
   and others' investment capital as being income and cash flows
   supposedly earned by the BIT.
2 The frequency of IPOs in Canada rises and falls. We regard them
   as the second most successful mechanism for a financial scam in
   terms of dollars lost, after Ponzi schemes. Their success depends
   on a combination of loose financial reporting rules governing such
   practices as related-party-transactions and absent oversight by so-
   called independent directors and biased business valuations that
   reward the manipulators at the expense of the investor.
   In Canada, it is not uncommon to hire a valuator who will
   assess private companies at the highest possible value when
   they're dumped into a public company. As a result, the people
   who sell the private company receive more shares at a price that is
   higher than warranted. Overly weak financial reporting allows
   manipulators to bury the excessive value of these acquired assets

on a balance sheet with other bloated intangible assets. The intangible assets continue to be valued at an inflated level to avoid expense write-downs in later financial periods. With the share price inflated, the schemers ultimately sell their shares and make a tidy profit.

3 Companies that buy other companies can easily inflate income and cash flow from operations and re-value assets. They can do this because, before they became public companies, they operated as a number of individual private companies under private-company reporting rules. As public companies, they can resort to all sorts of games to restate values to reflect the transition from private to public entity. IFRS has produced a whole new field of potential problems, by allowing management to attach bloated values to assets.

A LEARNING OPPORTUNITY

Hydro One initially issued shares to the public representing 17% of the company through an IPO in 2015. Until then, Hydro One had been owned by the Ontario government. The IPO was for $20.50 per share. In the subsequent 12 months, the price rose by more than 10%. The government said it would sell more shares in Hydro One to the public, which it did in 2016.

An interesting question is whether a price of $20–$26 per share is valid. By continuing to watch Hydro One, investors can learn some valuable lessons. Here's what to watch for:

1. Is the price currently being promoted by underwriters in anticipation of further sales of Hydro One shares? (Underwriting fees and more are likely forthcoming.)

2 Hydro One is supposed to pay an annual dividend on its outstanding shares, including those still owned by the Ontario government, of about $500 million. Can its cash earnings support such a significant sum?

3 To replace aging assets and to expand, Hydro One will have to borrow large amounts of cash. Will the bond market support

Hydro One's bond sales? Will the market demand a higher interest rate? Will it place other conditions on Hydro One's debt?

4   Ontario's utilities regulators prefer a financial structure of 60%
    debt and 40% equity in operating companies. If Hydro One sells
    more bonds, it will also have to sell more equity to maintain this
    ratio. Is the stock market prepared to simultaneously buy shares
    from both Hydro One and the Ontario government?

5   More shares sold will require more dividends to be paid. Can
    Hydro One's earnings support the additional dividend demands?
    Meanwhile, by issuing more shares, Hydro One could dilute the
    values of previously issued shares.

6   Will the greater financial risks of the next four to five years
    require Hydro One to renew its debt at higher interest rates?

7   Hydro One has a large unfunded pension plan (i.e., over $1 bil-
    lion) and will have to use available cash to purchase assets for
    the pension plan. It will have to invest these assets elsewhere to
    earn interest and dividends used to pay pensioners.

8   The Province of Ontario already charges relatively high power
    rates compared to other regions in North America. Can it raise
    power rates without losing industries and jobs to other provinces
    and the US? Will customers protest?

9   Hydro One's approximate $500-million annual dividend may
    have been set at an artificially high price. Some Canadians base
    share-price calculations on the amount of the dividend and
    ignore whether the dividend can be maintained over the future
    years. Will Hydro One have to reduce its dividend rate to pre-
    serve cash?

10 Will slow economic growth add another risk? If so, with what
    degree of impact?

Investors should monitor these types of issues in the coming years
and see what they can learn from a live example IPO, like Hydro One.
A utility company is highly unlikely to go bankrupt; thus, the focus in
analysis has to be on the dividend rate in the future, and effects on the
Hydro One share price. Hydro One has to exist in one form or another;
but, at what price per share?

SUMMARY

To avoid being conned in an IPO, investors have to consider the following points:

1 Do the promoters of the IPO have a history of arranging poor performing IPOs?
2 How were the asset transfers to the IPO valued?
3 Who valued the assets, and do they have a history or relationship with the promoters? How many valuations were obtained, especially from competing valuation firms?
4 What are the backgrounds of the individual corporate officers and directors?
5 Pay little attention to statements by external auditors. Many deficiencies can occur, as we've seen in previous chapters.
6 Watch for inflated amounts of goodwill and intangible assets appearing on the IPO balance sheet. Does any substance exist in the amounts?
7 Check benefits that have been granted to executives, such as large salaries, bonuses, stock options and similar perks.
8 What are the sources of cash for dividends? Cash earnings or other?

Always remember that no independent group in Canada is looking out for your interests. It's up to you to detect deceptions in an IPO, and elsewhere in the circumstances that we have described.

20

Watch for the Usual Suspects

In previous chapters we've discussed the financial deceptions in Canada that will only become more prevalent under lax regulation and deeply inferior IFRS. Among other matters, it puts pensions at serious risk and leaves the small investor vulnerable to the cheats and weak companies that exaggerate their financial position.

In this chapter, we'll briefly list some other traps that put unwary investors at risk. Space doesn't allow us to elaborate in much detail how these tricks work, but at the very least, we can draw attention to them so that investors can recognize these potential problems when they encounter them.

The absence of a strong unified investor-protection body in Canada to combat the lobby groups which continue to advocate looseness in financial regulation, tips the scales against investors. The Canadian imbalance of the large number of active cheats compared to fewer unorganized, individual, small investors should be obvious. Canadian governments have so far refused to step forward to combat the growing number of financial cheats; thus, we have to stress self protection for investors.

INVESTMENT ADVISORY ISSUES

We know many excellent investment advisors, but we also encounter some who emphasize sales above ethical service to their clients. Here are the Top 10 considerations to make:

1 Is the advisor registered and in good standing with the provincial securities commissions and/or relevant industry organizations? You can determine this by checking the various websites.

2 Have independent sources confirmed the advisor's credentials and reputation for service?

3 Did someone recommend the advisor? How well, or how poorly, did the advisor perform? Or is the advisor just a nice person? In an advisor, competence, ethics and results matter more than personality.

4 Does your advisor have access to fully independent research? Or do they merely use the firm's in-house research, some of which is designed to sell share issuances that the firm underwrites?

5 How does the advisor get compensated for selling mutual funds? Do they receive an up-front or ongoing fee from the mutual fund company? How much? How much is the annual fee that you pay to the mutual fund company? In Canada, these annual fees are relatively high. Some are passed along to your advisor. Ask how much. And, for how many years?

6 Does your advisor call frequently to pressure you into buying or selling an investment? Are they trying to increase your wealth or are they just "churning your portfolio" to generate trading fees?

7 Does your advisor sell only their own firm's mutual funds? Sometimes it's not evident which products are in-house funds, especially if they are branded under a different name. Make sure you know whose mutual funds you're buying.

8 Does your advisor know how to detect Ponzi schemes? Does she or he recommend that you play the yield game to compensate for low interest rates? As discussed, Canadian companies may inflate their reported income to justify a high dividend rate while actually engaging in a Ponzi scheme. Ask your advisor whether the company can sustain its dividend yield over many years.

9 Make sure that you avoid trading arrangements that you do not fully understand, such as margin accounts, puts and calls, and short selling. Short selling can carry huge risks in Canada. You should also avoid buying new stock issues of untested

companies, especially if the advisor receives higher compensation for the new issue as opposed to an alternative investment.

10 It is a significant risk to not understand all of the fees associated with your account. Some fees are hidden. You have to ask your advisor many questions to be able to understand.

In addition to the Top 10 you should think about:

11 Stock market cycles. The market rises and falls. Your advisor should help you to avoid following the herd mentality, and act as a sober influence.

12 Hype and exaggeration. Just because the media have jumped on the bandwagon to promote a high-flying stock, your advisor shouldn't urge you to climb aboard. How knowledgeable is your advisor about the company and about the suitability of the stock for your portfolio? Stock prices can rise on nothing more than rumours, including those spread by the media. Most of the failed companies that we've discussed, such as Nortel and Livent, were once darling stocks.

13 Mortgaging property to raise investment funds. We've encountered far too many unscrupulous people who convince clients to increase their borrowing on real estate to invest the money in risky stocks. Then they churn the portfolio to generate commissions for themselves while eventually losing money for the client. You should also be wary of reverse mortgage propositions. Some people unfortunately buy into the reverse mortgage concept when it does not make sense for their situation. At the very least, you should understand that the interest you pay on the mortgage might quickly erode the equity in your home over time.

14 Telephone cold calls from people offering to manage your money. Calls can come from untrustworthy individuals or from US bucket shops offering high returns on questionable investments. If you are going to hire a new advisor, get recommendations from several of his or her clients first.

15 Advisors who recommend revamped tax shelters: Vehicles such as limited partnership units in the ownership of a yacht may

sound attractive, but they usually work to the benefit of someone other than the investor. You need expert tax advice before you make such an investment.

16 Investment clubs. Before you join such a group, ask if the members have similar long-term objectives and attitudes towards risk.

17 Some advisors are willing to charge annual fees, instead of a commission on each purchase and sale. Calculate the effects of an annual fee on your desired trading pattern.

18 Family law issues cannot be ignored when building an investment portfolio. A variety of issues often arise:

   a Having sufficient liquid assets to pay lawyers.

   b Perhaps having offshore entities for creditor and other protection.

   c Considering the effects of long-term pay-off situations (i.e., not yet matured business operations) that cannot materialize on a timely basis because the assets have to be sold as part of a divorce settlement.

   d Valuation of private businesses held by the family; significant disagreements about value tend to occur.

   e Taxation issues related to the above; and more.

In short, too many investment advisors are basically salespeople. Finding a person who has your interests in mind is vital. Especially watch for those who merely sell high-priced mutual funds that generate years of fees to themselves at your expense.

OTHER CONCERNS

Wealthier investors should do their due diligence and engage a high net worth investment advisor, who conducts better research through independent sources of information. Often, such advisors can also provide tax planning and other services.

No matter how much money you have to invest you should pay attention to investment diversification. Instead of putting all your investment eggs in one basket, spread them over stocks and bonds in different industries, different countries and different currencies. Consider adding real estate and commodities to your portfolio.

TROUBLESOME SCENARIOS

We are often asked to identify the most troublesome situations that we encounter in our forensic investigations. Some of these problem areas can be difficult to detect, especially in their early stages. It doesn't help that Canadians often get lulled into a sense of complacency, unwisely believing that we live in a country that protects investors through laws and regulations, when in fact the opposite is the case. That's how Canadians fall into deceptive traps, such as Ponzi-like business income trusts.

Having said that, we've listed below some of the most common ways in which Canadians get duped.

Trick 1: Yield Worship

Canadians are attracted to dividend yields, but often ignore many other factors occurring in the company. For how long will the dividend rate be maintained? In an era of low interest rates, yield traps play into the hands of financial cheats who can cook the books by inventing revenue, altering expenses and creating assets. Then, the company deceptively increases the dividend rate. Mesmerized by the yield, Canadians will buy the shares, and the price will tend to rise beyond its worth.

As we've discussed, the deceptive company then borrows money to pay for the increased dividend while personally selling shares at the inflated price. Given the silence of regulators on this type of trap, it's no wonder that manipulators continue to use it with impunity. (See the previous discussions about business income trusts.)

A high yield that may exist for only a year or two is all too common in Canada. The source of cash to pay the dividend must be traced very carefully. Lenders will not finance Pyramid schemes forever. Good collateral to be pledged against bank loans eventually gets exhausted.

Trick 2: Nortel Clone Variations

Again, as we've discussed, companies like Nortel and their clones get away with this trick by claiming in their annual and quarterly reports that typical financial reporting does not do justice to the company's so-called potential. The company then invents its own reporting rules "to better reflect the company's value". As the company emphasizes its own version of reality, the media accepts the story, referring to fabricated figures such as adjusted EBITDA or adjusted earnings. Using such figures, companies ignore many expense categories, such as selling and administrative expenses. They may also incorporate future hoped-for revenue into the current year's figures. The overall effect is to produce an inflated picture of profit that does not exist under conventional reporting methods.

As gullible investors buy the stock, the share price rises. Company insiders may receive bonuses based upon the company's phony profits. They might also exercise their stock options, acquiring shares at a low price and selling them at grossly inflated prices. IFRS makes this trick even easier to prolong because management has more ability to cook the books.

Trick 3: Resuscitating Declining Companies

Companies that are falling out of favour with customers and are experiencing declining sales and profits will often cook the books for a while. But, eventually they have to make major organizational changes. To buy time for a possible turnaround, a company might embark on a program of buying other companies. Sometimes, they're seeking additional revenue; at other times, they seek the strong cash flow of the target company. They may acquire one or more private companies to take advantage of higher earnings multiples that apply when these companies are swallowed into public entities. Investors have to determine whether a company is expanding for legitimate reasons or to cover up its own deficiencies. Under IFRS, temporary resuscitation of weak companies through timely acquisitions has become like child's play.

As explained, this trick works for the cheat who pays an excessive purchase price for the acquired company, then buries the excess as an intangible asset such as goodwill in the financial statements. Reporting rules are so loose that the scam can be hidden for several years in an IFRS-bloated balance sheet. Income statement results improve, but only because the reporting rules permit postponing the recording of write-downs of intangibles-based assets. Since reporting rules don't require companies to expense goodwill on a systematic basis, companies may choose to not write down bloated goodwill until the hot-air balloon of inflated value pops, leaving investors to deal with the losses.

Trick 4: Related Ownerships

Related-party arrangements can be productive and honest. They can also be outrageous diversions of shareholder money into the pockets of undeserving people. Once again, IFRS makes this trick easier to execute.

Transactions between related businesses should be recorded at fair market value. But under IFRS, a company can bury in notes to the financial statements the details about a company's related parties, including corporate executives, directors, joint venture partners and family members. As we've discussed, investors can sometimes find these details by scouring numerous corporate financial disclosure statements. As an alternative, investors should simply walk away from such dubious companies and look elsewhere for better investment opportunities.

Trick 5: Believing the Company's Numbers

In our experience, investors in Canada place far too much reliance on published numbers. As we have stated previously, US GAAP tends to hold companies to a higher standard of reporting than IFRS and gives investors more reliable figures. But, US GAAP also has deficiencies. Under either system, investors should not place their complete faith in a company's published numbers.

Experienced financial cheats test the water by starting with elementary games such as using cookie jars to increase or decrease current liabilities and to alter revenue. If such games are not noticed, the manipulation escalates to much larger amounts, usually with a different trick.

Even if they get caught, financial cheats are often penalized by securities commissions with nothing more than a no-contest settlement.

Sometimes, in exchange for a relatively small payment, the accused just walks away. By agreeing to settle the matter, the manipulator reduces the commission's expenses, eliminating the requirements of a hearing and all the bureaucratic red tape that goes with it. But the investing public remains unaware of important details about the nature of the scam, and the cheat knows that he or she can do it again, facing only a minor penalty if they get caught.

SUMMARY

Canadians need to be aware of the games that are being played by financial cheats, especially under IFRS. Persistence is necessary in analyzing financial statements to uncover these tricks. Canadians have to be more willing to judge certain management actions and to call into question the deficiencies behind a company's reported results. Just because a stock rises in price, investors should not believe that it reflects a company's appropriate value. Stocks rise on hype and rumour as much as performance sometimes. The best advice is to sell when you feel suspicious, and uncomfortable, even if the price continues to rise.

The worst decision to make is to fall back into a belief that the situation "cannot be that bad, because authorities would have acted to stop the financial tricks." A long line of Canadian cases tells us that authorities did *not* act, time after time. You have to learn to protect yourself.

21

Canada's Slippery Slopes

The main purpose of this chapter is to show that Canada's investor protection system was in a dismal state prior to the introduction of IFRS, and that IFRS has made it much worse. Why this additional decline is not alarming to lawmakers could easily mean that white-collar crime is not on their agenda, and is not being monitored through independent sources.

We'll also look at some of the financial fiascos that have occurred over the last 40 years to see how they've contributed to the dismantling of investor protections in Canada. Weaknesses in several areas are now combining into troubling times.

While lawmakers and securities commissions have sat back over that period, leaving the partially-official alleged regulators to regulate themselves, we've seen case after case of corporate failures leading to multi-million-dollar losses that confirm that investors can depend on no one but themselves for protection. The rigidity of our lawmakers is especially baffling.

From Hercules to Nortel to Livent, investors have been left with no reliable sources on which to evaluate investments, while lawmakers have essentially made no serious effort to pass corrective legislation. Instead, lawmakers continue to promote self-regulation of groups such as external auditors despite investors having to incur multi-million dollar thefts from unchecked corporate scammers. Canada's reputation is suffering, but Canadians seem to be unaware.

Investors have no choice but to pick carefully who is managing their savings and corporate pension plans by asking questions, which we'll list later in this chapter and beyond. Too often, the motivations of people who are managing your savings or providing investment commentary are contrary to your interests. They do not merit your trust until they demonstrate loyalty to you.

CURIOUS PATTERN?

Here are just a few of the more noteworthy events that have led to investor losses over the last few decades. They confirm that our lawmakers are ignoring a growing crisis at great expense to you, your family and friends, other investors and the country itself.

1980

- A recession begins. Many corporate consolidations occur. Too many investment professionals and Canadian business leaders abandon any pretence of statesmanlike leadership. Sell, sell, sell becomes their mantra.
- Failure of Hercules Managements, a Manitoba-based mortgage company, financed primarily with publicly held debt, but also with some privately-held family equity. A similar fate occurs for Victoria Mortgage. [These failures to monitor corporate liquidity are dangerous; and adds to IFRS being scary, because it downplays cash operations.]

1985

- Failure of two Alberta banks, Canadian Commercial Bank and Northland Bank, after not disclosing data on liquidity problems in their audited financial statements.

1985–1988

- Failure of Principal Group, an investment firm operating primarily out of western Canada, leading to significant investor losses. Inadequate financial reporting was a serious factor.
- Two public inquiries to investigate the failures of Northland, Canadian Commercial and Principal Group lead to the formation of the Office of the Superintendent of Financial Institutions

(OSFI) to supervise banks in Canada. These are the last public inquiries in Canada to draw public attention to questionable financial reporting. The Federal government quickly alters legislation to deal with bank failures, but essentially ignores lost investor money; direct causation affecting external auditors is not addressed.

- Failure of National Business Systems, a public company listed on the TSX, after the company attempted to prop up its stock price with related-party transactions leading to discrepancies in reported revenue, and alleged dubious stock sales.

1990–1999

- A rash of financial failures; including: Castor Holdings, Confederation Life, Confederation Trust, Standard Trust, Livent, Philip Services, Victoria Mortgage, Teachers' Investment, and YBM (which includes some billion-dollar corporations).
- Supreme Court of Canada's Hercules Managements decision strikes a major blow to investor rights, and investor protection in general. Analysts do not know where they can obtain trustworthy financial data for a company.
- Many mining company failures and reorganizations and subsequent investor losses pile up.

2000–2005

- Media reports about Nortel Networks, based on its audited financial statements, pump its stock price higher, which later collapses. Investors lose billions. Financial reform seems urgent, but nothing of significance occurs in Canada.
- Business income trusts, inflated on media hype, collapse causing multi-million dollar investor losses. Once more, the investment crowd's opinion is extensively wrong, because basic Ponzi schemes were in operation and were not publicized as such.
- External auditors loosen the Canadian rules affecting the reporting of goodwill, intangibles and financial instruments. Financial manipulation is thus simplified and is seized upon by cheats. Overstated assets, mainly intangible, remain on audited financial statements for years.

- To meet a deadline in 2005, Europe adopts a hastily prepared, inappropriate common financial reporting system to replace a range of country-specific, philosophically-different systems. Incorporating major compromises, the system is called International Financial Reporting Standards (IFRS). To obtain multi-country agreement by the 2005 deadline, it is based upon a lowest-common-denominator concept. All sorts of conflicting bases for reporting are welcomed into the IFRS club, and are labelled as being in accordance with IFRS.
- External auditors incorporate into their contract letters with corporate clients clauses excluding them from responsibility in Canada for detecting various fraud, related-party and other valuations and transactions. Investors are thus more vulnerable than ever. (See Appendix 3.)
- Despite all the investor losses, Canadian lawmakers leave crucial matters related to investor protection in the hands of seriously conflicted self-regulators. The bias is extreme.

2006–2010

- Ignoring the potential consequences, and without serious debate, Canadian lawmakers accept the external auditors' recommendations to adopt IFRS, effective as of 2011–2012 for public companies. Companies may elect, as an alternative, to use US Generally Accepted Accounting Principles (GAAP).
- Extensive Ponzi schemes continue, made easier to prolong by IFRS (for the many reasons to be analyzed later).
- Education of investors about the especially serious limitations of IFRS is minimal at best in Canada. Many financial analysts' writings display extensive confusion, which continues to this day. Investors are forced to absorb the losses for lawmakers' support of archaic self-regulation.

2011–the Present

- Collapse or deterioration of Sino-Forest Corporation and some other Chinese companies listed on the TSX, leading to more investor losses. Some out-of-court settlements are reached. Related cases are ongoing.

- IFRS is adopted for public reporting purposes by many Canadian public companies. Financial manipulators clue-in quickly to take advantage of new powers granted by IFRS to corporate management, to cook the books.
- Most of the claims of promoters about IFRS prove to be deeply misleading. At the time of adoption by Canada's lawmakers, no independent body challenged these misleading claims on behalf of investors. Power accesses with lawmakers remained with the conflicted external auditors.
- Poseidon Concepts, a public company based in Alberta, collapses after alleged misreporting of revenues and accounts receivable under IFRS rules. Despite some out-of-court settlements, investors lose millions.
- Real estate and other companies take advantage of loose IFRS rules to significantly inflate their profits and cash flow from operations, which would not have been permitted under old Canadian GAAP. Analysts and the media refer to favourable profit and cash trend lines by comparing balance-sheet-based IFRS figures with figures reported under old Canadian GAAP.
- Decisions involving Castor Holdings are released. The Supreme Court of Canada declines to hear the appeal by the external auditors.
- Livent Entertainment's civil court and appeal decisions are published. The external auditors appeal to the Supreme Court of Canada, which agrees to hear the case. (The Supreme Court's response should be informative.)

Throughout the period of the late 1980s to 2015, lawmakers discussed the formation of a National Securities Commission. No concrete plans are made to replace archaic self-regulation or to address financial reporting deficiencies. Investors remain unaware of IFRS's many limitations. A gloomy future looms for investor protection.

Lawmaker silence has clearly led to massive investor losses and huge gains for financial manipulators. Extensive buck-passing continues among lawmakers, which prevents progress, as we discussed in this book's Preface and Chapter 1. In Canada, investors remain on their own, and have to contend with tainted financial information on potential investments.

IMPLICATIONS

Except in Quebec, where the courts' decisions in the Castor Holdings case extended some support, investor protection in Canada continues to decline, and seriously so. Loyal to a dubious philosophy of self-regulation, our lawmakers do nothing to alter this course while denying the prevalence of continuing financial reporting games. How much must investors lose before lawmakers decide to act?

Lawmakers did not investigate the nature and implications of IFRS and the effects of excessive power that it has granted to corporate managements to publish their biased dollar figures. Lawmakers hardly reacted to court decisions involving Hercules, Livent, and other cases in which auditors have largely remained unaccountable for alleged materially misleading audited financial statements. And, securities commissions apparently reacted only after prompting from the US in the case of Nortel Networks. In our view, lessons that ought to have been learned have been ignored. Without the availability of various cover-ups, self-regulation blunders and biases would be more evident, and the urgent need for securities reform would be clearer.

Based on the following observations, lawmakers are obviously *not* directly addressing the glaring matter of how investors are supposed to make decisions about public company investments:

1 Virtually no oversight of officers and directors of public companies exists in the current Canadian legal system except when major, easily proven alleged frauds are brought to light and can no longer be ignored.
2 Even when these glaring alleged frauds exist, where is the assurance that they will be investigated and then prosecuted? Provincial securities commissions do not seem to have the leadership and talent to win cases. Many Ponzis continue for years. Complaints receive little attention, based on what we are frequently told by clients and what we continue to see.
3 The purpose of audited financial statements as it is being interpreted by the courts is close to pointless. Shareholders can *easily* be led astray by management applying our weak reporting rules. External auditors seem not to object sufficiently to financial

manipulations. Court decisions have granted them immunity from responsibility to investors, even though they claim outside of court that they are gatekeepers for investors.

4 Investors cannot expect protection from external auditors and securities commissions because:

  a External auditors supported an ill-considered anti-investor choice in advocating the adoption of IFRS rules for financial reporting. Such soft rules are easily circumvented to mislead investors.

  b External auditors require public companies to sign audit engagement letters that excuse them from detecting frauds and other basic deceptions.

  c Securities commissions in Canada, unlike their US counterpart, do not require essential supplementary corporate disclosure for the many financial activities not covered by weak financial reporting rules such as for valuation assumptions and inappropriate interest/discount rates. Without such supplementary requirements, an external audit is of minimal benefit for investment decisions, and can easily be misleading.

  d External auditors also act as consultants and advisors for their clients, raising additional serious conflicts of interest. How can they possibly be neutral for investor purposes? Nor can an organization financed by external auditors remain independent, despite their claims about these conflicted Standards Boards. (See the Preface and Chapter 1.)

  e By promoting IFRS, external auditors were fully aligned with corporate management, who gained significant powers from the new standards. While IFRS accommodates a so-called "principles-based" approach, the guiding principles remain vague and open to considerable management interpretation (e.g., choice of interest rates).

  f In the Hercules Managements case, external auditors urged the court to restrict their responsibilities to *shareholder* evaluation of corporate stewardship, even though their own CICA rule book at the time (as well as today) extended that responsibility much further. How can the public have any faith in what they say?

g Despite all of the above, external auditors choose to offer advice to the audit committees of the Boards of Directors. Trickery can be reinforced.

Summed up, claims that external auditors are gatekeepers for investors are without substance. Nor can conflicted external auditors play a meaningful role in designing a National Securities Commission based just on their track record of repeatedly objecting to audit quality improvements. Similar reasoning can be applied to many provincial securities commissions. Their track records show little concern for investors, and negligible objections to the usage of easily manipulated IFRS choices.

5 Securities commissions across Canada have demonstrated little interest in pursuing financial deceptions and offer no criticisms of the worst portions of IFRS, despite clear evidence of its harms.

6 As for directors of public companies, in our experience, the vast majority of directors know very little about IFRS or the extent of reporting tricks. Many directors are honest, but many more merely rubber stamp corporate management's decisions.

As forensic reporting investigators, we see far too much thievery to come close to believing that matters are getting better. We hear promises of change, but we see no progress, and also we observe steps backwards, such as the treatment of leases. Meanwhile, multi-million dollar scams are being ignored. Investors are being misled by pronouncements of trivial reform while regulation remains mediocre at best, and clearly ineffective.

TIME TO HELP YOURSELF

The fact that you have to protect yourself should now be more than obvious. With this in mind, you need to pose questions to the people who invest your money. For example, if they try to push you into some high-fee mutual fund, ask why. Where is the benefit to you? Whether you meet in a coffee shop with a person who is not employed by a known investment firm, or consult one of the robotic people who make a living by selling high-cost bank mutual funds, you can lose money in a range of situations. The undernoted should be added to our previous commentary on the subject of learning to manage your money. Ask about:

1 Excessive annual fees charged by certain mutual funds. (Why pay 2.5% in fees when you are only earning a 5% return?)
2 Fees to extract yourself from some locked-in, multiple-year fund.
3 Frequent trading in speculative stocks and other unsuitable investments, without adequate research having been conducted.
4 Turning over all of your decision-making to an advisor, who makes money from frequent trading of your securities.

Thus, you have little choice but to ask a few of the following questions and to listen carefully to the answers:

1 If I had invested $10,000 five years ago in the mutual fund that you are recommending:
   a how much would the amount invested be worth today? (Does the amount include interest and dividend income? How much?)
   b how much would I have paid in fees for management of my money over the past five years?
   A brief silence or an imprecise answer should be regarded as a strike. Ask for proof on paper of year-by-year performance. And remember, in the stock market, the past is not necessarily a good indication of the future.
2 How much revenue does this company generate in Canadian vs. US dollars?
   A good advisor should be able to approximate the sources of the company's revenue based on minimal research. But most robotic salespeople will not have an answer. If they say, "I don't know," at least they're being honest.
3 How long have you been advising clients on investment choices? How long have you worked for this company? What about your employment at other investment companies? What experience did you have in other sales positions?

The answers will determine whether your advisor has much experience in investments, as opposed to sales. If you don't get the answer you want, regard it as another strike.

4 What is your source of ideas for companies that you recommend that I purchase? Are you a portfolio manager, and do you conduct your own research? Or do you buy into what your in-house research department recommends?

As we have stated previously, an analyst's sell-side research is often tainted by his association with the stock's underwriters, another potential strike, unless the advisor has other reliable and credible sources of information.

5 Do you use audited financial statements in your analysis? If so, how much faith do you place in the audited numbers?

After reading this book, you should know how someone should answer this question. (Audits are typically of little comfort to investors.) If the advisor is not clued-in to prevalent financial games in Canada, you'll be exposed to greater risk than is necessary.

6 Where possible, do you choose US-based stocks that utilize US GAAP and have some US investor protection? Or are you indifferent to US-based GAAP vs. Canadian IFRS-based reporting?

A qualified advisor will be on guard for easy-to-manipulate IFRS reporting tricks involving intangible assets, cash flow from operations, switching expenses into assets, pointless lease capitalization, and similar.

7 Do you pay attention to court cases in Canada that involve manipulation of reported profit and cash flow from operations? With this in mind, do you think investing in the Canadian stock market is risky? Why, or why not? Do you know about the Sino-Forest case? How much?

Most investment advisors will suggest that they will control the risk for you, which may or may not be credible. Watch for statements that a company's profits and cash flows are not important and that other issues such as export sales are more vital. Such comments play directly into the hands of people who con analysts with faked numbers that the analysts pass along to the unsuspecting investment advisors.

8 Could you explain how a Ponzi scheme works?

Ponzi schemes work by inflating profit through various methods, as we described earlier, such as reporting operating expenses as assets and then using the inflated profit figures to attract lenders and more shareholders to provide additional cash. The cash is then used to pay high dividends, which attract more shareholders and sell more shares. As the Ponzi attracts more money, the corporate manipulator sells her/his shares at the inflated price and exits with the cash.

Assess the quality of detail that the advisor provides to explain how financial reporting can be utilized to build Ponzi schemes. Many advisors were not able to detect the serious Ponzi element in business income trust scams between 2000 and 2010. Glib responses tell you all that you need to know, to look elsewhere.

9 What do you look for in judging whether a company's dividend rate will be cut? Won't a dividend rate reduction lower the market value of the shares that I hold in the company?

As we have discussed previously, dividends have to be cut when cash is not readily available to pay them. In a Ponzi scheme, that means more money may not be available through borrowing or selling inflated shares, while insufficient cash is being generated from the company's daily sales and service operations. An astute money manager will look for the overstated profits and cash flow from operations, and understand how IFRS allows considerable manipulation.

10 How did changes in Canadian financial reporting in 2011–2012 affect reported income and cash flow figures and financial analysis in general?

If an advisor does not comprehend why IFRS is dangerous for investors, she/he should not be managing your money.

Most advisors will explain that they are being policed by various investment or mutual fund oversight bodies. This is true, but often the oversight extends only to outright theft. Incompetence and ignorance of financial games is not especially scrutinized.

SUMMARY

You must learn how to protect your financial health. Organizations that claim that they are looking after your interests as investors are not being sincere, and are not coming close to doing the job. Too many conflicts of interest and loyalty exist. Too many financial failures have occurred in Canada. Matters are not under control, and that is why we have provided several examples.

Canada needs a larger, more powerful body to replace the self-regulators. Lawmakers have to end 80-plus years of procrastination and step up to the plate to legislate on behalf of investors. Self-regulators have had years to take action, and they did not act. It's time for Canada to move forward with serious regulation before deceptive reporting leads to the collapse of even more suspect companies. Your savings vanish because of lawmaker neglect.

22

The Party Line

Canadian lawmakers and securities commissions continue to leave investors unprotected while claiming that self-regulation in the securities industry is adequate. As Canadian investors, including seniors, continue to believe this face-saving evasion, sophisticated US pension funds are becoming more aware of Canada's regulatory deficiencies. Having pursued litigation against Canadian-based financial failures, they have begun to view Canada more and more as an investment casino.

We have discussed the role and impact of Canadian regulatory authorities with people convicted of financial deceit, usually after US, not Canadian, authorities have identified them. They regard Canada's regulatory environment with contempt. They say there are massive un-policed areas in the Canadian regulatory system. While lawmakers of Canada toe the party line, the problems remain unaddressed and investigations are too often toothless.

While a few legitimate independent investor groups function in Canada, such as the Small Investors Protection Association (www. sipa.ca), too many such groups parrot the accepted wisdom that all's well with the world. These groups have some of the following characteristics:

1 The group was formed by people with serious conflicts of interest and having only a tentative relationship with authentic investors.

2 The group is largely funded by other groups in similarly conflicting circumstances. You should try to find the sources of funding
   for such groups before you decide whether to believe them.

3 Instead of tracking causes and effects when an embarrassing
   Canadian financial failure occurs, the group sweeps the underlying issues under a rug of deceptive reasoning. Strong corrective
   action is not recommended to lawmakers.

4 The group's annual reports include elaborate explanations in the
   first few pages about their supposed intended goal of "ridding the
   world of all evil."

5 When contacted by investors who have lost money in scams, the
   group bounces them from person to person and department to
   department until the victims get fed up and leave.

6 The group describes investor scams in such vague and inoffensive
   wording that it often is not possible to recognize what an investor
   has lost or how a specific scam works.

7 Situations that ought to be prosecuted instead have simply been
   permitted to grow stale and irrelevant, over time, through deliberate obfuscation and procrastination.

8 The group weakly investigates a few token cases for show, to
   claim that progress is being made.

9 Well-intentioned advisers promise to consult such victimized
   groups on investors' behalf, but become disillusioned and cannot
   deliver on their promises to the swindled investors.

The solution is to form a separate, fully independent organization
in Canada similar to the US Securities and Exchange Commission
(SEC), to represent investors' positions in cases involving deceit.
Provincial securities commissions remain toothless and need new
leadership, as well as commitments from lawmakers.

In the meantime, our lawmakers routinely consult with these party-
line organizations and conclude that *no change* of regulations is
required. They ignore evidence of blatant financial manipulations and
repeat the mantra that everything is under control.

The beneficiaries on such "do nothing" attitudes are the financial
swindlers. You know who the losers are.

AN EXAMPLE

Provincial securities commissions give the appearance of taking investor protection seriously. But let's look at what they actually do.

The most powerful of these bodies, the Ontario Securities Commission (o s c), says in its Annual Report of 2014 that:

o s c Mandate
To provide protection to investors from unfair, improper or fraudulent practices and to foster fair and efficient capital markets and confidence in capital markets

o s c Organizational Goals
1 Deliver strong investor protection
2 Deliver responsive regulation
3 Deliver effective enforcement and compliance
4 Support and promote financial stability
5 Run a modern, accountable and efficient organization.

On page 16 of the o s c's report the enforcement director states:

We're making the o s c as effective, active and visible as possible by taking more cases before the Ontario Court of Justice, targeting fraudulent activity and recidivists, going after people who don't comply with Commission orders, expanding our enforcement tools, tailoring enforcement to fight different misconduct, and strengthening our partnership with the Ministry of the Attorney General.

The objectives and goals of the o s c are certainly admirable. It is also interesting to see the o s c claim that protection to investors is their top priority. But how exactly does the o s c proceed day-to-day to attain its Organizational Goals?

When we reach page 68 of the o s c's Annual Report, an Appendix provides some statistics:

	Number of matters assessed	Number transferred for investigation
2013–2014	289	41
2012–2013	238	18
2011–2012	210	21

The number of cases transferred for investigation almost doubled, to 41 from 21, between 2011–2012 and 2013–2014.

But, on page 69, under "investigations," we see a small decline in "number transferred for litigation."

	Number of completed investigations	Number transferred for litigation
2013–2014	42	24
2012–2013	36	25
2011–2012	39	29

By 2016, as we write this chapter, by now we should know something about the 29 litigation cases from 2011–2012. Some cases must have been resolved. How much money is involved? But we know little. Why? How does secrecy help with investor education?

Again, on page 68 we are told that: "Total contacts from investors to the osc Inquiries & Contact Centre amounted to 6,035 in 2013–2014."

Most of the 6,035 contacts appear to involve less serious matters. Still, the "number transferred for litigation" (24, 25, 29) would appear to be relatively low. And according to page 16, the osc laid *only three* criminal charges between May 13, 2013, and March 31, 2014. Three?? Involving whom? What were the charges? Why so few?

Yes, of the over 6,000 contacts to the osc in fiscal 2014 only three so far have involved criminal charges. Not mentioned are the full numbers from 2011–2012. How many resulted in convictions, and what were the sentences? Only fines?

What is osc's *conviction* record of the past five to 10 years? This crucial piece of information is not explained. Why? Does it say something about the validity of the osc's Organizational Goals?

Outcomes on some cases may not be available for years. Traditionally, the o s c has settled cases such as Nortel for trivial amounts compared to investor losses. A troubling question is whether such o s c behaviour serves as an incentive to manipulators? What do they have to lose by engaging in financial deceit?

In our experience, the US often has to prod Canada to act. Sometimes the media helps to publicize the deceptions. But often it merits barely a mention. As a financial cheat, where would you prefer to live?

SUMMARY

Securities commissions and external auditors clearly do little to help to protect investors. So what is left? Access to the courts is expensive and, for investors, the results are dismal, outside of Quebec. Canadian investors have to seize the initiative and educate lawmakers and the media about the extreme imbalances in Canada's securities and investment world.

Evidence of shabby treatment of investors is readily available and has existed for many years. Your savings and pensions are being attacked on a daily basis. Why wait to be swindled? Misleading advertising involving financial matters has to be curtailed.

·Ask yourself how lawmakers can keep allowing conflicted external auditors be the persons who set an "appropriate level" of Canadian financial reporting standards? The external auditors once were credible, but since the 1980s:

1   They have signed audit reports for dozens of larger Canadian corporations that failed shortly afterward.
2   Their published material states that financial statements are designed to help investors and creditors. Yet they have successfully argued the opposite in court.
3   They have not pushed lawmakers to reverse the 1997 Hercules decision, which immunizes them against allegedly legitimate investor actions.
4   They are parties to the writing of reporting and auditing rules that are close to toothless, especially I F R S, with its long list of

grandfathered cop-outs that produce multiple ways of reporting identical transactions.

5 Above all, they pushed IFRS into Canada on the basis of qualities that do not exist and that are causing havoc in Canada.

Their best friends in all of the above have been the provincial securities commissions and corporate directors as well as lawmakers.

Investors and lenders have been abandoned. Financial cheats and manipulators reign. Canadian authorities remain silent, as the evidence, and losses, pile up. Worst of all is the direction in which we are headed: clearly downward for investors.

23

IFRS in a Nutshell

Canada's recently adopted accounting regime, International Financial Reporting Standards (IFRS), has so many serious deficiencies that it is difficult to decide where to begin our analysis.

Before IFRS was adopted in Canada in 2011–2012, our lawmakers accepted it without conducting much research. IFRS's shortcomings were obvious. Yet our lawmakers followed their self-regulation beliefs, and allowed seriously conflicted external auditors to impose IFRS on Canada. Our lawmakers then described, and shockingly still do, external auditors as "independent" standard setters. The facts strongly indicate otherwise. (See Chapter 1.)

Here are some of the main deficiencies of IFRS:

1 IFRS extended power to corporate managements to choose the dollars that they report to the public, as well as the words they use to describe their reasoning. This material is well beyond the logical limits that had been negotiated in Canada over the 50 years before 2011. A fundamental concept of having checks and balances on the activities of corporate management was discarded by IFRS.

2 The Supreme Court of Canada in its decision in the Hercules Managements case in 1997 had already given corporate managements extensive opportunity to mislead investors. The decision tacitly enabled managements to write their own report cards and, in relieving external auditors of any worthwhile duty to

investors, deprived them of an *independent* assessment of a public company's performance.

3 The court restricted the basis of investment decisions in Canada to whatever corporate management published in their so-called audited financial statements. Honest portrayals? Perhaps yes, perhaps no.

4 In granting many additional powers of choice to corporate managements, IFRS reduced the legal responsibilities of external auditors even further. Responsibility was diverted to boards of directors, which external auditors could then rely upon, according to their adopted standards. Meanwhile, IFRS gave external auditors opportunities to earn additional fees for advising boards and managements about the implementation of the standards while reducing their own legal liability. The "independence" of external auditors in assessing IFRS on behalf of Canada's lawmakers is more than questionable.

5 The devastating combination of IFRS in softening financial reporting requirements and the court's decision in Hercules Managements compromised the credibility for investors of audited corporate data, especially about income and profit and crucial cash operating flows. We saw such in the cases of Sino-Forest and other Canadian financial failures. Ponzi schemes have flourished as a result, with many still being in progress.

6 IFRS focuses heavily on corporate balance sheets, which often include intangible assets and financial instruments that are difficult to value, while downplaying the importance of the income/profit and operating cash flow statements. Both of the latter are critically important in business valuation because they help to identify trends.

7 Previous standards of financial reporting distinguished investors' subscribed capital from subsequent earnings on this invested capital. IFRS seriously weakened this distinction, enabling managements to muddle today's cash transactions with their optimism about tomorrow, and thereby inflate a corporation's income figures. With higher dollars of reported income, manipulated corporations can attract more investor dollars to their

Ponzi and other schemes. Is this really what our lawmakers
wanted to happen from rubber-stamping IFRS?

8 While many financial analysts and investors apparently do not
understand the negative implications of the combination of IFRS
and the Hercules decision, financial manipulators certainly do.
They can turn a mediocre company into a glorious investment
opportunity, thanks to IFRS's loose, ill-considered financial
framework, with its imaginary profit.

9 With such extensive choices granted to corporate managements,
IFRS does not meet one of the important objectives identified by
lawmakers of achieving a uniform reporting standard throughout the world. In fact, while government ministers accepted the
assurances of alleged independent self-regulated auditing and
accounting organizations that Canada would join a world-wide
regime of financial reporting uniformity, such a proposition was
impossible to achieve. Evidence to the contrary showed that
IFRS supporters were willing to include contradictory reporting
within the IFRS umbrella, just to "sign on" another country
for IFRS. Hence, a major initial objective of IFRS was self-
destroyed at its outset.

10 The United States, Canada's major trading partner, has rejected
IFRS for its registered domestic companies partly on the grounds
that its loopholes and impracticalities could eventually lead to
another major stock-market crash.

11 Meanwhile, Canada has not only adopted IFRS but has also
failed to address the standards' deficiencies within IFRS.
Independent evaluations of IFRS by securities commissions
in Canada is non-existent.

The losers, as always, are the investors. Their pensions, mutual
funds, private portfolios and savings are at risk. It is time for Canada
to wake-up.

BACKGROUND

A frequent statement made by supporters of IFRS is: "Many countries
besides Canada have adopted IFRS."

While such a comment is correct, it does not prove much or address vital issues that affect Canadian investors. Consider the following factors:

1 A large number of IFRS adopters are small, non-industrialized countries that did not have an adequate reporting system previously. For them IFRS was indeed an "improvement."

2 Many European countries were forced by the European Union to accept IFRS arbitrarily, in order to further the EU's political agenda.

3 Canada is a resource-based country. At some point, its financial reporting standard must accommodate our cross-section of resource industries. IFRS tends to be general, not industry-based, often implicitly emphasising retailing and manufactory enterprises.

4 The US has reluctantly tolerated foreign securities filings based on IFRS but domestic companies must stick to US Generally Accepted Accounting Principles in their principal financial statements. Attempts to have IFRS and US Standards Setters work together have been mixed. Conceptually, the two reporting systems are worlds apart.

5 Some larger countries that have adopted IFRS have also imposed their own variations and exceptions, while Canada has simply followed IFRS virtually to the letter, regardless of its inadequacies. Independent thinking is absent in Canada.

6 Many countries have prescribed better governance and investor protection legislation and Court oversight than exists in Canada. Such governance serves to keep "creativity in financial reporting" somewhat limited, or at least partially under control in these other countries.

7 To Canada's embarrassment, the US has come to our rescue in helping to control financial reporting frauds based primarily in Canada. As IFRS encourages such frauds, do Canadian lawmakers and IFRS supporters seriously expect the US to continue to police such IFRS-based scams?

8 IFRS was sold to lawmakers in Canada as a world-wide uniform system. In fact, numerous exceptions have been made by

individual countries in applying IFRS, which has undermined the possibility of such uniformity. Even for Canadian-only companies, multiple choices exist, and for many issues, especially "valuations."

9 In its training of external auditors, Canada now emphasizes the memorization of rules while minimizing the application of principles, leaving them ill-prepared to apply even the poorly defined, incomplete generalized principles of IFRS.

10 Many rules that once governed the way Canadian corporations accounted for certain of their transactions can now be interpreted loosely under IFRS. By essentially de-regulating financial reporting, IFRS has brought an "anything goes" mentality to Canada.

11 IFRS avoids dealing with many issues, such as the measurement of self-dealing transaction effects, which are commonplace in Canada. This raises another challenge to any serious claim to uniform treatment of financial reporting throughout the world.

In brief, IFRS brought many more problems to Canada than it resolved. Several of them were foreseeable even before Canada officially adopted IFRS.

Just because some countries have adopted IFRS proves nothing with respect to its suitability in Canada. Nor can Canada ignore its main trading partner, whose financial reporting standards are clearly superior to IFRS.

Unlike the US, Canada has no oversight body to monitor the effects of its grossly inferior reporting system. Instead, we have only the activities of our self-regulated auditors, which are repeatedly rubber-stamped by provincial securities commissions. For lawmakers, this provides a convenient way to pass the buck. For investors, as we've shown in previous chapters, it amounts to no protection at all.

CONCEPTUAL AND PRACTICAL FLAWS

Conceptually, IFRS has major incurable flaws, especially for investors. It often allows past, present and hoped-for future transactions to be jumbled together in one figure. The time dimension that should be inherent in periodic financial reporting has thereby been destroyed. Poor operating results in the current year can be covered up by including management's optimism about the future, in one composite figure. Vital emerging trends and evolving financial problems can be hidden from investors for a few years and perhaps longer.

Here's an example: Under IFRS, interest expense can incorporate a mixture of cash-based interest on long-term debt; imputed interest on capitalized liabilities, which offset capitalized leased assets; amortizations of selected present value estimates, and other non-cash items. Worse treatment for the Cash Flow Statement occurs. With all these expenses jumbled together, reasonable trend lines of arm's length cash reductions in the most recent period cannot be established. (We'll explain this in more detail in a later chapter.) Tricksters can take advantage of this weakness in IFRS to make a declining company look robust, or adequate for several years.

Many analysts think that a cash flow statement will give them an accurate picture of a company's financial condition. But we've already discussed the ways that people can manipulate a cash flow statement. In the case of Sino-Forest Corporation, for example, few analysts caught on to the distortions in its cash flow statements, which extended over many years.

The same distortions allowed by IFRS also make company-to-company comparisons almost pointless, because each company's management has so many choices, assumptions and interpretations available in preparing their financial statements. Even within one company, changes in management's probability estimates from 51% down to 49% can change sales revenue, tax assets and more. IFRS allows for many such oddities.

And while advocates of IFRS, including external auditors, claim that it's investor-friendly, the Supreme Court's decision in the Hercules Managements' case asserts that investors should not rely on financial statements in making their decisions. In fact, if external auditors in Canada really believed what they told the Supreme Court of Canada in the Hercules case about the purposes of financial statements, they should never have pushed IFRS into Canada. Advocacy of IFRS by the external auditors sent a huge signal to investors that they were close to irrelevant.

MAJOR PRACTICAL FLAWS

In the list that follows, we identify several practical flaws in IFRS, which we will discuss at greater length in the next few chapters.

1 *Excessive Management Control*

Without clear rules for handling troublesome situations, IFRS typically gives final decision-making power to individual corporate managements. They decide in many cases how and what to report to investors. Being allegedly principles-based (but with the principles unclear), IFRS assumes that all managements are honest and have no personal stake in financial reporting. This alone brings into question the credibility of IFRS, since the bonus plans and other rewards of many company managements are based on IFRS dollar numbers.

How many corporate officers in Canada have incentive plans that are *not related* to profits, sales, or adjusted EBITDA? How many managers receive turn-around bonuses for guiding a company from losses in one year to profits in the next? (Nortel had such an incentive plan.)

In our opinion, managers who receive bonuses and other reporting-based incentives tied to sales or other figures should *not* be making financial reporting Standards. Reporting rules that cannot be easily circumvented are required. Yet, securities administrators and external auditors repeatedly do not accept that IFRS has serious shortcomings.

Canadian proponents of IFRS, believe it or not, have argued that oversight of corporate management is *not* an accounting and reporting responsibility, but is a governance obligation. If such were the case, external auditors could wash their hands of their obligation to validate management choices, including the magnitudes of reported corporate dollars.

External auditors would serve a purpose to Canadian society if they would be designated to prevent management from violating an enforceable *rule*. But since IFRS is so-called principles-based, and allowing of management to make broad choices, few such enforceable rules exist. Could this have been a reason for advocating IFRS in Canada? If so, why should our corporate and securities law require external auditors at all? What can they possibly accomplish? On behalf of whom?

Hasn't the time arrived for Canada to revamp a regulatory system that is so riddled with contradictions, loopholes and vague responsibilities?

IFRS seems to suggest that corporate directors should assume all responsibility for governance, including analyzing the details of reporting policies and practices. How many boards in Canada have the time or the talent to do this? If such responsibility were legally imposed on directors, who in her or his right mind would join a corporate board? Independent, specialist assistance would be needed, from other than conflicted auditors.

In the meantime, we've discussed the way that securities commissions have washed their hands of responsibility for detailed corporate governance. So who is checking up on corporate management? How could they possibly have been granted such corporate reporting freedom?

A major reason for originally having securities regulation in Canada was the concept that management's reporting should have various levels of governance oversight to minimize false reporting. It is precisely this basic checks-and-balances mechanism that has severely broken down in Canada. And, circumvention of oversight is being aided by IFRS, by lawmaker-approved delegation.

Canada's system was already weak when IFRS extended significantly more freedom to management to cook the books. Instead of tackling the growing crises, our lawmakers permitted greater protection to the very people who were causing these problems. IFRS made financial tricks that much easier to employ. Yet, none of the original gatekeepers on behalf of investors are requesting the drastic reform that has become urgent in Canada.

2   *The Old Way: Realization, Matching, and Conservatism*
   a Realization
Before 2011, and IFRS, Canadian GAAP was grounded on three conceptual foundations:
   • Wherever possible GAAP required *realization* or actual dollar confirmation of transactions with *third parties* before a

company recorded results of the transaction for financial
reporting purposes, including income measurement. When
doubt existed, a conservative approach applied. The recording of the transaction's outcome was delayed until the facts
were sufficiently clear to provide adequate comfort to investors.
- Profit is defined as revenue less matched expenses. Where
possible, when computing income/profit for an enterprise,
accountants attempted to *match* to recorded revenue the
expenses incurred in earning that revenue.
- Under a conservative approach to financial reporting, no
changes in value were recorded until sufficient and appropriate evidence was obtained to validate the appearance of
income and cash flows.

In contrast, IFRS emphasizes current value accounting. Instead
of emphasizing the old GAAP's realization concept, current value
reporting allows the recording of increases in current values,
based on management's dollar choices. Under the old GAAP, a
company would have to complete the sale of assets such as land
and buildings, for example, to a third party before it could pass
the realization requirement test. Under IFRS, such an independent, completed third party transaction is *not necessary*.

This raises some critical issues: Does the offset to an increase
in long-term assets get recorded on the income statement or elsewhere? How much evidence is needed to justify an increase in current or fair value? What level of proof is required under IFRS?
Not much.

Old GAAP generally did not allow the recording of certain current values, because it could lead to excessive manipulation of
financial statements. Instead, the credibility of accounting reports
required a level of reporting discipline. For example, GAAP would
regard as credible the market prices of frequently traded stocks
listed on a well-operated and regulated stock exchange. Estimates
of value made by managers of a company whose shares traded
infrequently or not at all would carry less credibility, perhaps none.

Too frequently IFRS is reminiscent of the financial reporting
that led up to the 1929 stock market crash. Sources of "valuations"

were from speculation, with little logical basis and research. Nonsense dollar amounts compounded into a bubble.

Since old GAAP was often regarded as deficient for investor decision purposes, rules about the realization of value were relaxed over the years to make financial statements supposedly more useful for investment decisions. When Canada adopted IFRS, the relaxed GAAP rules were abandoned for the sake of what could be viewed as an irresponsible leap of faith. Under IFRS, definitions of current value are too ill-formulated and highly speculative.

Instead of basing current values on substantive or credible information, IFRS flung open the doors to all sorts of pie-in-the-sky estimates that management could choose, and the choices especially extended to intangible assets. Under pressure from certain countries, the standards governing current-value calculations under IFRS were tightened somewhat, but still allow for a wide range of management judgment.

For example, a company's land, buildings, and equipment may realistically attract a sale price of $10 million, net of selling expenses. But based on some medium-term profitable contracts, the company's management believes that the assets are worth $18 million. In Canada, IFRS allows management to use the higher figure in its financial statements. This "value in use" or value to the owner is wide open to abuse. Management will likely attribute much of the $18-million in value to the land, because it does not require the recording of a depreciation expense and therefore does not reduce the company's profit.

As schemers take advantage of a loose interpretation of the concept of realization under IFRS, they can be viewed as pulling figures out of the air in valuing real estate, and other assets and liabilities. The tricks extend to mutual funds holding shares in private companies and to financial institutions. Inventory figures can also be shuffled up and down.

The departure in IFRS from the realization concept under GAAP *significantly* changes the definition of income and affects the reporting of cash flow from operations. With such room for manoeuvring, the gates are wide open for people to construct more elaborate Ponzi and other frauds.

b *Matching*

IFRS has also re-defined the concept of matching. Under the principle of matching, a company reports certain expenses on its income statement in the same period as the related revenues. Other expenses, such as insurance and utilities are recorded in their time period of incurrence, or usage. These items are not directly related to revenues.

Under old Canadian GAAP, *income* statements had three main categories:

a Cash transactions, such as cash revenue, and cash expenses;
b Accruals for uncollected or prepaid revenue and prepaid, or yet-to-be-paid, expenses, including accounts payable; and
c Non-cash adjustments for amortization expense, for example, and extraneous gains and losses from selling land or similar manufacturing assets.

Under GAAP, companies had to back out the non-cash adjustment to get to cash flow from operations. As we discussed earlier, the analytical process could become a nuisance, but rough conclusions were usually possible, minimizing the effects of management manipulation of operating cash flows.

IFRS relaxes the concept of matching so that it becomes almost meaningless. In some industries, management can treat the income statement as a broad accounting garbage can, where it can stuff discards from adjustments to each balance sheet account, such as inventory upward valuations. A company's cash and accrual-based profit-generating activities become difficult to distinguish from management's own value judgments based on nothing more than its optimism or pessimism about the future. IFRS allows extensive grouping and netting of numbers, which can have a direct effect on a corporation's profit/income, creating a golden opportunity for Ponzi and other schemers. Management can summon profits out of nowhere, which may or may not eventually be earned. If they're earned, they could still be far into the future. Trend analysis may not be possible because financial items can be shuffled from period to period.

Many analysts do not detect these valuation adjustments made under IFRS. This limits comparisons with other companies and renders them misleading. Equally misleading are attempts to demonstrate future trends over five years or more within a single company. While IFRS-based financial statements show improvements in a company's performance, they could be nothing more than management-based gimmickry. No real dollar trend may exist, and the "values" reported could be unrelated to operating cash flows.

The most troublesome aspect of the abandonment under IFRS of matching is that income inflation can occur from speculative revaluations. The same assets that previously showed valuation gains can end up being sold at a loss, well below original cost. (See the Mainstreet Equity commentary, and Appendix 4.)

Investors have to track corporate management's non-cash optimism/pessimism quarter by quarter and separate management's judgment calls from actual cash and accrual-based results of the company's sales and service operations. Otherwise, investors can get distracted by management's fluctuating opinions of values and make bad investment decisions. Unfortunately, such separation is difficult if not impossible in many companies' reports.

Likewise, current balance sheet values are of use to investors only at the current moment and lose their usefulness as time passes. For instance, a December 31, Year 1 balance sheet figure for real estate could become materially different by February 28, Year 2, the date when the company releases its financial statements for Year 1. Interest rates may change in the interim, for example, affecting values recorded on the balance sheet.

c *Conservatism*

As for the concept of conservatism, it declined in importance over the past 50 years, and now, under IFRS, every company can easily have a different definition of the concept. For financial manipulators, conservatism may not even have a place in their accounting lexicon.

When just the three concepts of realization, matching and conservatism are compared under old GAAP and IFRS, their definitions and applications are worlds-apart. Hence, advocates of

IFRS who state that it is an improvement over old GAAP, and
IFRS is just an extension of old GAAP are outrageously ill-
informed. Entirely different financial statement amounts can
appear. (See Appendix 4.) Most investors are unaware of the
potential problems.

3 *Inadequate Prohibitions*

The wording used in IFRS often is neither specific nor strong
enough to dissuade determined manipulators from plying their
trade. Corporate managers in Canada seem to believe that, without clear concrete rules, they can report virtually anything.
Instead of concrete rules, IFRS is loaded with vague phrases
and general guidance. Surely, a term such as "economic benefits"
(an IFRS favourite) might be defined endless ways across countries and within Canada, and even within one company.

For external auditors, who may need to substantiate their objections to management's sneaky portrayal of a transaction by referring to specific accounting standards, IFRS often gives them only
vague guidelines. Whether auditors object or not, IFRS allows
management to interpret phrases such as "value" in a way that
portrays their company in the best possible light, based on the
slimmest of hopes. Perhaps there really is a pot of gold at the end
of the corporate rainbow. With IFRS, management can claim for
years that value is there, until their company really needs it, and
investors discover that it was never there to begin with.

Hastily written and permissive wording made IFRS acceptable
to member countries of the European Union, enabling them to
adopt alleged uniform accounting standards even though cheats
had been evading similar standards for the previous 30 years. In
their haste to meet a deadline for adoption, authorities did nothing to close the loopholes or strengthen the vague guidelines
incorporated into IFRS.

The goal of having a common reporting system in Europe was
accomplished by allowing multiple ways of accounting, but by
saying they were all in accordance with IFRS. Unfortunately,
the naïve believed the advertising nonsense.

In its search for the lowest common denominator, in order to
meet the 2005 European deadline, IFRS tossed out nearly
100 years of evolution of reporting, including that which was

imposed to curtail repeats of previously existing frauds. The replacement material by IFRS handed over power to those people who had major responsibility for such schemes. Was this our lawmakers' real intentions?

This embracing of IFRS has had embarrassing consequences. When a rogue trader lost billions of Euros for his employer, for example, the flexibility of IFRS mysteriously permitted the company to record the loss in the year *before* it occurred.

With little protection offered by IFRS, Canadian investors can look to the US to invest in companies that use US GAAP to prepare their financial statements.

4 *Disappearing Protection*

As we previously stressed, Canada held one of its last serious inquiries into a corporate financial failure in the mid-1980s. In his report on the collapses of the Canadian Commercial Bank and the Northland Bank, issued in August 1986, Justice Willard Estey of the Supreme Court of Canada said:

> The auditors, on the documentary and testimonial evidence before the Commission, clearly failed to apply in their judgment on the fairness of these financial statements as prepared by management in the year 1984, and probably as well in the year 1983, those accounting and auditing principles and practices pertaining to the audit of banks. The Northland Bank statements did not, on the basis of the information revealed in this record, fairly present the financial position of the bank at the 1984 fiscal year end, and probably at the 1983 fiscal year end as well. Accordingly, the auditors should not have issued their certificate of approval of these statements for 1984, and probably should not have done so for 1983. This is not an assessment of circumstances exercised in hindsight and based upon loan reviews after the appointment of the curator, but rather a judgment which must necessarily be passed on the basis of the record as revealed and known to the auditors by 31 October 1984.

In response to this scathing criticism of the banks' auditors, Canada incorporated an entire new section into its accounting and reporting handbook standards in the mid-1990s. Section

3025 specifically addressed impaired loans on the books of financial institutions in this country. But when Canada replaced GAAP with IFRS in 2011, the new standards did not include a similar comprehensive section. Instead, the loopholes that Section 3025 had plugged were once again wide open to manipulate.

While lawmakers, auditing authorities and provincial securities commissions sat back and adopted IFRS, investors thereby lost several of the few protections they'd enjoyed under the old GAAP system and thus were abandoned to their own devices.

5 *Choices*

As we've argued repeatedly in previous chapters, IFRS relieved external auditors of certain legal liabilities and helped them to generate larger fees. Our lawmakers took the advice of external auditors and adopted IFRS without much question. Combined with the Supreme Court's decision in the case of Hercules Managements, IFRS has greatly impaired the credibility of corporate reporting for investors and financial analysts. While politicians discuss the adequacy of Canadian pension arrangements, they seem to make no connection between pension-plan shortfalls and the financial thievery made possible by IFRS. Why save money so that it can be turned over to thieves?

To the detriment of Canada's investors as well as its reputation as a secure investment destination, financial reporting by public companies under IFRS is becoming increasingly unreliable, misleading and treacherous. Yet, our lawmakers astonishingly continue to place their misguided faith in those who forced IFRS into Canada.

Here's just one glaring example of the way the ill-conceived system of IFRS makes life especially hazardous for investors. IFRS 1, the version first put forward in 2003 and later amended slightly, says that corporate managers can prepare financial statements under IFRS using information that "can be generated at a cost that does not exceed the benefits." It does not elaborate on the nature of those benefits or identify specifically who should enjoy them.

Another paragraph called "First-time Adoption of International Financial Reporting Standards" says:

An entity may elect to use *one or more* of the exemptions contained in Appendices C–E. An entity shall not apply these exemptions by analogy to other items. (emphasis added)

Appendices C–E are lengthy. Appendix D, for example, lists 19 exemptions (although one of them was subsequently deleted). Appendix C focuses upon "Exemptions for business combinations." Appendix E deals with "short-term exemptions from IFRS."

With companies taking advantage of such a lengthy list of exemptions, comparisons of financial results between companies or from year to year within the same company become exceedingly difficult, or treacherous. Yet the organizations and individuals who advocated for the adoption of IFRS in Canada emphasized the world-wide comparability of financial statements as one of the major benefits of IFRS. Credibility of such claims has to be zero.

We'll continue our analysis of IFRS in the next few chapters.

SUMMARY

The more analysis that is conducted of IFRS the greater its incurable (yes, beyond a cure) deficiencies become obvious. Yet, our lawmakers refuse to address the fact that only they can call a halt to the use of IFRS in Canada. Only they can prevent the steady thievery from Canadian savers. Passing the buck is disingenuous when those who have received the "passed buck" have displayed, over many years, that they intend to do nothing worthwhile for investors.

24

Conceptual Flaws of IFRS

INTRODUCTION

A main purpose of this long chapter is to explain why much of IFRS financial reporting in Canada is causing huge investor losses. Bluntly stated, IFRS is so conceptually flawed that it cannot be sufficiently re-formulated or repaired over time to become useful for financial decisions by investors. Prompt corrective action must occur.

This chapter commences a several-chapter process of trying to explain that, unfortunately, Canada's IFRS is a road to nowhere. Additionally, further proceeding down the IFRS road cannot result in accomplishing a world-wide uniform basis of financial reporting, or some similar goal. IFRS contains too many examples of difficult or impossible to correct problems, and has granted extensive alternatives and exemptions.

The bottom line is that IFRS chose to entice as many countries as possible into the IFRS family by allowing each country and their followers to continue with their popular conflicting reporting choices. Virtually all of these alternative methods subsequently were permitted to be labelled as being in accordance with IFRS. Not only was a uniform reporting goal across the world extensively sacrificed or destroyed in the enticement process, but so were investors, who still have little or no idea which method a particular company has adopted. What a chosen method purported to convey can be a mystery. Adopting IFRS for Canada was an especially serious mistake for investors and lenders.

What is needed by investors and business decision-makers is largely being fogged-up by alternative available measurements, and IFRS phrases having unknown meanings and purposes. Cash effects are being obscured in IFRS too many times. Illiquidity brings forth fraud schemes and financial failure.

De-cluttering IFRS to obtain the nuggets is typically not possible because essential information has not been provided under IFRS's requirements. Credibility of the numbers varies considerably in IFRS. Investors, especially, should not be being asked to suffer such mediocrity.

Over the next chapters observe the following reasons why Canada should not be part of any IFRS association or grouping, with its deregulation of financial reporting agenda.

1 IFRS figures are too often a combination of
   a cash-based transactions;
   b near-cash items such as current receivables and payables;
   c non-cash figures such as amortizations;
   d management's valuation adjustments to the balance sheet
      amounts, wherein widespread freedom has been granted for
      the recording of management's optimism and pessimism.
   It is this widespread management choice (1d above) that prevents investors from knowing what actually happened in a recent
   financial period. Widespread management choice encourages
   deceit.
      The more credible (but not perfect, by any means) cash and
   near-cash based financial activities (1a and 1b) can be difficult
   if not impossible to trace under IFRS. Mainly these cash-like
   transactions would involve third-party actual financial activity.
   (1a and 1b), which is more credible.
      Quite simply, corporate management is being permitted by IFRS
   to "cover-up" previous ineptitude, or worse, with hard-
   to-quantify and especially difficult to verify, personal opinions,
   which are provided from management. Many dollars could flow
   from bonuses calculated from management-biased figures.
2 The consequences of IFRS in Canada are likely to approach an
   extreme at some point because IFRS is essentially not being

policed or monitored. Various frauds can easily be carried on for several years before the company suddenly collapses. Cash and borrowing ability simply dry-up. The stock's price tumbles as its liquidity crisis unfolds.

Previous chapters have shown that buck-passing at the cabinet level in Ottawa downward, along with self- regulation favouritism from Canada's courts have erased Canadian investor protections. Yet, Canada's investors are being forced to rely upon heavily-biased IFRS numbers for their personal investment decisions. Prior to IFRS, many Canadian analysts had learned how to handle 1a, 1b, and much of 1c.

3 Further cover-ups than balance sheet adjustments also exist under IFRS because a variety of common transactions have not been addressed by IFRS, or the wording permits a wide list of alternative treatments (e.g., related party transactions; provisions). Steps to prevent or curtail many of these cover-ups of financial failures are likely to conflict with IFRS's goal of having a "current value" balance sheet. Hence, IFRS has become incurable, because it has spread itself across too many diverse directions, which collide with each other.

4 Long-standing beliefs about the value of an asset or entity are based upon the appearance of expected future operating cash flows. Extensively, IFRS hides cash operating results. Investors want to be able to estimate such cash flows from operations by using numbers that are not contaminated by widespread management biases. Balance sheet valuation adjustments and management-created solutions to situations where IFRS is silent, present major interpretations problems.

5 Over many years, Canada has demonstrated that an important percentage of corporate management will take advantage of weak financial reporting requirements and negligible oversight monitoring of published financial reports. The IFRS's permitting of corporate management to fill the gaps or holes with flattering figures flies in the face of desirable humanity, and Canada's history. If the IFRS's sudden cure for excessive management freedom were to be to add prohibiting rules, fair value balance sheets of today would have to change dramatically. The valuation of intangible assets

would require considerable re-thinking. De-regulating IFRS in Canada would have to be abandoned as being incurable. Much of "fair value" accounting makes sense for internal management decision-making. But, it can be dangerous for public reporting if its inclusive assumptions are hidden from decision-makers.

6 Whereas Canada's pre-2011 GAAP concentrated upon reporting third party consummated cash-like transactions, and attempted to minimize management speculation, IFRS comes close to being the *opposite*. IFRS simultaneous embracing of many of the reporting systems having different objectives or purposes in Europe at the pre 2005 time period creates a monumental problem. Too often investors have no idea what is being served-up by a financial report containing unreported assumptions and an unclear purpose. Pretending otherwise can thus lead to troublesome losses.

7 Canadian investors are being deceived by IFRS and do not realize the extent of management creativity that has been built into the IFRS dollar amounts. IFRS represents a massive rejection of the system that previously existed, and was heavily based on third party independent transactions having to occur before such dollars would be reported.

In short, Canada allowed management speculation to become a significant component within IFRS financial statements. A vote was not held on such a significant matter, because our lawmakers blessed self-regulation by external auditors. Compounding the problems are the absences of education, at all levels, of what has occurred.

Elaboration of the foregoing themes follows. IFRS should never have been allowed into Canada. Unfortunately, its dangers are multiple times its possible benefits, and effects are likely to occur over many years.

INVESTORS' DECISIONS

IFRS includes phrases that state clearly the main purpose of a financial statement is to assist investors and creditors in making decisions. (Elaboration follows shortly.) Before we can determine whether IFRS achieves this purpose, we need to define the information that investors and creditors, as well as financial analysts, require to make informed decisions. According to our research and experience, they need information about trends and variations over time in a company's income/profit and operating cash flow. They also need to feel confident that the dollar figures in a financial statement are credible. To this end, they need to know specifically what the figures measure and how the company makes these measurements.

Unfortunately, IFRS allows management such a wide range of choices not only in reporting its measurements in dollar figures but in the way it makes those measurements – what it includes, what it leaves out, how it interprets vaguely worded concepts, that the final results that appear in a corporate financial statement become almost useless for investors, creditors and analysts in their decision-making.

To undertake comparisons for purposes of making decisions, *at least two* pieces of information must be compared from the following list:

- this year's results versus last year's, for the same company or entity; or
- same year results for two competing companies; or
- budgeted results versus what actually happened, for specific transactions (such as for sales, income or cash generated from service operations); or
- other similar comparative activities (such as results before and after a corporate acquisition or sale).

Sadly, IFRS is so loosely worded and so subject to management manipulation of its dollars that none of the above comparisons may be attainable. Even for comparisons within the same company, the analytical measuring stick can change, making comparisons difficult or impossible. As we saw with Nortel, management may loosen the credit requirements for buyers of its products. Receipt of cash for delivery of products thus becomes less important. The company consequently records sales revenue over time using different definitions of revenue, which leads to confusion.

Granted, the same thing can happen to some degree under most countries' accounting and reporting systems. But while other systems restrict such manipulation, IFRS gives management far more leeway. While other systems explicitly state that management can or cannot go beyond a certain point in its interpretation of events, IFRS too often leaves the final decision to management.

As a consequence, we have the equivalent of a highway sign that says, "No speeding," but no number to define the term speeding. We also don't know if it's measured in kilometres or miles per hour. Basically, you can frequently just make it up as you go along.

Under IFRS, financial comparisons between or among companies become impossible, because each management has its own ideas and employs its own judgment, based on its own levels of optimism and pessimism. For investors, interpreting IFRS requires extensive guesswork.

Recent revisions to IFRS's lease capitalization rules allows lessees to apply a wide range of judgments and rate measures in making their calculations. Under IFRS lease reporting, balance sheets are fattened by adding assets and liabilities, while cash rent expense gets turned into non-cash amortization and non-cash interest expense. In the process, actual cash receipts become obscured, leaving investors in the dark, regardless of what IFRS supporters say about helping investors to make decisions.

IFRS allows management to include future, hoped for, receipts, based on their status as "economic benefits," whatever that means, with today's actually collected cash. Thus, management can roll the past, present and future into a single reported number, which appears in the audited financial statements as a measure of activity during just one recent time period. Magical; but not very practical for investors who do not want management's hoped-for sales numbers contaminating actual third party transactions.

To measure a company's performance, investors, creditors and analysts want to know what actually happened in legitimate third party transactions between the company and its customers in a recent quarter or year. Under IFRS, they have to guess how much the numbers have been padded because everything has been lumped together.

Canadian GAAP, which preceded IFRS, was not perfect, but it contained far fewer loopholes and was far more suitable for analytical purposes. For example, GAAP required companies to report transactions such as amortizations as non-cash transactions. Under IFRS, companies like Sino-Forest could include balance sheet valuation changes in their aggregated financial statements numbers side-by-side with cash transactions involving third parties.

But even now, after we've seen how companies have manipulated IFRS to their own purposes while bilking investors out of millions of dollars, promoters of IFRS have yet to admit to lawmakers and the public that bringing IFRS to Canada was a massive blunder. Integrity of the numbers become materially suspect.

IFRS: FRIGHTENING IMPLICATIONS

IFRS has so many major flaws that it is difficult to decide which ones to address in this book. One of the most alarming flaws is that it assumes the complete and uniform honesty of corporate management. It takes no account, for example, of a behavioural pattern called the "Endowment Effect," which inclines individuals to give a higher value to an asset that they own than they give to an identical asset that they might acquire.

Under IFRS, management may be naturally inclined to give a much higher value to a corporate asset than the value that a third party would place on the same asset. Even when management thinks it is behaving honestly, it may still overstate corporate assets and equity. Under dishonest managers, such bloating or exaggeration can occur for years and provide the basis for an extended Ponzi scheme.

IFRS repeatedly makes such distortions possible, because it emphasizes the balance sheet over income and cash flow statements. Dependent upon the industry and the company involved, the dollar effects of third-party arm's-length transactions can have less impact on a financial statement than corporate management's balance-sheet valuation biases. Instead of providing resolutions to specific technical complexities in financial reports, IFRS often leaves the resolution up to management, whose bonuses may depend directly on an asset valuation. In the absence of adequate regulations, Canadian corporate managers can make choices with little or no oversight.

Being human, corporate managers will have different opinions and apply different values even under the same conditions. At best, this makes it impossible for investors to compare one company with another with any confidence. At worst, IFRS plays directly into the hands of financial manipulators, who wish to promote the company with exaggerations.

Without direct government intervention to create a regulatory body with the power to enforce a high standard of financial reporting and auditing the financial crises that have already occurred under self-regulation will only continue. A typical Canadian compromise solution that permits external auditors to still set the standards of financial reporting and auditing will not stop the financial cheats or protect investors' mutual fund and pension savings. Setting levels of standards is a lawmaker decision, and cannot be delegated to those possessing serious conflicts-of-interest.

The US addressed external auditors' conflicts-of-interest many years ago. In Canada, lawmakers accepted the advice of external auditors and adopted IFRS, which simply exacerbated the conflicts-of-interest and further isolated investors.

CONCEPTUAL ISSUES

We've already discussed in previous chapters the reasons why IFRS makes international comparisons of corporate results either difficult or frequently impossible. Despite its claims of simplifying comparisons and providing an international financial reporting standard, IFRS is so wide open to misinterpretation and major abuse that international comparisons become meaningless. IFRS's treatment of multiple currencies, for example, is by necessity so permissive that interpretations differ from company to company and country to country, and even within one company from time period to time period.

The following conceptual flaws seriously inhibit the effectiveness of IFRS in Canada:

1 Objectives and purposes: IFRS's conceptual framework states:

The objective of general purpose financial reporting is to provide financial information ... that is useful to *existing and potential*

investors, lenders and other creditors in making decisions.
(emphasis added)

As we've stated repeatedly, IFRS gives extensive freedom to
corporate management to choose from a wide range of possible
reporting treatments. As a result, management can easily manipulate dollar figures and explanations, rendering them inappropriate
for investment decisions. IFRS thus goes beyond the Hercules
court decision and falsely presumes that the needs of potential
investors are being addressed in IFRS's financial statements.

Accordingly, IFRS has set an objective that it cannot possibly
attain. Management can easily manipulate financial statements
to frustrate "existing and potential investors, lenders and other
creditors."

2 Balance sheet emphasis: IFRS focuses on fair value balance sheets
as its fundamental starting point, thereby downplaying income
and cash flow statements. Yet these operating period statements
are critical for cross-checking the values that appear on the balance sheet. What is the value, for example, of an asset that does
not produce future cash income?

As a result of IFRS's emphasis on the balance sheet, the following problems arise:

a Many corporate balance sheets contain considerable soft assets
such as intangibles, goodwill and hard-to-value financial instruments. In the 2008 financial crash, for example, organizations
priced credit default swaps and similar financial instruments in
a way that often defied reason. In such cases, achieving a fair
value balance sheet becomes impossible, leaving it easy to
manipulate owners' equity, among other matters.

b Dollar cast-offs in fair-valuing the balance sheet can end up on
the income, or comprehensive income, statement. To de-clutter
an income statement to arrive at bargained arm's-length income
transactions of the current period, which investors need,
becomes as difficult as unscrambling an egg.

c What is value? Conventionally, value is defined as reflecting
future net cash receipts. This is the way a bond is valued, for
example, adding annual interest to residual principal. But as we

showed in our discussion of Nortel, IFRS allows management to contaminate cash receipt information with non-cash estimates from adjusted and fair valued balance-sheet choices. Thus, it becomes almost impossible to use figures on cluttered income and cash flow statements to cross-check balance sheet values.

d Comparison hindrances: Investment decision-making typically involves a comparison of at least *two* sets of dollar amounts. By allowing a multitude of reporting choices, measurement systems and management interpretations, IFRS makes comparisons almost impossible, even within the same company. Under IFRS, management can vary its optimism and pessimism levels, hindering comparisons and decision-making. (Admittedly, other reporting systems have similar limitations, but to a much lesser degree.)

e Temporal limitations: As we stated earlier, IFRS increases management's opportunities to mix financial transactions of the past, present and future into one set of reported financial statement numbers, enabling management to cover up mistakes. Investors need to measure a company's performance in achieving its objectives. When too much management optimism is combined with actual arm's-length current events in, for example, one reported interest expense account, current period performance cannot be evaluated. Investors need a record of discreet arm's-length activity in a period. They need to know what actually happened in a company for the set of third party, independently-bargained transactions on their own (as uncontaminated as they possibly can achieve) before they can make an informed decisions.

As an aside, we wonder whether Nortel would have had to restate its original audited financial statements if IFRS had been adopted by Canada at the time of the company's demise. IFRS would have given management far broader reporting choices that would have continued for several years. Eventually, Nortel would have run out of cash, but not before it could have taken advantage of IFRS tricks to lose more money over an extended period.

f   Worldwide weakness. To recruit as many countries as possible into the IFRS regime, prohibitions under previous standards were relaxed and reporting choices expanded. Several reporting treatments once prohibited in Canada were once again allowed under IFRS.

This one response of gathering-in as many countries as possible, with their wide diversities of financial reporting being acceptable under IFRS, virtually automatically destroyed the credibility of IFRS. Words that have multiple definitions and interpretations inhibit understanding. The same applies to financial reporting. IFRS cannot function on its alleged "principles" basis, especially when the "principles" are not known nor well defined. Personal beliefs and value systems obviously vary widely across a world.

g   Perpetual Ponzi schemes: The vague and excessive management estimates allowed by IFRS make ongoing multiple-year Ponzi frauds far more likely. As we discussed, the confusion under IFRS of what constitutes original capital versus what represents real, earned income directly encourages such schemes. Slippage that allows capital investment to become labelled as earned income is extensive under IFRS, and directly feeds the Ponzi schemes.

Combined with a lack of government oversight and court decisions such as Hercules Managements, IFRS becomes even more unsuitable for Canada as time passes. In our opinion, the system as it now stands cannot be modified to eliminate these deficiencies, because they are built into the fundamental principles of IFRS. Further adjustments to IFRS are unlikely to work, because many permitted reporting choices would have to be prohibited, thereby alienating multiple countries. IFRS just does not have a logical and solid enough conceptual base to build upon. A balance sheet emphasis directly conflicts with investor needs for third-party tabulations of current period profit and operating cash flow. Balance sheet adjustments, clutter from cookie jars and inventory and similar, certainly muddy the waters.

FURTHER DISCUSSION

Under IFRS, investors simply cannot take at face value the numbers that they find in a company's financial statements. Dollar amounts for profitability and operating cash flow, for example, easily may not be credible, for reasons that we have previously provided. Under IFRS, management can focus on the balance sheet, even though credible fair value information for many balance sheet items such as goodwill and intangibles may not be readily available. Instead, IFRS allows management to make estimates without much substance and to report financial information that may be seriously misleading (e.g., ignoring The Endowment Effect).

By downplaying the importance under Canada's previous GAAP standards of concepts such as third-party revenue recognition and matching of revenue and expenses, among others, IFRS has opened the door to even more estimation, more management choices and more speculation about the future included in a company's audited financial statements. By combining optimistic predicted values with the current period's cash and near-cash financial results, management can disguise cash losses and create fake assets simply by calling them future "economic benefits."

Frustratingly, too much of IFRS mixes management biases with actual cash-like believable results. Investors cannot distinguish unwarranted hype from the basic information they need, such as, "Which entity bought which products or assets at which prices." "Did the buyers pay cash?" This is vital information that investors can use to determine trends in a company's bargained third-party transactions. "Trends" cannot be what management decides to create for some bonus or other purpose.

To make sound decisions about a company's progress, investors ideally need clear-cut tabulations of what financially happened in a specific period. For example, a corporate division's budget may allow it to spend $1 million cash in the month of September, but it actually spends $1,408,975 cash. What caused the overspending? Wastage? Incompetence? Or, was a legitimate asset acquired? Theoretically, you could find out what happened by comparing actual results to some form of budget. To do this you would need at least *two* pieces of information, calculated using *similar measures*. But when one piece of information is non-cash-based and has been arbitrarily selected by management, useful comparisons become difficult or impossible.

Budgeted versus actual cash that was spent are but *two* of the crucial pieces of information required by decision makers. Biases obviously occur when management reports one set of figures for comparison to another vague set of figures based primarily on management's imagination. More trouble occurs when both sets of figures, such as the most recent year versus the previous year, have been assembled by an unknown management team with different members at different times. They could use two different optimistic or rosy estimates of future possible events, depending upon their chosen purpose at the time. In any case, when management can manipulate one or both sets of numbers, credibility evaporates. Worse, the degree of dollar tampering can be difficult to ascertain under IFRS.

Why Canadians tolerate such a deficient IFRS reporting system is difficult to fathom. It should be obvious that the more freedom that is granted to corporate management the increased risk of faked numbers arises. Temptation to increase management bonuses cannot be ignored. In an important sense, adopting IFRS in Canada was akin to abolishing Canada's criminal code.

IFRS allows many situations like this, giving management a licence to muddy the financial waters by making the final reporting decision and depriving investors of the third-party information they need to evaluate a company's performance. With hundreds of exceptions and oddities available to management in dozens of countries, IFRS has rendered audited financial statements, for comparison purposes, as practically meaningless, and certainly dangerous.

IFRS simply allows too many management guesses about fair value, for example, while making it impossible to ascertain the dollar magnitude of such distortions. With so little credible information available from management, investors, shareholders, lenders and analysts cannot measure the dollar degree to which optimism has distorted revenue or asset and liability values. By allowing individual managers to use their personal judgment, which inevitably varies from one person to another based on their character, experience, optimism and a wealth of other factors, in preparing financial statements, Canadian investors face the distinct possibility of suffering significant financial losses from IFRS.

Financial disasters in Canada already make this a critical issue for investors. Nortel, Livent, Castor Holdings, Hercules Managements, Confederation Life, Northland Bank, Canadian Commercial Bank, Victoria Mortgage, and many other failures over the last 25 years confirm that unrealistic management decisions have led to some serious losses for Canadian investors. And for this we have to thank Canada's external auditors for ignoring the readily available evidence and bringing inept, contrived IFRS to Canada.

OLD CANADIAN GAAP

Some of the same problems existed under Canada's previous accounting and auditing standards as they do under IFRS, but to a much smaller degree. That's because IFRS allows management to move much further in its financial reporting from recording short-term accruals and purely cash-based transactions. Instead, IFRS allows management to include a range of subjective non-cash figures and estimates in their calculations without identifying and tabulating the extent or magnitude of their estimates, making financial analysis difficult or impossible. Unaware investors are left to evaluate recommendations of undeserving stocks based on worthless or contrived numbers.

In addition to pure cash transactions, Canadian GAAP allowed management to include in its reports of third-party transactions the following:

- Non-cash accruals for such accounts as relatively short-term receivables and payables, including estimates of how much of the receivables would eventually be collected in cash;
- Various GAAP-defined non-cash items such as amortization, cost allocations arising from the purchase of another company, interest/ discounting rates, and several but limited management judgments; and
- Restrictions or prohibitions to reduce some of the deceit that was inherent in the above non-cash activities. GAAP set limits, or

disclosure obligations, for example, on interest rates utilized to measure pension and other liabilities.

There's no question that investors had to keep their eyes open for excesses in management judgment under GAAP reporting. At times, investors would have their hands full trying to pick out the credible numbers. But compared to IFRS, which extends an almost endless range of choices to management, GAAP was still a relatively useful and often manageable system. Investors tended to know what they did not know about crucial topics. They could look for other sources of information or take management's financial statements with a grain of salt.

IFRS has made this much harder to do by adding all sorts of additional ingredients to the original GAAP stew of management choices, such as annual or quarterly updates in valuation, balance sheet adjustments and others that we've discussed in this book. It has now become impossible under IFRS in many companies to determine what management was thinking when it chose a particular value and whether we should regard it with scepticism or simply toss the entire stew down the drain.

Allowing the acceleration of recording of revenue and recognizing income in anticipation of future profits, IFRS has made it impossible to define exactly the period over which the data in a company's report have been measured. Financial statements may specify dates, but under IFRS many more numbers on the balance sheet incorporate management's optimism about a long future. How then can we measure the reliability of a manager's judgment in a specific financial period? How can we compare figures for one period to figures for another period when each set of figures incorporates different management judgments? What actually happened with respect to just the company's third-party transactions? This basic arm's length information is not readily available to investors who use IFRS figures.

Investors have to know what happened in a particular period. Such is inherent in quarterly and annual financial reporting. They want to know the actual bargained-transaction results, uncontaminated by management bias as much as possible. They can then compare the results to managements' promises or budget plans, outlined in other documents (such as press releases), to judge trends for themselves and identify unwanted departures. Instead, IFRS resembles an ongoing dollar-revision machine that makes this analysis impossible.

Too many hoped-for management estimates have been given the same credibility as proven, completed, third party bargained transactions when the future has been permitted to be brought forward into the present day's figures. Hence, what was prohibited by old Canadian GAAP is being encouraged by IFRS's balance sheet emphasis and loose revenue recognition wording.

Management teams within the same company can contaminate financial statements from one period to the next, as occurred with Nortel, without having to quantify the extent of the damage. In cases of deliberate deception, the more financial difficultly a company gets into, the more manipulation it adopts, and investors can never determine how much exists from period to period. IFRS may assume as a basic premise that management is 100% honest, with good judgment and total loyalty to shareholders. Investors in Canadian companies like Nortel, Livent, Castor Holdings, and dozens of others know better.

ADDITIONAL CONSIDERATIONS

Many financial analysts and media journalists disregard the inherent assumptions and value adjustments that managements build into their IFRS income and operating cash flow statements. This is a serious mistake for decision-making purposes. These inherent assumptions must be identified so that the numbers can be adjusted accordingly. Otherwise, analyst and media reports that X Co.'s earnings per share doubled last year are meaningless. The increase could be based on a mere change of a management assumption.

Before analysts crunch the numbers, they need to establish whether the dollar figures are *worthy of belief*. Are the reported figures on an income statement based significantly on management's estimates? Or, are changes from one period to the next based on legitimate arm's-length third-party transactions?

When we evaluate IFRS for its strengths and weaknesses for financial reporting purposes, we ask:

258 Easy Prey Investors

- prepared for which specific person or group?
- prepared for which type of investment decision? and
- relative to which other reporting systems?

We try to look beyond the inherent assumptions or estimates used in IFRS reporting to determine the sources and credibility of the numbers. In assessing management's estimate of an asset "value in use," for example, we have to estimate the effects on future years. We have to consider whether management is double counting across present and future periods. We try to determine the way that management has made its assumptions. We look at the notes for explanations. Often, though, the notes are silent on crucial matters.

As we've discussed, external auditors have to assume responsibility for bringing IFRS to Canada. But this isn't the first time that they've tried to force Canadian companies to adopt an ill-considered reporting system. In the 1970s, external auditors promoted another system called General Price-Level Restatements (GPLR), which enabled a company's managers to apply a series of variables and estimates to determine the numbers they used in their financial reports. Unlike IFRS, the deficiencies of GPLR became apparent within a year, and it faded away before investors lost money.

CONCEPTUAL REVISIONS?

So far we see no evidence that the conceptual and practical deficiencies of IFRS can be remedied. Recent changes affecting lease capitalization, for example, still allow extensive conversion choices. In the meantime, lawmakers have made no move to enhance investor protection in Canada. Government departments deny responsibility for the serious deficiencies in IFRS. Lawmakers ignore the fact that Canada has Corporation legislation, which requires an annual audit. Lawmakers' delegation of power to a non-independent body is baffling, and can be viewed as irresponsible.

CORE IFRS CONCEPTS

As we said earlier in this chapter, IFRS claims to provide management with a system for reporting "financial information about the reporting entity that is *useful to existing and potential investors*, lenders and other creditors in making decisions about providing resources to the entity" (emphasis added).

But by giving too much choice and flexibility to corporate management, IFRS makes it impossible for investors to distinguish honest management from the manipulators, As a result, realistically, investors can trust no one.

As we've discussed, income and accompanying cash flow from operating activities are vital for providing resources to a company. Borrowing and selling more common shares are also important, but income and operating cash flow that a company can generate in future years determine its value. The vital objective of any *business* is to earn income and generate enough cash to pay dividends and maintain its earning power.

But instead of giving equal weight to income and operating cash flow, IFRS places much more emphasis on the easy-to-manipulate *balance sheet*. Despite the relationship that should exist between a company's cash earnings and its overall balance sheet values, IFRS has badly muddied that relationship. By allowing management to make highly subjective adjustments instead of reporting hard, credible data, IFRS has led to serious disconnects between corporate balance sheets and operating cash flows. (See Appendix 4.)

Under IFRS, many balance sheet numbers are based on estimates and speculation involving basic matters like the possible collectability of receivables before recognizing revenue. Only a 50.001% likelihood of collection is adequate under IFRS for revenue recognition. Such estimates can be minimized and controlled, but IFRS does not require that evidence. Instead, for investment purposes, these numbers can be contrived. Without having sufficient, reliable cash-based figures, investment decisions have to be based on non-cash balance sheet estimates. We've shown repeatedly throughout this book that such information often cannot be trusted. (Nortel, Sino-Forest, Poseidon, and many others.)

Here's an example of a standard comparison used by investors and analysts:

Step One: Determine dollars budgeted to be spent $5,000
Step Two: Tabulate actual dollars spent   5,675
Overspending $675

It's an important management function to determine and report on why the overspending occurred. Management needs to resolve problems so the company can move forward. Was the overspending a signal of a serious problem? Was it the result of a temporary, one-time issue? Under IFRS, management doesn't have to say. Instead, management can easily cover up overspending and hide the underlying problems by introducing optimistic forecasts. Under IFRS, management can describe the $675 in our example as a future economic benefit. This transforms it into an asset. It's no longer overspending, and an otherwise decrease in cash flow from operations.

As we've shown, IFRS allows a company to report repairs and maintenance as an asset instead of an expense. The company can obtain a valuation to show that repairs have contributed to an increase in a building's value beyond the figure recorded so far in the company's books. By applying a little magic, an operating expense for repairs becomes an asset, confirmed by the friendly appraisal value.

Admittedly, under GAAP, companies could record some portion of repairs as an asset. But IFRS allows companies to report many repairs entirely as assets. Overall, IFRS is just too loose.

IFRS TRICKERY

As we've already discussed in detail, IFRS offers management many choices to clutter their income and cash flow financial statements in pursuit of their objectives. Here are some of these especially popular choices:

- Capitalization rates: IFRS allows management to choose the rate applied to the valuation of rental property enabling them especially with REITs, to manipulate income dollars, the balance sheet's assets and shareholders' equity (Mainstreet Equity; Appendix 4);
- Revenue recognition: After 2002, proponents of IFRS and US GAAP worked together to create a common interpretation of revenue recognition, but they continue to differ in their interpretation of critical issues. For example, before revenue can be recognized in a financial statement, both the US and Canadian standards say,

"Collection of consideration must be probable." In US GAAP, "probable" means that management can say with at least about 70% assurance that it will collect the consideration; under IFRS, management merely has to believe that collection is "more likely than not." Interpreted to the letter, this allows management to record revenue if it believes that collection is 50.0001% likely. In other words, IFRS leaves ample room for the premature recording of revenue that may never be collected. Revenue documents have been drafted, but as of 2016, some changes were still being proposed. IFRS is allowing public usage of what exists in its 2014–2015 form. The US proposed an effective date of January 1, 2018, for US GAAP purposes. Some further changes in wording and dates are possible;

- Interest rate assumptions for pension liabilities: Management chooses the rate, with few restrictions;
- Future economic benefits: Perceptions by management of vague IFRS words such as the likely "future economic benefits" are wide open to interpretation and abuse;
- Financial instrument values: IFRS gives management wide leeway to determine values of derivatives and other instruments:
- Goodwill and intangible assets: IFRS allows management to manipulate values to avoid expense write-downs. Goodwill can be attached to different segments of a company's operation and thereby can be valued differently. In some public companies, goodwill and other intangibles can be over 50% of total assets. Thus, valuing a balance sheet under IFRS can become pointless;
- Environmental restoration: Under IFRS, management can make provisions for estimated liabilities guided only by vague rules;
- Tax asset collectability: Management can base its estimates on the weight of the slimmest probability and can vary its estimates widely from period to period;
- Inventory: Write-ups and write-downs allowable under IFRS enable limitless cookie jar adjustments to inventory and liabilities. By contrast, Canadian GAAP virtually prohibited write-ups of inventory, in order to minimize income manipulation;
- Capitalized expenses: Another favorite trick of management.

In a nutshell, here's what IFRS enables investors to do:

| Compare a set of estimates made by management one year ago, | TO: | Another set of estimates by management that were made more recently |

When management has everything to gain by manipulating the numbers, why should investors rely on numbers prepared under IFRS by management? What possible valid conclusion can an investor reach? IFRS allows management all sorts of room to generate a fat bonus, con a banker, or bamboozle a shareholder.

Those who think that Securities Commissions or external auditors are restraining management should refer to earlier chapters, which discuss obligations and track records of such parties. Simply, in Canada, investors are largely on their own.

Under IFRS, investors can never determine whether cover-ups occurred in one or more financial periods, if bonuses are at stake or if management is pursuing other suspect objectives. For example, third-party bargained transactions ought to be separated in financial statements from non-cash management estimates. Otherwise, analysts do not learn what actually occurred in the most recent financial period, and cannot establish credible trends. Likewise, management could arbitrarily decide to reverse a previous write-down/expensing of inventory. Such a reversal would increase inventory on the balance sheet and increase income by lowering expenses, such as costs of goods sold. But investors usually cannot tell how many dollars of manipulation have occurred over time in various financial accounts. Thus they do not have a hard measurement for decision-making purposes of what actually happened in a particular period. Did the written-up inventory sell for its usual gross margin in the next financial period? If not, the write-up on the balance sheet probably was too high. Why? Perhaps a management bonus scheme was involved. Dozens of similar examples can be cited. As for external auditors, they can relinquish responsibility for detecting management tricks, and if IFRS doesn't allow them to do it, Canada's court system apparently will.

These examples are precisely what affects crucial income and cash flow dollars used in business valuations. Without requiring hard information, IFRS gives Ponzi schemers a free ticket to plunder investors' money.

With all of this in mind, Canadians should be much more concerned by blatant manipulation of their savings and pension investments. Written protests to lawmakers could be a starting point to force necessary change.

WHAT IFRS DELIVERS

With a few adjustments to an income statement, prepared under Canadian GAAP, investors could obtain a relatively useful result for third-party-bargained transactions and then compare the results against forecasts to track trends over the years and to recalculate the value per share of a company's stock. The numbers were more believable under old GAAP because it was clearer what had actually been included in the totals, and how dollars had been counted.

Under IFRS, depending on the industry under review, it's no longer possible to determine conclusively what actually happened to a company's income and operating cash flow, especially when management does not document its estimates and assumptions, or their impact on current income and operating cash flow.

SUMMARY

IFRS focuses on balance sheet valuations that are frequently *not* helpful to investors. Changes in value made by management under IFRS guidelines may have no connection to goods and services sold to third parties for a cash profit.

The balance sheet foundations of IFRS especially have serious conceptual flaws. The information needed to prepare a credible balance sheet is frequently just not available. Contaminating estimates occur. Extended years of cover-ups are thereby possible.

By allowing management hype and fuzzy estimates IFRS is practically useless for investment decisions in many companies because credibility ranges are not known to investors. IFRS makes it impossible for investors in most situations to strip away the biased estimates and uncover the underlying hard cash-based figures. Balance sheets prepared under IFRS simply contain too many intangibles with unknown values, which fluctuate quickly.

IFRS is ill-conceived for investors and is not reparable. Year after year of taped-together management-manipulated figures make it impossible to evaluate what actually happened in the latest financial period. Investors cannot reliably determine the financial outcomes of a company's dealings with arm's-length participants. Is the company under consideration actually making progress? Under IFRS, investors can only rely on management propaganda that incorporates optimism into hard dollar figures. ("We are making progress; trust us.")

The application year-after-year of repeated management estimates in reports prepared under IFRS can cover-up a weak company for years. A company does not have to come clean *until the end is near*. A short-term financial gain for management in Canada could easily result in large losses for investors over several years into the future.

IFRS opted for signing-up as many countries as possible to its reporting system. Virtually endless concessions were made to allow peculiarities or traditions within those nations to become accepted reporting under the IFRS umbrella. Several of these oddities have been noted in previous chapters. The consequence is that investors do not know which of the multiple available IFRS-approved alternatives have been chosen by a particular company for a specific time period. Interpretation becomes impossible. Bargained third party transactions are being combined with extensive management biases. Cover-ups are unlimited. Where lies reality?

Disturbingly, several portfolio managers in Canada are blissfully accepting the biased, reported, audited figures. Peoples' savings are consequently being eroded before their eyes. Yet, lawmakers continue to pass the buck to those who are benefitting from biased IFRS. To call the situation shocking, and lacking in courage is not doing justice to the matters of open thievery. Lawmakers may be advised to read a childrens' classic: "The Emperor's New Clothes."

25

Deficient IFRS

IFRS claims that its objective is

to provide financial information about the reporting entity that is useful to existing and potential investors, lenders and other creditors in making decisions about providing resources to the entity. Those decisions involve buying, selling or holding equity and debt instruments, and providing or settling loans and other forms of credit. (Conceptual Framework, Chapter 1, OB2)

Lenders are obviously especially interested in trends and dollar amounts of operating *cash* flows and legitimate *cash*-equivalent income/profits. Existing and potential investors are seeking magnitude and trend information on realized income/profit, and its composition. None of the financial statement readers would want to see the figures being contaminated with management's current or futuristic estimates of *non-cash* changes in inventories, intangibles, long-term asset "values," current and longer-term liabilities, and other balance sheet non-cash adjustments. Such non-cash information could be reported separately, especially those hoped-for financial effects.

IFRS clearly does not achieve its objectives.

As shown several times previously, the income and operating cash flow statements become cluttered with balance sheet cast-offs. Separation of already-achieved cash-equivalent results from management's hopes and estimates and cover-ups are often either difficult or impossible to isolate. Trends in cash liquidity are being obscured by the IFRS clutter.

Additionally and deeply troublesome about IFRS is that it fails to separate owners' capital investment dollars from the dollars of income that hopefully becomes earned by wisely using the invested dollars. It is this income versus investment separation that is crucial to protecting against Ponzi and other related frauds. In this respect IFRS is a dismal failure.

On top of the foregoing, which should be viewed as devastating criticisms of IFRS, comes the matter of "can IFRS be restructured in order to attain and maintain its described objective?" The answer is "no," for a variety of reasons that we will introduce or repeat in this chapter and those that follow.

For example, in recent years, IFRS has studied two large issues: revenue recognition, and capitalization (to the balance sheet) of leases. For the former, overall, an appetite to clamp down on revenue games has not been established, especially with regard to the importance of cash receipts. For the latter, an IFRS balance sheet emphasis was reiterated without seriously addressing the downsides of capitalization having cast aside cash effects. Financial cheats are forever trying to convert cash expenses, such as rent, into non-cash amortization. (See the Sino-Forest variation.) IFRS has played directly into the hands of manipulators. Accordingly, here come more Ponzi schemes.

Summed up, the message being sent by IFRS proponents is that they are unfocused, and are moving farther away from IFRS's published objectives. Too many personal agenda issues are receiving attention instead of dealing with mainstream problems that require tightening-up. It is not realistic to assume that Canada does not breed financial predators.

In thinking about this chapter, readers should focus upon the number and magnitude of problems that IFRS has not dealt with adequately, or at all. Parts of the chapter constitute repetition, but they have been repeated as vital reminders for reaching an overall assessment of IFRS. Our point is that IFRS is *not* worth trying to save. But, that is precisely the stall for time approach that is likely to be taken by our lawmakers and external auditors.

IFRS is seriously harming the very people whom its objectives claim that IFRS is trying to help. A Plan B, which casts aside IFRS, is required, and soon. IFRS is too scattered in its permitted choices to be able to rehabilitate. Too many of the claims about the alleged benefits of IFRS cannot be demonstrated. Such has been obvious for years.

LATEST REPORT CARD

Whatever IFRS was designed to accomplish is still not sufficiently clear, other than it was supposed to meet a European Union financial reporting uniformity deadline for 2005. What is clear, however, is that IFRS has extensive deficiencies and in Canada is not a work in progress. IFRS makes financial analysis by investors exceedingly difficult, if not impossible, especially for industries and companies in which soft assets play a major role. Both the conceptual and practical limitations of IFRS are more than just troublesome. Conceptually, IFRS is planets apart from the Canadian GAAP system that preceded it. This makes comparisons difficult between financial statements prepared under each regime, although comparisons are also difficult even for statements prepared by the same company under IFRS.

Here's a brief summary of the criticisms we've made of IFRS so far:

1 IFRS allows management to choose, from a long list, the numbers and explanations that are included in their audited financial statements. IFRS was a major step backward for Canadian financial reporting.

2 Conflicts-of-interest involving external auditors make self-regulation of reporting standards in Canada unworkable. Lawmakers need to legislate a system of thoroughly independent setting of financial reporting standards that takes into account investors' needs and rights. The Hercules decision in particular has been financially devastating for investors. IFRS adds to their woes because it permits extensive choices for reporting most financial transactions, thereby leaving bewilderment in its wake. Cash and non-cash adjustments can be mixed together.

3 IFRS emphasizes balance-sheet values while downplaying the importance of income and operating cash flow statements. Especially for companies that hold huge intangibles, goodwill and financial instruments, balance sheet valuations of these assets are wide open to manipulation, as we discussed in the previous chapters. For soft asset industries and companies in particular, the emphasis by IFRS on balance sheets can be misleading, especially when soft assets are increasing year after year and are accounting for a large percentage of total assets. Investors have to watch the dollars whenever a series of corporate acquisitions are being finalized. Large amounts of intangibles often appear, and cause difficulties for many future years.

4 IFRS's tendency to mix in a single account a concoction of cash transactions, accruals of receivables and payables, non-cash amortizations and management's fair-value balance sheet adjustments produces an unpleasant financial cocktail. The ingredients and their proportionate values in the mix are impossible to ascertain. When corporate management wants to change the taste and dollar value of the cocktail, it simply makes a few arbitrary adjustments without adequately explaining its decisions to investors. Management can do this every quarter, extending the company's survival until it eventually collapses. Cash and non-cash effects are simply tossed together on one pile.

5 As we discussed earlier, IFRS has seriously worsened the financial reporting problems associated with self-dealing in Canada by giving more power of choice to corporate management to repeat its deceit. IFRS does not require bargained, third-party evidence to permit the recording of a dollar figure for a revised balance sheet valuation.

6 Under IFRS, a corporation can easily cover up unfavourable trends in its liquidity, especially involving cash flow from operations. Using non-cash IFRS balance sheet adjustments for recording appraisal amounts, for instance, can help to disguise marketing and similar expenses that have been inappropriately placed on balance sheets as assets. Consequently, faked expense reductions can serve to bloat cash flow from operations, thereby leading to overvalued companies and exaggerated capacity to

generate future cash flow from operations. Another favourite IFRS trick for inflating cash flow from operations involves including interest expense as part of Financing Activities. This inappropriately bloats cash flow from operations.

7 Valid comparisons can be made only by utilizing two or more pieces of information, as long as they are measured in the same way. Under IFRS, comparisons in financial terms may have to be made between one figure measured in centimetres and another figure measured in feet. While old GAAP had similar problems, they were kept to a minimum by rules and prohibitions, many of which IFRS does not impose. An arbitrary change of interest rates by management can have significant effects on the dollars of financial instruments, pension liabilities, liability provisions and long-term asset value, for example.

8 IFRS enables Ponzi schemers to confuse investors' capital dollars and the legitimate income earned by those dollars. Tricksters can pay dividends from borrowed money, for example, while overstating earned income. Corporate risk can thereby significantly increase.

Too much of IFRS involves hiding the cash items from non-cash valuation adjustments. Serious financial problems are destined to arise whenever interest rates on borrowings increase by a few percentage points.

9 A company may obtain a price for a product today that, for various reasons, it cannot obtain tomorrow. This makes current-value accounting useful for daily corporate management purposes, where today's third-party purchase or sale may depend on the estimated current value. But current values calculated months earlier, as allowed by IFRS, have little utility for shareholders if conditions under which those values were calculated have materially changed, especially when management does not explain the assumptions behind those chosen values. Increases in value on a balance sheet can vanish by the time financial statements are published. A value based on the price of oil in 2014, for example, would have declined precipitously by the end of 2015. Some companies are more forthcoming than others in providing the crucial assumptions behind the current values recorded on their balance sheets.

Management can obtain their desired current values by selecting the "right" type of business valuators and appraisers. They can
record these optimistic values even if they're far off the eventual
sale price of the asset. Investors must read notes to financial statements carefully to ascertain whether figures arise from credible
sources or from management's guesses. Unfortunately, all too
often, investors are not told what they need to know, even in the
financial statement notes. Investors in Canada have frequently
been misled by distorted valuations of financial instruments and
private companies, as shown on financial statements. Exaggerated
values in the statements of Crocus Investment Fund, in Manitoba,
for example, led to serious investor losses.

These are just the most glaring conceptual problems and practical
deficiencies of IFRS. There are others. The point is that Canadian
lawmakers and regulators have to recognize these deficiencies and
their impact on Canadian investors. Instead of enabling them to make
informed investment decisions, IFRS forces investors to gamble that
a company has honestly reported its results. Such gambles don't
always pay off, as we have noted in our writings for over 25 years.

Many more deficiencies of IFRS can be listed; more will be covered
shortly. As stated, it is the breadth and depth of these serious concerns
that cannot be ignored when reading IFRS-based financial statements,
and when evaluating whether Canada is inviting more financial failures by tolerating IFRS. Pretending that IFRS is not "an accident
waiting to happen" is hardly wise.

IFRS AND INVESTOR SURVIVAL

Can investors survive the presence of IFRS in Canada? We have deep
concerns. Lawmakers and securities commissions could help, but they
seem either disinterested or ill-equipped to act:

1 Lawmakers: The silence from lawmakers speaks for itself.
  Lawmakers have supported self-regulation of external auditors
  for over 80 years. Influenced by strong and relentless lobbying by
  the self-regulators, lawmakers are unlikely to budge in a helpful

way. Nearly 20 years ago, lawmakers could have reversed the Supreme Court of Canada's decision in the case of Hercules Managements, but chose to do nothing. More recently, they have seen the unfortunate impact of IFRS on investors in this country, and still they do nothing. Lawmakers should feel deceived by the exaggerations and fanciful tales spouted by promoters of IFRS, and they should question the claims to the contrary of auditors who testified in the Hercules case that they owe no responsibility to investors. Unfortunately, all it apparently takes to prevent change among our lawmakers is a few self-serving complaints from lobbyists, and they'll ignore investor protection.

2 Securities commissions: While they fight amongst themselves over territorial powers, these provincial bodies continue to ignore the plight of investors. As we've discussed, their claims to "deliver strong investor protection" are continually contradicted by their inaction in pursuing investor claims. The Ontario Securities Commission, which often sets precedents for the rest of the country, has made extensive promises over the past 30 years, but has delivered little of consequence on those promises. Other provincial bodies are not doing much better.

What Canada desperately needs is a clued-in, designated independent oversight body to head off another calamity. Answers must be demanded to questions about IFRS, whether they're asked in Quebec, Alberta, or other provinces. Instead of accepting the reassurance of self-regulators that "everything is fine" and then rubber-stamping IFRS, securities commissions have to demand tough supplementary reporting beyond IFRS while a new system can be devised. Otherwise, the widespread manipulation will continue.

Having supported a hugely-flawed IFRS, securities commissions should be embarrassed. Yet, they seem unaware.

ISSUES TO RESOLVE

Here are some of the issues that securities commissions, other independent bodies and investors need to address before they can begin to correct the deficiencies in IFRS and decide whether it should be heavily reinforced or abandoned altogether in order to curtail repeated thefts from investors. As previously stated, our view is that IFRS permits too many diverse treatments, such that it cannot be revived for Canada:

1 Regarding self-dealing/related party/non-arm's-length transactions: Securities commissions should require a public company to submit, at least annually, the names of people and entities that it regards as related parties and make this information available to the public. Failure to include a related party on the list would expose the company to a serious penalty.

2 Self-dealing: Public companies should submit details of all related party transactions that occur in a period or a quarter or a year above a specified amount of perhaps $1 or so million. Details should include the valuation methodology, crucial definitions, parties involved, dollars involved, names of appraisers, dates, and similar information. The filing would exclude certain transactions such as those between 100% owned subsidiaries. Canadian securities regulations once required such information when appraisal values were being used in financial statements.

3 Pro forma financial statements: After considering the issue of pro forma financial statements, securities commissions arrived at a disclosure resolution, but it was weak and ineffective. Canadian companies continue to create their own accounting numbers and reporting systems, including under loose IFRS rules that lend credibility to their deceptions in the minds of unaware investors. The issue of pro-forma reporting must be re-visited. (Further details are noted in the chapter for Nortel and its clones.)

4 Criminal investigations: Even pursuing cases before 2011 under GAAP, RCMP investigations of corporate deceit seldom led to convictions. Now that IFRS has opened the door to even more tricks, such as greater capitalization to the balance sheet of expenses, weird conversions to non-cash expenses and distortions in reporting of goodwill and intangibles, the RCMP or an equivalent must be given the training, political support and legal

authority to pursue financial manipulators to the full extent of the law. (Probably laws as revised and updated.)

5 Loan losses, revenue recognition, etc.: As we've discussed, IFRS allows companies to recognize revenue when they adopt a 50.0001% probability of receiving a mythical economic benefit. US GAAP sets the bar much higher. Although US regulators might discuss a compromise, IFRS in Canada opens the door to deceit. Until IFRS is replaced or significantly repaired, scams will continue, as will similar problems involving faked interest revenue, realization, matching and reporting of troubled loans.

6 Asset write-downs: IFRS imposes a variation of a two-part test to determine whether a write-down is in order. Part one can be interpreted to give the power to corporate management to decide whether an asset write-down is needed. Part two applies for calculating "recoverable value" in case corporate management decides that an asset impairment exists. Otherwise, no write-down occurs. Some amendments are being considered. The autonomy granted to management under IFRS has become especially problematic in Canada's energy sector. Despite the precipitous drop in oil prices between 2014 and 2016, many companies have dragged their feet in reporting timely asset write-downs and related declines in operating cash flow. Since IFRS allows such games, securities commissions have ignored the problem instead of demanding prompt asset write-downs. Despite substantial declines in asset values, some energy companies continue to show much higher values on their financial statements. So-called gatekeepers, as we've described in our list in earlier chapters, from securities commissions to boards of directors, allow this to happen.

SUMMARY

Left to their own devices, investors can search for companies with honest management, whose performance has been substantiated by independent researchers, preferably reporting under US GAAP. In the meantime, they must contact their provincial and federal elected representatives and hope that the lawmakers might start to pay attention. Eighty plus years of neglect is compounding the problems and increasing investors' losses.

IFRS has added what can only be described as a frightening burden on investors and creditors. By ignoring the dreadful decision to impose IFRS on Canada, with its benefits to financial manipulators, and not correcting the extensive negatives, drops Canadian financial reporting down to where it should not be trusted until proven otherwise, company by company.

26

REITs and Cash Flow:
More Misleading IFRS

Standard phrases in auditors' reports state that they provide "reasonable assurance" that the financial statements are "free from material misstatements." In terms of auditing standards, "reasonable assurance" means a high level of assurance, but not a guarantee. Although these reports are usually addressed to existing shareholders, prospective shareholders, lenders and others may inappropriately derive comfort from these reassurances by external auditors. Few people realize that, based on the Supreme Court's decision in Hercules Managements, they should not rely on these financial reports for investment purposes. (Which sources of information does your investment advisor use? Do they know about the effects of the Hercules' decision?)

Even though the Hercules decision says they shouldn't, investors and others may also mistakenly take reassurance from the objectives and purposes of financial reporting under the IFRS framework. According to the framework's first chapter, entitled "The objective of general purpose financial reporting":

OB 2 The objective of general purpose financial reporting is to provide financial information about the reporting entity that is *useful to existing and potential investors, lenders and other creditors* in making decisions about providing resources to the entity. Those decisions involve *buying, selling or holding equity and debt instruments*, and providing or settling loans and other forms of credit.

OB 3 Decisions by existing and potential investors about buying, selling or holding equity and debt instruments depend on the returns that they expect from an investment in those instruments, for example *dividends, principal and interest payments or market price increases*. Similarly, decisions by existing and *potential lenders* and other creditors about providing or settling loans and other forms of credit depend on the principal and interest payments or other returns that they expect. Investors', lenders', and other creditors' expectations about returns depend on their assessment of the *amount, timing and uncertainty* of (the prospects for) *future net cash inflows to the entity*. Consequently, existing and potential investors, lenders and other creditors need information to help them assess the *prospects for future net cash inflows to an entity*.

OB 4 To assess an entity's prospects for future net cash inflows, existing and potential investors, lenders and other creditors need information about the resources of the entity, claims against the entity, and *how efficiently and effectively* the entity's management and governing board *have discharged their responsibilities* to use the entity's resources from unfavourable effects of economic factors such as price and technological changes and ensuring that the entity complies with applicable laws, regulations and contractual provisions. Information about management's discharge of its responsibilities is also useful for decisions by existing investors, lenders and other creditors who have the right to vote on or otherwise influence management's actions.

OB 5 *Many existing and potential investors, lenders and other creditors* cannot require reporting entities to provide information directly to them and *must rely on general purpose financial reports* for much of the financial information they need. Consequently, *they are the primary users* to whom general purpose financial reports are directed. (emphases added)

While this may sound reassuring to "potential investors, lenders and other creditors," the Supreme Court of Canada, in its Hercules decision, directly contradicts these claims. In the court's opinion, informed by testimony from lawyers engaged by external auditors, investors should not rely on financial statements to guide them in making investment decisions. The financial statements merely enable existing shareholders to determine (at least in theory) whether the company in which they own shares is being managed properly. Given that management prepares the financial statements, picking from among IFRS's choices, the "theory" of the Supreme Court is not valid.

In the nearly 20 years since the court's decision, no one – including external auditors themselves as well as the lawmakers who took the word of external auditors in adopting IFRS for Canada – has taken any steps to overrule the court's judgment by passing corrective legislation.

While most Canadians falsely believe that they are being protected by IFRS and by external auditors, that protection simply doesn't exist unless the auditors and the companies that they audit demonstrate extreme negligence or deliberate fraud. Then, a lawsuit may commence, which could take a dozen or so years to resolve.

In short, investor protection in Canada is a myth. Keep this in mind as we discuss further inadequacies of IFRS.

MORE CHOICES

In IFRS, the European Union (EU) sought an adequate level of uniformity in member countries' financial reporting. But even as they adopted IFRS in 2005, that uniformity was compromised by the extensive power of choice extended by the IFRS system to individual corporate management. Nevertheless, when the promoters of IFRS turned their attention to Canada a few years later, they emphasized the global scope and uniformity of IFRS and its "principles-based approach" to financial reporting. They knew, or should have known, better.

Other highly misleading descriptions applied to IFRS such as "user-friendly" and "cost-effective" were widely spread. Investors and creditors who "used" IFRS had to be mind readers to determine management's interpretation of vague concepts like economic benefits. Likewise, IFRS "principles" were primarily borrowed from US

GAAP, which supports these principles with detailed rules, many of which were not adopted in Canada.

While most financial practitioners would be hard-pressed to list, and then explain these alleged IFRS principles, lawmakers, business reporters, investment analysts and many others accept at face value such IFRS catch-phrases. They issue misleading interpretations to investors based on their erroneous belief that IFRS compels companies to be principled in their reporting. As we've shown throughout this book, this is simply not close to reality.

Long before Canada adopted IFRS, lawmakers had already seen what happened when corporate management received uncontrolled power over its reporting choices. In 2001, rule changes gave discretion to management to determine goodwill valuations, and reductions. Between 2002 and 2007, goodwill was rarely expensed in Canada. But, when the recession hit in 2008, bringing deep value declines, expense write-downs slowly began to appear, years after they should have been recorded. It then became obvious that managements had overpaid to buy other companies and had buried the excesses under the word goodwill on the Balance Sheet. In the interim, shareholders bought and sold the stock of companies long before management disclosed the bad news. Did they get value for their money? Did investors deserve the consequent losses?

IFRS has allowed this type of behaviour to continue since 2011, to the detriment of investors in Canada. Without an independent oversight body in Canada to ascertain whether published financial statements have materially misled investors, and with only vague, largely unenforceable reasonable assurances from auditors, how can an investor distinguish a recommendation to buy a stock from management hype repeated by an analyst? Another example may assist those who still have doubts about the major shortcomings of IFRS.

REAL ESTATE INVESTMENT TRUSTS (REITS)

Canadian reporting by REITs is one of the easier-to-explain examples of the absurdity of IFRS. At first, financial manipulators probably could not believe that they had struck gold with IFRS. (Appendix 4 provides further details.)

IFRS generally does not specify the issues that companies in a particular industry should address in their financial reporting. This lack of specificity is a major drawback to IFRS. With few rules, and only vague principles to apply, accountants may have to resort to applying Canada's discarded Generally Accepted Accounting Principles (GAAP) to a company's reports, even though IFRS is conceptually far removed from GAAP. We see this, for example, when corporate management wants to record expenses as assets to match them later with hoped-for future revenue.

In the case of Real Estate Investment Trusts (REITs), IFRS is equally nonspecific. REITs are heavily financed with debt. Interest expense on debt can be a huge subtraction from the amount that is ultimately being earned by shareholders. Logically, from a *shareholder's* point of view, the income statement should record interest as an expense. Similarly, cash flow from operations on the cash flow statement should be reduced by interest expense.

So much for logic. Here's what IFRS says:

Interest paid and interest and dividends received are usually classified as operating cash flows for a financial institution. However, *there is no consensus* on the classification of these cash flows for other entities. Interest paid and interest and dividends received *may be classified as operating cash flows* because they enter into the determination of profit or loss. Alternatively, interest paid and interest and dividends received may be *classified as financing cash flows* and investing cash flows respectively, because they are costs of obtaining financial resources or returns on investments. (emphasis added)

Under IFRS, in other words, management can bloat a company's cash flow from operations by excluding interest as a cash-type expense.

Again, as we've discussed, the same manipulation is available to management in reporting the replacement of a financial period's worn capital assets, recorded as maintenance CAPEX. It should be subtracted from cash flow from operations before calculating overall company value. This overall value would then have to be split into debt and equity components. Variable IFRS can help to distort maintenance CAPEX, resulting in a grossly unrealistic overall company value.

Given the choices available under IFRS, investors must try to determine the ones that a company's management have selected. Otherwise, nonsense conclusions could arise. Then they have to adjust the reported numbers accordingly before they can analyze the company's investment suitability. You might find some contradictory information in the notes to the financial statements. Or you might not. Under IFRS, management doesn't have to tell you much about its choices.

While IFRS offers little help, the Real Property Association of Canada has issued some guidance for analysts, including a list of 20 (yes 20, but there could be more) adjustments that can be made to IFRS-calculated net income for REITS. Until these adjustments are made, operating cash flows of individual REITS may not be anywhere near comparable. And to make these adjustments, the REIT must make the necessary figures available. Some do, some don't.

We previously explained how interest rate changes applied to assets such as rental properties, causes their balance sheet valuations to change. Lower interest rates produce higher values for properties. IFRS for REITS magically permits the alleged value increases to be labelled as income (but, non-cash). The income statement becomes bloated, but in reality the cash flow statement should not be affected. (See Appendix 4.)

Long before Canada adopted IFRS, information about its severe limitations was readily available. Problems with current values had already arisen in other countries, and the number of guess work valuation estimates required to prepare financial statements under IFRS was common knowledge. Canada's lawmakers and regulators also knew, or ought to have known, that the country did not have the financial infrastructure to monitor the manipulators who would use and abuse IFRS to their advantage. Yet Canada went ahead and adopted IFRS based on the ill-considered decision of the conflicted external auditors.

Average Canadians owning pension plans, mutual funds and other savings arrangements remain exposed to such unreasonable risk. Canada still has insufficient resources to clamp down on widespread

IFRS-based trickery. And when lawmakers ask a select few people if we have a problem with financial reporting under IFRS, our self-regulators insist that all is well. The deceit has to end.

CASH FLOW STATEMENT IMPLICATIONS

As we've discussed in earlier chapters, investors have to pay close attention to the way a company calculates its cash flow from operations. IFRS gives management choices in the way it records long-term debts that are coming due, for example, and when it should record some debts as current liabilities. This enables a company to falsely bloat its cash flow from operations with a temporary increase in accounts payable and other liabilities at the end of a quarter or year.

In addition, IFRS is too flexible in allowing management to categorize cash flows on the cash flow statement as arising from more than one of the three categories: operations, financing or investing. Tricksters may increase cash flow from operations by hiding offsetting amounts under financing or investing. (See Sino-Forest.) Management may include periodic scrap values of machinery and equipment in a company's revenue, for example, and then add those values to cash flow from operations. Since the company's primary business has nothing to do with selling its machinery year-after-year, such sales do not qualify as revenue or contribute to cash flow from operations. Cash flow from operations should measure only transactions that are repeatable year after year. Obviously, non-cash "valuation adjustments" should not be part of cash flow from operations.

A PRECAUTIONARY NOTE

Academics at Fordham University, Temple University, the University of Colorado, and the University of Texas (San Antonio) studied the impact of IFRS-based financial reporting of interest expense on cash flow from operations. Based on samples from 13 European countries, they concluded that 23% of companies using IFRS did not deduct interest expense from cash flow from operations. As a result, these companies reported falsely inflated cash flow from operations, which had "beneficial effects" on the companies' stock prices. Canadian investors aren't the only ones at risk from IFRS.

SUMMARY

IFRS is far too loose to be labelled as a financial reporting system that aids investors and creditors in their decision-making. Trickery designed to mislead investors is just too easy to formulate. In short, dollar amounts arising from IFRS cannot be trusted.

The consequences are also clear. Audited IFRS too often can be lacking in credibility. Auditors cannot object to strange dollar figures when IFRS permits such. Yet, too many financial analysts in Canada sadly accept the figures as being reliable. Investors thus become the victims.

IFRS is thus not some innocent alternative way of financial reporting. Instead, it is dangerous, because it aids the two most commonly utilized games of bloating income and exaggerating cash flow from operations. IFRS's obsession with turning cash expenses (e.g., leases and lease capitalization) into non-cash amortization is being ignored by too many analysts and lenders. Actual cash flow is needed by corporations to survive.

27

IFRS and Extractive Industries

Extractive and resource industries play a significant role in the Canadian economy. They also account for a majority of the public companies listed on Canadian stock exchanges. Like all industries, mining, oil & gas, forestry, farming, fisheries and related industries present unique challenges and circumstances to participating companies. But in its pursuit of unattainable, illogical uniformity, IFRS does not acknowledge many of these industry-specific issues.

As a result of its vague and open-ended terminology, differences in interpretation of IFRS as it applies to a specific industry like mining can cause great confusion. We directly learned this ourselves in a court case involving the environmental restoration of an exhausted mine site. The case raised so many contradictions and so much confusion that it seemed, at one point, to involve 15 different interpretations from 10 different lawyers and accountants about the dollar value of the liability in question.

Part of the problem arises from the obsessive focus of IFRS on current valuing balance sheets instead of reporting important cash-like matters such as operating cash flows. When it comes to Canada's resource industries, ore and oil & gas in the ground cannot be estimated closely enough in dollars to be recorded with any certainty as assets on a current value balance sheet. Selling prices change by the minute. Recoverable volumes vary, based on an area's geology and other factors. Yet companies in resource industries prepare financial statements based on IFRS that contain hard numbers based on significant guesswork. Whether these companies are run by honest management or manipulators, investors have to rely on these statements in making their decisions. Why? In Canada, where do you search to obtain credible financial information for specific companies?

Describing what actually happened from period to period to a company's revenues actually received and expenses actually incurred was the objective of financial reporting in Canada for over 50 years, until IFRS came along. By enabling management to record extensive estimates of balance sheet values, IFRS has drastically changed the information flow between a company and the people who have to know how it's doing. By allowing management to mix up certainty with estimates in reporting a single number for past, present and future transactions, IFRS enables executives to prolong their schemes until a company's cash becomes exhausted and the entity fails.

IFRS also gives excessive freedom to corporate management to invent its reporting policies. International Accounting Standard 8, for example, says:

> In the *absence of an IFRS that specifically applies* to a transaction, other event or condition, *management shall use its judgement in developing and applying an accounting policy* that results in information that is:
>
> a) relevant to the economic decision-making needs of users; and
> b) reliable, in that the financial statements:
>   i)   represent faithfully the financial position, financial performance and cash flows of the entity;
>   ii) reflect the economic substance of transactions, other events and conditions, and not merely the legal form;
>   iii) are neutral, i.e. free from bias;
>   iv) are prudent; and
>   v)   are complete in all material respects. (emphases added)

These words sound reassuring. But without strong and consistent oversight and enforcement of management decisions under IFRS, they're practically meaningless. They leave management free to create accounting policies that suit their personal objectives, which may or may not be honest. This freedom comes at the expense of IFRS-desired uniformity in financial reporting and leads to confusion, manipulation and investor losses.

In resource industries, IFRS enables management to make choices that present a company in the best possible light based on estimates of ore bodies and mineral reserves that eventually disappear, long after investors have bought the company's stock at inflated values. This is a particular problem with smaller companies in Canada, which account for about three-quarters of the public listings in the resource industries.

As we've discussed, problems of dubious asset values existed under Canada's former financial reporting system. But in resource industries, GAAP users ignored asset figures because they were known to be based upon historical cost.

Under IFRS, the balance sheet of a company in the resource industries does not tell investors and lenders about its principal assets of oil, gas or ore in the ground. Reported owners' equity, for instance, becomes close to meaningless.

Instead, investors would like to know about a company's future expected production volumes, year-by-year, and the expected selling prices, with ranges. Under GAAP, this type of information was beyond the realm of accounting and reporting, because it directly deals with a future based on nothing more than management hope, or hype. GAAP dealt with what has actually happened. It focused on verifiable transactions with third parties. IFRS allows management to include its unknown biases about the future so that what actually happened becomes confused with what management hopes will happen.

Investors would also benefit from information about a company's recent cash-based extraction and marketing/distribution costs. This information would appear on the income statement, not the balance sheet, and it would be helpful in investment decisions as long as cash expenses were separated from other adjustments and non-cash-related accruals. Investors could then compare the cost of extraction, refining and delivery to current sales revenues to determine the company's viability within selling price ranges. Under IFRS, investors have to wade through a clutter of cash and non-cash items on the income statement, and they may never be able to separate one from the other to make a well-informed decision based on hard numbers rather than management hype.

The balance sheet of a company in the resource industries would potentially have some relevance if it played down asset "values" but still presented a credible estimate of liabilities, and related future expenses. In particular, companies could quantify on their balance sheets their financial obligations to restore the environment once they complete the extraction process. These estimates would have to be compiled and verified by independent sources, and they would have to be revised from time to time as better information became available. (We'll discuss this in more detail later in this chapter.)

Crucially, companies in resource industries should describe in notes to financial statements the amount of refined metal or other commodity that they have sold in advance and the prices at which they've sold it. If a company has sold 90% of its refined metal in advance at a low price, it could face cash flow issues in the future.

SO-CALLED PRINCIPLES

As many accountants and auditors have remarked, IFRS may be principles-based, but the corporate managers who apply it often lack principles. Even people who have ethical principles sometimes search in vain for guidance from IFRS. Here's an example that involves the resource industries.

As we said earlier, a mining or oil & gas company has to address the eventual cost of restoring the environment around the site of its operation. But by the time the company searches through IFRS guidelines to determine the applicable reporting requirements, the operation may have shut down long ago. Managers would begin their search by locating passages that address estimated liabilities or provisions. They might begin with paragraph 10 of IAS 37, which defines "provision" and "liability" as follows:

A *provision* is a *liability* of *uncertain timing or amount*. (emphasis added)

A *liability* is a present obligation of the entity arising from past events, the settlement of which is expected to result in an outflow from the entity of resources embodying *economic benefits*. (emphasis added)

This definition of a provision seems to capture the fundamental characteristic of a liability: the expectation that it will result in an outflow. So far, it does not address the issues of timing or amount except to say that they are uncertain.

So we press onward to paragraph 14:

> A provision shall be recognized ... (or recorded and reported)... when:
>
> (a) an entity has a present obligation (legal or constructive) as a result of a past event;
>
> (b) it is probable that an outflow of resources embodying economic benefits will be required to settle the obligation; and
>
> (c) a *reliable estimate* can be made of the amount of the obligation.
>
> If these conditions are not met, *no provision shall be recognized*. (emphasis added)

This paragraph raises some confusion. Surely, a restoration cost is not likely to be zero. Paragraph 10 says a provision is a liability of uncertain amount; but paragraph 14 says we can recognize a provision only when we can make a reliable estimate of the amount. What does "reliable" mean? Since the amount is uncertain, we may not be able to make a reliable estimate. In that case, paragraph 14 seems to give us the freedom to not record a dollar provision.

If we were cheats who wanted to overstate income, this gives us a handy way to do it. We simply leave out from our financial statements any mention of this uncertain expense while referring in a vaguely worded note, written in small type and buried under a blizzard of other notes, that our company may face a possible future obligation sometime.

As we've discussed in previous chapters, IFRS overflows with vaguely defined words and leaves it to management to interpret them. In paragraph 14, critical words such as "reliable" and "probable" and the annoyingly unclear term "economic benefits" are left to management's discretion to define as they see fit.

In the case of a mining company, a law may specify that a company must arrange a bank line of credit or deposit in trust for a minimum of $10 million to cover the cost of environmental restoration. Ideally, a restoration cost liability could become recorded simultaneously with the recording of a year-by-year expense. The expense reduces income, and theoretically would lower a stock's price. Again, theoretically, expenses of restoration should be accrued over the life of the mine's ore being extracted.

Yet in its financial statements, the company records no liability and no expense, justifying this decision by referring to paragraph 14 and arguing that it cannot make a reliable estimate of the restoration costs.

There's more. Paragraph 23 says:

> an outflow of resources or other event is regarded as probable if the event is *more likely than not* to occur, ie the probability that the event will occur is greater than the probability that it will not. Where it is not probable that a present obligation exists, an entity *discloses* a contingent liability. (emphasis added)

As we've said before, under IFRS, a probable outcome is one that has a 50.001% chance of occurring. That 0.001% makes it more likely than not to occur. If an outflow of resources seems only 49.999% likely to occur, then a company does not have to record a present obligation. Who decides on the likelihood? The company's management does.

Other passages in IFRS refer to situations whose recording depends on a "high level of reasonable assurance." This phrase is still vague, but if the words "high level" had been added to the conditions governing the recording of provisions, then management could more easily justify recording no provision. In our example, if management needed a high level of assurance rather than a reliable estimate about the amount of its liability for environmental restoration, we could feel more confident in its decision not to record a provision. Needing only a 50.0001% probability, management has far more room to make judgments in its own favour.

Likewise, the dates when a company expects to incur restoration costs are critical in valuing a mining or oil and gas company using discounted present value techniques. Environmental restoration costs can be huge. If resource companies can postpone or manipulate these costs in their financial statements, as IFRS allows, they can deceive investors and bring Canada's resource-dependent economy into question. Canadian taxpayers would have to pay for environmental clean-ups, and not the shareholders of a mine.

We understand in certain circumstances the need to make best estimates in preparing financial statements. But IFRS gives management such wide choices in making these estimates that investors can never determine whether management is doing what's best or what's convenient personally for managers. Even by closely observing changes in the numbers in a company's statements from year to year, investors can never be certain that management is not continuously manipulating the numbers under IFRS. Why the lawmakers continue to ignore such blatant problems is troublesome.

THE IFRS PUZZLES CONTINUE

Now we turn to the word "contingent." Paragraph 23 says, "Where it is not probable that a present obligation exists, an entity *discloses* a contingent liability."

To what does the contingency apply? In our example, is the recording of a restoration liability contingent upon management's frame of mind at the moment? One day it might feel confident that it can estimate the liability; the next day, for one reason or another, it may feel less confident. Or does the contingency involve some external event such as the passage of a new environmental law?

As we keep emphasizing, too much management choice allows endless cover-ups of mistakes or manipulation or both. An example common in Canada is overpaying to acquire another company. The terms within IFRS need more extensive explanations. Instead, IFRS tells management and financial practitioners to apply principles. But precisely what principles, from what part of IFRS, and with what precise meaning, IFRS barely says.

Our analysis continues. As paragraph 14 says, a company does not have to make a provision for an obligation if it cannot make a reliable estimate of the amount involved. Certainly some costs involved in restoring a mine site to its original condition, such as the removal of contaminants from the soil, cannot be reliably estimated until the mine ceases production. But other costs such as the dismantling of buildings can be reliably estimated, and a company can make a provision for such a cost, recording it as an expense, which therefore becomes a payable of some variety.

Perhaps IFRS provides some guidance in this respect? Let's look at paragraph 25:

> The use of estimates is an essential part of the preparation of financial statements and does not undermine their reliability. This is especially true in the case of provisions, which by their nature are more uncertain than most other items in the statement of financial position. Except in *extremely rare cases*, an entity will be able to determine a range of possible outcomes and can therefore make an estimate of the obligation that is sufficiently reliable to use in recognizing a *provision*. (emphases added)

Fair enough. But then we come to paragraph 38, which casts confusion on the issue:

> The estimates of outcome and financial effect are determined by the judgment of the *management of the entity*, supplemented by the experience of similar transactions and, in *some cases*, reports from independent experts. (emphasis added)

In other words, management determines the estimates based on experience and, in some cases, by independent expert reports. And who determines the cases when those expert reports are necessary? Management, of course. Nowhere does IFRS state categorically that estimates need to be validated by independent experts. In the final analysis, management prevails.

We could refer to dozens of passages that lead to similar confusion and to the inescapable conclusion that management makes the final decision in preparing financial statements under IFRS. Despite conflicts of interest and self-enrichment arising from compensation arrangements tied to financial statement numbers, IFRS allows management to apply its judgment with little guidance and little supervision and little corrective oversight from directors or external auditors. At the very least, different people will interpret the vague words of IFRS differently, making comparisons and decisions difficult if not impossible for investors. Under IFRS, the ultimate boss is corporate management, be they honest or not.

So far, our example and analysis applies only to companies in the resource industries addressing the potential cost of environmental restoration. We could extend this analysis much further. Management can apply its judgment under IFRS to intangibles, pensions, tax assets, financial instruments and much, much more. Provisions are only one example.

WHICH PRINCIPLE?

How did IFRS become so vague, confusing, contradictory and non-specific? Was it deliberate? Did its creators hesitate to step on somebody's toes? Or did they merely aim for the lowest common denominator necessary to convince the most countries possible to adopt IFRS in the shortest conceivable time? Regardless of the reasons, we find it disturbing, to say the least, that Canada chose to accept such inferior reporting standards.

Worse still is that Canada has not embarked on a program of upgrading IFRS when it is clearly wide open to manipulation. Canada typically rubber stamps whatever IFRS churns out. Accordingly, Canada's reporting standards, or quality thereof, are being decided largely in Europe, based on what the European politicians in power at the time want to see. Must Canadian courts act, to set Canadian reporting fairness?

To return to our earlier example, if a resource company's management applies the so-called principles of IFRS in reporting a restoration provision/liability and the cost involved, here are the possibilities:

1 Let management decide everything;
2 Record zero liability until the absence of the liability becomes so apparent that management has to record something;

3 Record the lowest possible amount as a liability and append a note to the financial statements explaining that the amount of the liability could be higher; .

4 Let management define the rare case when an expert opinion is required, and then ignore it;

5 Pass a law that overrides IFRS and forces management to record a liability;

6 Record the estimated liability or else, knowing that "or else" is rarely enforced in Canada;

7 Disclose little or nothing about any liability, based on the IFRS principle that allows such a choice.

So far in Canada, IFRS allows such a range of financial reporting treatments of environmental restoration expenses and liabilities that managements are using this vagueness to do whatever they want to accomplish their personal and corporate objectives. For every honest manager, there's a cheat waiting to pounce.

OVERALL

Investors have to examine resource companies' financial statements to detect expenses and liabilities that are either unrecorded altogether or recorded in trivial amounts.

When an attendee at one of our conferences doesn't want to hear this message, they tend to say: "you have chosen rare exceptions which are unrelated to Canadian situations." Our responses vary with the circumstances, including: "how many examples would you want to see, to convince you that investment losses are actually very large?"; and "why do you assume that these situations are rare?"

At this point, it is wise to ask yourself how well your investments are being protected. Canada really does not need any more Nortels, Sino-Forests, Livents, Castor Holdings, or Valeants. Your opinions on the matter should be heard by lawmakers.

28

IFRS Financial Analysis

As we've pointed out, the financial statements of individual companies tend to be different, despite desires of IFRS for some form of uniformity. In addition, companies in different industries face different reporting challenges. Despite these extensive differences between companies and industries, we have identified throughout this book some of the common IFRS problem areas that investors should consider when examining any company in any industry.

As an obvious first step, you should consult the external auditors' report to ensure that the company under analysis has utilized IFRS rather than US GAAP. Analysts often make comparisons between companies that don't use the same reporting system, but differences between the two can be substantial. Philosophically, IFRS and old Canadian GAAP could easily be viewed as being from two different planets.

We've only touched in the previous chapter on industry-specific reporting challenges. We could have looked at other industries besides mining and oil & gas. In the construction industry, for example, IFRS apparently does not permit a company to defer profits when uncertainty exists that risks could readily materialize, so corporate managers resort to other tactics such as manipulating the dates of recording costs.

Investors who want more industry-specific information should examine financial statements from the industry in question. They can begin by looking at the undernoted more general areas of a financial statement that may reveal management tricks and manipulation. The

list has been updated from previous commentary to include more
IFRS implications:

1 Revenue recognition and reporting: As we've discussed, tricks
  involving the non-collection of cash and bad receivables are common in Canada. Companies can rely on woefully deficient IFRS to
  record revenues based on a 50.001% probability of eventual collection. Changes are continuing, and US authorities are working
  on the problem to find a possible better solution. But for the time
  being, the overall manipulation problem has not been fully
  addressed and continues to pose a risk for investors.

2 Self-dealing and related-party transactions: IFRS does not require
  management to fair value measure and report for excessive profit
  made by corporate management on sales from management-
  owned private companies to the public company. Instead, IFRS
  focuses on note disclosure, and not on verifiable fair value dollar
  measurement.

3 Balance sheet valuation changes: IFRS does not require a separate
  listing of all non-cash adjustments made in each financial period.
  Instead, management can change valuations simply by altering its
  judgment on interest and discount rates, and other matters such
  as inventory write-ups and write-downs.

4 Manipulation of cash flow from operations and income/profit:
  IFRS allows management to attribute interest expense to financing activities instead of operations, as well as income statement
  manipulation and receivables/payables cookie-jar movements,
  thereby potentially deceiving investors and lenders.

5 Overstated goodwill and intangible assets: Management can use
  this trick to hide excessive acquisition costs and delay expense
  write-downs. Investors should determine for themselves the
  percentage of total assets represented by soft assets. The higher
  the percentage, the lower the credibility of the balance sheet.
  Capitalization of leases is a recent example of IFRS's obsession
  with balance sheets, and the ignoring of fogging up liquidity and
  cash flows. (Cash rent expenses become converted into non-cash
  amortization and dubious interest expense.)

6 Adjusted EBITDA and related games: Management can draw
   attention to a company's adjusted EBITDA and similarly vague
   figures that may disguise a variety of tricks from interest-rate
   manipulation to faked fair values. All of these types of distractions are aimed at boosting perceptions of income and operating cash flow in order to inflate the amounts artificially.

7 Understated CAPEX: By understating capital expenditures
   required to upgrade and maintain equipment and property, companies can manipulate their free cash flow upward, enhancing
   their stock valuation. Investors should compare amortizations
   recorded on a company's cash flow statement with annual
   CAPEX reported in the financial statements. In addition, the
   Cash Flow Statement's "Investing Activities" may be helpful in
   determining what was actually being spent on investment maintenance in recent periods. Differences can then be examined.

8 Understated liabilities: It is possible to manipulate interest and
   discount rates to understate liabilities. Investors should confirm
   and evaluate a company's long-term liabilities, such as expenses
   recorded by mining companies for the cost of site restoration,
   and scrutinize provisions for such liabilities recorded on the
   company's balance sheet. Pension liabilities can be fictional
   even in large companies.

9 Expenses reported as assets: Companies use this trick to inflate
   income/profits by converting regular cash expenses into capitalized and amortized non-cash expenses. Investors should compare
   the company's larger dollar expenses over several quarters and
   watch for variations in the proportions of each period's revenue
   and expenses.

10 Bloated owners' equity: Under IFRS, management can easily
   overstate assets and understate liabilities. Investors should look
   at company statements from previous periods to determine
   whether the change has arisen from gimmickry or real cash-like
   profits.

11 Manipulation of profits and losses: Investors should watch for
   changes in current assets and current liabilities, and specifically
   for changes reported under accrued liabilities, provisions, other

liabilities and similar terms. (These are called the "cookie jar" manipulations, and can be desperation cover-up techniques.)

12 Reporting of acquisitions: Management can manipulate asset values and hide over-payments for acquired companies by disguising the over-payment as goodwill or intangibles. This has become especially easy under IFRS, which does not require management to obtain a serious independent valuation of the acquired assets and liabilities. Investors should look for increases in goodwill and intangibles in the financial statements, and ascertain exactly what was acquired. Financial games can also be played with inventories, current liabilities, provisions and similar, to bloat income in the periods after the acquisition.

13 Income tax assets: Management can pad their balance sheets and income statements by applying the "more likely than not" test under IFRS. As we've observed, a 50.0001% likelihood is all it takes to determine whether a tax asset can be recorded.

14 General and administrative revenue and expense: Manipulation of reported dollars for revenue and expenses under the term "general and administrative" is common under IFRS. Investors should determine whether notes in the financial statements provide an adequate explanation of recorded data in this category. The vaguer the notes, the more suspect the numbers. Over expenditures for bonuses can be hidden by placing expenses on the balance sheet as fake assets.

15 Ponzi schemes: Investors in Canada have always had to look closely to see whether a company is paying dividends from borrowed money, while overstating income to disguise the source. Under IFRS such Ponzi schemes have become more common than ever. Investors' capital is being re-categorized as income, by running dubious gains through the income statement. The ratio of dividends to income is inappropriately lowered to fool investors.

16 Transfer prices: Management can enrich itself by manipulating the price of goods transferred to a public company from private subsidiaries in which they have an interest. Minority shareholders can be easily deceived, although they can launch minority oppression lawsuits if they later detect the deception.

17. Manipulation of executive bonuses: Investors should investigate and confirm the way management earns its bonuses, especially in mid-sized companies. If bonuses are tied to corporate profits, for example, investors should examine the ways management has reported profits to detect one or more of the games that we've described in this book.

18 Financial instruments: IFRS gives management considerable freedom to select fair values for infrequently traded instruments in order to increase income/profit. Investors should read notes to the financial statements that describe the way management determined these values. Often, considerable estimation has occurred.

19 Timing of transactions: This is another common trick made easier by IFRS. Management times the recording of transactions, usually around the end or beginning of a period, to bloat or decrease income/profit for the period. Investors should look at financial statements to detect delays from one period to the next in recording losses, the dates chosen to record a corporate acquisition and similarly time-sensitive information.

20 Deferral and amortization: By extending the capitalization of a lease, a company can record rent expenses as non-cash amortization, which enables it to manipulate assets and liabilities on the balance sheet. Interest on the faked liability then becomes another non-cash interest expense that corporate management can manipulate. The result for investors is a distortion of the company's income and operating cash flows. Since 2011, the same trick has been applied to short-life assets. For years, these items were expensed as cash disbursements. With IFRS and claims of future "economic benefits," the expense becomes a fake asset to be spread over several future periods. Both income and cash flow from operations becomes distorted.

21 Realization and matching: IFRS allows management much more freedom than its GAAP predecessor to manipulate the matching of revenue from the sale of goods or services with the expense involved in producing it. Once again, IFRS allows management to apply the "more likely than not" rule (50.0001% probability) to record revenue from doubtful accounts, with a subsequent

distortion of reported income dollars. By ignoring third-party contracting to achieve realization, IFRS widely opened the door to the self-dealing that was mentioned for Sino-Forest. IFRS helps to invent mysterious buyers somewhere off in the future; hence, expenses of acquiring these "future" customers become distant "economic benefits."

22 Emphasis on the balance sheet: IFRS places a far higher priority on balance-sheet numbers than cash flow from operations and its impact on cash flow from arm's-length transactions. Although many corporate balance sheets lack credibility, analysts inappropriately rely on these dollar figures to assess a company's value. Such manipulation can disguise growing liquidity deficiencies in companies. Bankers especially have to be on guard for unjustified borrowings.

23 Unusual gains: These should always be analyzed to determine their legitimacy and sources. The years-old problem of recording gains on the income statement while losses become buried on the balance sheet has been greatly facilitated by IFRS.

24 Restructuring: As with unusual gains, restructuring costs must be analyzed to ascertain what became buried in net or consolidated amounts. Often, the net costs include funerals for previous bad management decisions.

Some of these tricks, and others, were possible under GAAP. IFRS has enabled them to continue, or blossom because management has been granted greater power to cover-up. New scams have been introduced in response to the loose and vague terminology of IFRS. In any case, these games can pose a serious threat to investors whenever they are overlooked. They also continue to bamboozle many financial analysts, who remain unaware of the vast scope of manipulation available under IFRS. In fact, we cannot stress analyst unawareness enough. Every day we are forced to read misleading financial data in their reports.

Investors should also keep in mind that most Canadian companies that have adopted IFRS are not registered with or monitored by regulators in the US. Some of the biggest cases against Canadian-based companies have been initiated and pursued by US, not Canadian, authorities, but these companies were listed on US as well as Canadian stock exchanges. Companies that sell shares only on Canadian exchanges do not fall under US jurisdiction. Thus, investor protection against deceptions could be negligible, and has to be factored into buy, hold and sell decisions. Without pressure from outside Canada, the chances of prosecutions within Canada quickly diminish.

Also, as we've mentioned, US authorities are working to tighten and harmonize their respective revenue recognition requirements. These revised requirements are supposed to become effective on January 1, 2018 but delays are possible. Until then, old rules apply. When the requirements change, investors and analysts will have more difficulty than ever determining trend lines in a company's performance.

The revenue notes in IFRS-based financial statements for the years up to 2018 will have to be read especially carefully. Choices exist under IFRS for implementation dates. Analysts must ascertain which sets of the changing rules have been adopted, and which have been deferred under IFRS.

FURTHER CONCERNS

Many items on the list in this Chapter are more easily utilized under IFRS simply because corporate management is frequently permitted to make the final reporting decisions. For example, both the degree of note reporting (but of not dollar quantifying) for self-dealings and the choice of interest/discount rates essentially are dependent on corporate management's judgment. These two items alone give corporate management wide dollar freedom to feather their own nest and should always be given close attention.

We would prefer to give investors more specific information about the games that specific companies have used to deceive them. Unfortunately, Canada's laws make it very difficult to expose the companies that have pursued these tactics. Oppression of critics is made too easy by Canadian laws. All we can do is provide hints of where to look in a company's financial statements for clues. Investors themselves have to follow up on the hints.

Over the years we have frequently observed that Canadian investors have a high tolerance level in support of those holding power positions. That is why the billion dollar financial losses occur. Adopting a position that is contrary to the crowd is what helps the most in avoiding losses. Contrary to the alleged gatekeeper party lines, Canada has experienced huge losses, such as Nortel and the business income trusts, and more since then.

29

IFRS Analysis in Action

By recognizing the manipulation allowed in Canada under IFRS, investors may be able to avoid or sell a stock in advance of a decline in share price. Unfortunately, most Canadian investors, in our experience, will hang on to and support the stock of a dreadful company for months or years after they should have abandoned ship. Among other matters, this procrastination enables cheats to maintain a manipulated stock price by paying a Ponzi-like dividend that has little chance of being sustained into the future.

Admittedly, it's difficult to detect when a decline in market confidence is imminent. Financial manipulators can stabilize a stock price for weeks or months after serious financial problems in a company have surfaced, which should have led to its decline. Examples are Sino-Forest and Nortel. This can be done in a number of ways. For example, they can force short sellers – those who borrow shares and sell them in the belief that their price will fall, and then buy them back at a lower price before they have to repay the lender – to buy back shares prematurely. In buying the shares, the short sellers sustain the company's stock price, even if its overall financial condition has deteriorated.

In this chapter, we'll look at examples of problems in financial reporting allowed by IFRS. In our opinion, these treatments can potentially put investors' savings and pensions at serious risk. In none of these cases, unless the facts state otherwise, do we suggest that the company has broken the law. On the contrary, we have included these cases to emphasize the wide range of possibilities that current Canadian law and IFRS allow.

EXAMPLE 1: MAINSTREET EQUITY CORP.

Mainstreet Equity Corp. (MEC) is listed on the Toronto Stock Exchange. It owns rental apartment properties, mainly in Western Canada.

Dramatic differences in MEC's financial reporting occurred when old Canadian GAAP was replaced by IFRS in 2011–2012. Although we've acknowledged the deficiencies in GAAP, these differences under IFRS raise far greater risks for investors. (See Appendix 4, for financial details.)

Here are MEC's condensed financial results, prepared under GAAP, for the years 2009 and 2010:

	September 30	
	2010	2009
	($thousands)	
For the year ended September 30:		
Rental revenue	53,117	51,661
Expenses	58,680	61,557
Net loss	(3,863)	(3,026)
Cash from operating activities	10,462	4,627
At September 30:		
Real Estate Properties	384,342	342,001
Total assets	399,440	381,167
Share capital	26,214	25,422
Deficit	(37,924)	(33,854)
Shareholders' equity	(8,523)	(5,063)

According to the old Canadian GAAP, which had its deficiencies:

1 Both years, 2009 and 2010, showed a net loss.
2 Both years showed positive "cash from operating activities."

3 At the end of each year a noticeable equity deficit existed.
4 In both years, the company showed negative shareholders' equity.

For financial reporting purposes, MEC switched to IFRS on October 1, 2011, for its year end of September 30, 2012. It also prepared comparative reporting data for October 1, 2010 to September 30, 2011. It engaged appraisers, who valued the properties for IFRS purposes, based on management-approved estimated interest rates. Overnight, MEC's reported investment properties increased in value to $743,265 (in thousands). That overnight increase amounted to $359 million:

	(millions)
October 1, 2010	$743
September 30, 2010	384
Increase, in millions	$359

Shareholders' equity increased, as well, from negative $8.5 million to positive $293.4 million, an increase of over $300 million.

In the three years from 2011 to 2013, a combination of additional purchases of property and updated valuations increased the value of MEC's investment properties even further. As of the September 30 year end in each year, MEC recorded investment property values of:

2011	$908 million
2012	$983 million
2013	$1,128 million

Hence, in the three years from September 30, 2010, to September 30, 2013 the audited, reported investment properties increased in value by:

September 30, 2013	1,128 million
September 30, 2010	384 million
Increase in $millions	$744 million

In other words, by switching to IFRS and acquiring some further assets, MEC almost tripled the reported value of its real estate properties.

Over the same period, MEC's rental revenue increased by less than 50%:

Rental revenue ($millions)

2010 old GAAP	53
2011 IFRS	56
2012 IFRS	66
2013 IFRS	77

A look at MEC's stock price shows another curious and dramatic increase after the company switched to IFRS reporting. Until the end of MEC's fiscal year in 2010, its stock traded at $5 to $17 per share. By the end of 2013 the stock price had risen to about $35 per share. By 2014, it was over $40.

MEC's stock price ($)
as of September 30 (in 2010 and 2013),
per share

2010	2013	2016
$17	$35	$35

These changes in share price raise some obvious questions:

1 Why did the value of MEC's investment properties increase so dramatically in value?
2 Why did this increase occur even though rental revenues increased by a much smaller percentage? Logically, revenue and income trends ought to bear a rough relationship to property values.
3 By answering the first two questions, can we explain the jump in MEC's stock price?

Let us look at what IFRS has done. In fiscals 2011, 2012 and 2013, MEC's income statements tell us:

	2013	2012	2011
	(in millions)		
Profit before continuing operations	$62	$50	$80
Less fair value gains on properties included in income (before future tax)	59	47	75
Profit, excluding fair value gains	$3	$3	$5

[Note that operating cash flow would *not* be close to the profit figure of $62 million in 2013. The $59 million is non-cash-based.]

What are these fair value gains that IFRS allows MEC to record on its audited income statement? They represent the alleged increase in fair value of the investment properties during the year as determined by a management-approved "independent" valuator. The previous GAAP system did not allow the recording of these gains on a company's income statement because they had not been verified through a third-party sale of the property. Without such a sale, there was no firm evidence beyond the word of management that an increase in property values had occurred.

The value of properties of a real-estate company like MEC is typically based on the cash flows that they generate from rental operations. (This principle applies, as well, to bond values.) Removing the non-cash fair value gains from the equation, MEC recorded a profit of $5 million, $3 million and $3 million in the three years of 2011 to 2013.

Even if we adjust for tax peculiarities applicable to real estate companies, MEC's investment properties, valued at $1.1 billion in 2013, earned a return of less than 2%. This seems woefully inadequate, especially when we consider that some financial institutions were offering higher returns on insured deposits.

So, why, under IFRS, might we end up with such unexpected property values? A closer look at the appraisal techniques applied to MEC's properties shows the values arise from MEC's IFRS-approved capitalization technique.

Over the three-year period of 2011, 2012, and 2013, MEC's management-approved valuators applied a continually lower desired rate of return in their calculations. By lowering the desired interest rate, the capitalization factor increases, resulting in apparent gains in value. Here's an example (multiplying the desired interest rate by the capitalization factors equals 100):

Rate of interest	Capitalization factor	Total
3%	33.33	100
4%	25.00	100
5%	20.00	100
6%	16.66	100

In other words, the lower the interest rate, the higher the valuation multiple for the investment properties. In the case of MEC, it reported property values of $384 million in September 2010. Three years later, after a few acquisitions and several updated valuations based on MEC-determined, lower multiples, the company's reported property value had increased to $1,128 million. Every time MEC lowered its estimated rate of return on its properties, it automatically increased the capitalization factor. Referring to our non-MEC example above, multiplying a figure using a capitalization factor of 33.33 produces a much higher number than a capitalization factor of 16.66. But that's what MEC did arithmetically, and IFRS allowed the company to do it.

What is the moral of this illustration?

1 Under IFRS, management has practically unregulated power to determine capitalization factors or multiples, sometimes based on little more than guesswork. The guesses can heavily influence the numbers on a company's balance sheet, and income statement.
2 Friendly appraisers, hired by management, can confirm optimistic management viewpoints. But, the appraisers tend to stay within broad limits.
3 Even if management records gains in property values based on improved cash flow from rentals, the relationship between a

building's value and the cash received from rentals, less expenses, should be reasonably close.

4 IFRS does not require the sale of properties to third parties before a real estate company records income. Hence, analysts' comparisons of IFRS to US GAAP and Canadian GAAP in effect prior to 2011 could be meaningless.

5 Until third-party sales confirm the value of property, gains in value recorded by a real estate company like MEC remain unknown, no matter what figures appear in its financial statements.

Many of MEC's properties were in Alberta. When the price of oil dropped in 2015, vacancies increased and MEC's rental income declined. The stock price fluctuated, and some investors lost money. How many of them might have been misdirected by MEC's IFRS-approved numbers?

EXAMPLE 2: LOBLAW COMPANIES LIMITED

The stance adopted by IFRS's proponents concerning self-dealing transactions is very difficult to fathom. Proponents want a current-value balance sheet, even though significant estimation is often involved. Yet, they refuse to *measure* self-dealing transactions to ascertain whether physical transfers were recorded at fair value. IFRS merely requires often too vague note disclosure, without any serious measurements at all. Wide latitude is generally permitted by IFRS with respect to what constitutes value, and self-dealing is yet another example.

One consequence of a grow-grow-grow or merge-merge-merge approach happens when the separate parts of a company are thought to become more valuable than the whole. This has led an increasing number of Canadian companies to split themselves up into separate publicly listed companies for stock trading purposes.

As an example, Loblaw Companies Limited sold off most of its real estate properties to a separate, related, newly formed company, being a real estate investment trust (REIT) called Choice Properties ("Choice"). The REIT was then listed on the Toronto Stock Exchange.

As often happens in these partial divestitures, this one involved negligible bargaining or a sales agreement with a third-party. Instead, the parent company basically bargains with itself over the transaction and makes arrangements that it hopes are sufficient to attract buyers of shares in the newly formed company.

In forming Choice REIT, Loblaw had to make the following considerations:

1 Which properties would it transfer to Choice and at what price?
2 What monthly rent should each property pay? (Based on store sales or some other formula?)
3 Which liabilities would Loblaw transfer to Choice?
4 Since each Loblaw store would have to sign a lease with Choice, which terms should apply, such as the lease period and the percentage by which rents would increase year by year?
5 Would Loblaw or Choice assume responsibility for operating expenses such as repairs and property taxes?

Crucially for investors, responsibility for answering all these questions lay with Loblaw's management. Loblaw owns well over 50% of the shares of Choice, while other shareholders rank as minority owners of the REIT. If Loblaw management turns to IFRS for answers, it finds little guidance. In other words:

1 Loblaw owns the majority of the shares of Choice REIT.
2 The vast majority of lease revenue earned by Choice comes from Loblaw.
3 In dollar terms, Loblaw determines the outcome of any negotiations with Choice.
4 Meanwhile, IFRS financial reporting requirements for such related-party dealings are pathetically loose or almost non-existent.
5 As a result, under IFRS, Loblaw can negotiate with itself to set prices that Choice pays for Loblaw real estate. Loblaw can also determine the terms of leases that apply to Loblaw stores on the Choice properties.

For investors, here are two significant consequences of such related-party dealings under IFRS:

1 In a multiple-year lease, rent escalation clauses usually reflect anticipated trends in inflation and costs over future years. Leases typically prescribe rent percentages tied to store sales, which may rise. This information is not always readily accessible in financial statements prepared under IFRS. IFRS focuses on note disclosure and carries few strict obligations to disclose dollar measurement or quantification of self-dealing transactions.

   In the case of Loblaw and Choice, Loblaw would incur an annual rent escalation of an average of 1.5% per year for the first five years, according to the Choice offering prospectus. The prospectus gives few details of this arrangement, although the 1.5% annual increase seems relatively low. The point is that Loblaw itself determines this figure and will continue to determine the rental increase in the future. This leaves minority owners of the REIT potentially vulnerable, but IFRS does not suitably address this exposure.

2 Under IFRS, Loblaw transferred its property to Choice at fair market value, which can vary widely depending on the appraisal reports. In addition, Loblaw reserved the right to share in the benefits of any improvements that Choice might make to certain of its properties. So even if the REIT paid fair market value on the date of transfer from Loblaw, it could have to pay more at a later date if certain types of renovations occur.

   The terms of the leases between Loblaw and Choice may be based on eminently reasonable grounds. But investors and minority shareholders will never know, because IFRS does not require disclosure of much information related to these terms. In any case the terms had been negotiated before Choice was listed as a public company. Before anyone else had become a shareholder, Loblaw's left hand had negotiated with its right hand to set the terms of the leases and many other pertinent details.

   Regardless of the companies involved, individual investors in a public company in Canada have little power. They simply have to hope under IFRS that directors and corporate management are honest and that they keep the interests of minority shareholders in mind at all times. When it comes to related party transactions, it's nothing more than a hope, though, because neither IFRS nor Canadian law sets out any well defined rules to make sure it happens.

By no means are we questioning the honesty of Loblaw's management. We're simply using this case as an example of the inadequacies of IFRS in dealing with non-arm's length transactions. As we've said, IFRS assumes that all corporate managers are 100% honest, 100% of the time. Such an assumption has frequently proven to be a mistake in Canada.

EXAMPLE 3: POSEIDON CONCEPTS CORP.

Poseidon Concepts Corp. emerged in 2011 as a public oil services company based in Alberta, after it was carved out of a larger company called Open Range Energy Corp. and listed on the Toronto Stock Exchange. Poseidon's initial offering prospectus contained financial data prepared under IFRS. Investors gobbled up the shares. A few months later, four Canadian banks lent money to Poseidon based in part on audited financial statements.

Trouble began less than two years later, when Poseidon announced that it had incorrectly recorded its revenues and may have to restate the figures. By the time the company collapsed a few months later, its value, based on its stock price, had fallen from a high of $1.3 billion to an initial liquidation value of $79 million. Poseidon's lenders suffered, recovering far less than Poseidon had borrowed, but its investors were left holding shares that were essentially worth nothing at all.

A blizzard of legal actions followed Poseidon's collapse and revealed many details of the way the company's management operated. For our purposes, we need to focus on the information provided to investors before, during and after Poseidon's rise and fall. In short, was it insufficient and misleading?

Investors should have been given more information, for example, on the basis on which assets and liabilities were split between Open Range and Poseidon to achieve fairness for each of the two companies and their shareholders and lenders. We're curious, as well, to know why Poseidon failed while the other company survived. Was it simply because of the comparative managements or was Poseidon deprived of cash?

In splitting one company into two parts, which constitutes a significant related party transaction, investors need information from independent third-party consultants to support reported figures about each company's performance and financial health. Liabilities, especially, have to be allocated so that one company is not overly burdened with obligations, especially with debts that are coming due quickly.

In the case of Poseidon, public documents indicate that much of the money raised in its initial offering was transferred to the other company. The money was used to pay a liability that arose from the split-off arrangement. Investors were not aware of much of this arrangement. Poseidon's prospectus stated that it would use investors' money to buy long-term assets. So, what happened? Was another related party transaction arranged?

A number of considerations emerge for investors from these related party transactions:

1 First, third-party bargained prices are often not readily available.
2 Second, data in the company's audited financial statements is not always reliable. Investors need far more evidence of the data's credibility.
3 Third, Poseidon failed within two years of its split from Open Range and its subsequent public offering. How could this happen so quickly to a company whose audited financial statements prepared under IFRS appeared at first glance to be so sound?
4 Fourth, as we've stated continuously, IFRS does not provide investors with sufficient and appropriate information to assess the risks of investing in a company.
5 Fifth, investors cannot treat self-dealing transactions lightly. Numbers assigned in IFRS-audited financial statements can be little more than guesswork. Documents have to be read especially carefully to ascertain the source of the dollar figures and to confirm the independence and trustworthiness of the valuators and appraisers.

6 Sixth, when crucial information is missing, investors should sell their shares or avoid the company in the first place.

EXAMPLE 4: NORTHLAND POWER INC.

In 2011, Northland Power Inc. completed a natural-gas-based power-generating facility in Saskatchewan and arranged a contract with the province's public power utility, SaskPower, to purchase the plant's output over a 25-year period. The agreement included a purchase option under which SaskPower could buy the facility at the end of 25 years for $1.

Under IFRS, the company recorded a $35-million increase in its income that year. It based the increase on the 8.4% yield recorded on the power-plant transaction with SaskPower. Every month over the next 25 years, SaskPower would pay Northland for a portion of the purchase and sale price of the plant equivalent, in Northland's calculations, to an 8.4% yield on its investment in the plant. Northland's cost of building the plant was presumed to be $35 million less than the discounted guaranteed payments that it would receive from SaskPower over the next 25 years, although full details were not disclosed. The agreement also allowed Northland to sell power beyond the contracted volumes with SaskPower. These additional revenues would raise the overall yield above 8.4%.

SaskPower paid for the natural gas that the plant consumed, and for some operating expenses. But Northland appeared to be operating the facility, in return for some reimbursement.

In calculating the $35-million profit, Northland had to apply discount and interest rates. In its reporting under IFRS, it also had to determine whether it would earn its $35-million profit in the first year or over the 25 years of the agreement. Obviously, it concluded that it would earn the profit immediately, and this is how it reported its results in its financial statements. The profit immediately increased Northland's owners' equity and added an impression of success and stability for the company.

A look at the relevant wording at the time in IFRS regarding a finance lease raises some concerns. It says substantially all the risks and rewards incidental to legal owner-ship...[must] be ... transferred by the lessor, and thus the lease payment receivable is treated by the lessor as repayment of princi-pal and finance income to reimburse and reward the lessor for its investment and services.

We have to wonder whether Northland transferred "all the risks and rewards" to SaskPower in return for an 8.4% yield. This is a rela-tively low return on such a project, which suggests that other reward opportunities likely were *retained* by Northland, contrary to IFRS guidelines.

In any event, by allowing management to choose the applicable discount yield rate, Northland was able to generate a $35-million immediate profit. Under the matching concept mandated by previous Canadian GAAP, management might have chosen a more appropriate discount rate and would have had to spread any profit over the 25-year contract. It would have had more difficulty separating the power plant itself from other parts of the power supply contract with SaskPower in calculating the benefits to Northland. As it stands, the $35 million profit did not likely arise in one or two years simply from building the power plant. Yet, the audited financial statements show otherwise.

Nevertheless, IFRS gives ultimate decision-making power to man-agement, which in this case results in the reporting of a curious up-front profit in its audited financial statement. Apart from management, no one can determine how it arrived at the 8.4% yield, when other percentages were possible.

SUMMARY

The examples in this chapter are merely a drop in a bucket of what IFRS has helped to produce. Canada's current financial reporting should be viewed as "the calm before the storm." Many Canadian-traded stocks are trying to appear more financially adequate by utiliz-ing the massive holes in IFRS. Unaware investors are likely to prolong the date of collapse of such many stocks. As we are repeatedly observ-ing, weak IFRS plays directly into the hands of opportunists.

Being able to easily inflate profits and operating cash flows under IFRS renders the IFRS system as being frightening for investors, and in need of constant vigilance. Simply stated, Canadian lawmakers and the Courts are protecting financial schemers by their procrastinations in ignoring white-collar crime, in general.

30

Typical IFRS Traps

While GAAP, the predecessor to IFRS in Canada, brought forth some financial reporting problems, IFRS not only retained many of these problems, it also added a large collection of its own issues to the mix. For example, as we've said before, IFRS allows management to cloud results of a poor current financial year by building unwarranted optimism into reported dollar amounts. Thus, especially income and cash flow financial statements become vulnerable in many ways. Management can mix the past, present and future together in one reported dollar figure, which makes it difficult for investors and lenders to distinguish what credibly occurred on an arm's-length basis in the most recent financial period. Separating cash or near-cash transactions from management's optimistic "value" estimates of future hoped-for transactions can become impossible in too many situations. If investors want to adjust the numbers to delete these management estimates, they probably will not find the necessary information in the vague notes to a company's financial statements.

This is one of the many reasons why we object so strongly to IFRS. Investors are forced to rely on biased dollars, or nothing at all. A financial reporting system should aim to measure as realistically as possible what happened in the way of confirmed negotiated transactions in each current period. To avoid confusion, management should report separately its unsubstantiated estimates or value adjustments. This distinction is necessary for investors' valuation and decision-making. Hoped-for future events could easily not occur, as we have repeatedly observed in Canada.

Under IFRS, in too many situations, it can be *impossible* for analysts to detect bargained profit and operating cash flow results in a current period. Monitoring trends is essential for analysts' evaluations. Companies could calculate financial results based on numbers in one or more of the following four categories:

Category 1   Cash-based or cash-like bargained, or third independent party transactions;

Category 2   Accrual-based near-cash transactions such as receivables and current payables; (plus Category 1, above);

Category 3   Non-cash items such as amortizations; (plus Categories 1 and 2 above);

Category 4   A set of management valuations that may approximate a management-biased current value but that could also disguise what actually occurred in Categories 1, 2, and 3. IFRS allows many adjustments under this category 4, including those affecting current accounts on the balance sheet (e.g., inventories).

The credibility of the reported numbers diminishes as we add more categories and estimates to the reported results. Credibility is highest when the results are restricted to bargained, completed transactions, although even then such information is partially limited in its usefulness (except in cash-only businesses). Adding information under category 2 raises the possibility of compromising the financial statements' credibility with the inclusion of uncollectible accounts and loans receivable. But, reporting rules can limit these dollar variations.

Categories 1, 2, and 3 existed for years under Canadian GAAP. They required some analytical adjustments to detect Ponzi schemes and unsustainable dividend yields. But IFRS gives financial manipulators many more opportunities to prey upon investors and lenders. By the time we add management estimates made under category 4, analysts and investors may have no clue about which transactions actually happened over the most recent financial period. Instead, they have to wade through IFRS-sanctioned management phrases like "economic benefits" to dig out figures for received cash and other important third-party numbers. Or they may have to try to measure a company's profit without obtaining from the financial statements a specific figure for the company's paid expenses.

As we've discussed in previous chapters, a company may include in its reported revenue figure the hope that it will sell future airplane flights in return for redeeming customers' accumulated loyalty points, with no certainty that this will occur. Such recording of premature revenue renders misleading all the calculations of income/profit and cash flow from operating activities. Yet some analysts use aggregate figures such as these to determine what has actually happened, thereby falling into the trap.

IFRS contains the fatal flaw of allowing management to combine too many hoped-for results with actual numbers. Such freedom allows them to cover up poor results or pull off other deceptions that work to their personal advantage (e.g., bonuses). Unable to separate hard facts from near fiction, analysts and investors suffer. All too often, the suffering occurs in silence over several years, until the company collapses.

REQUIRED SORTING

It is not necessary to learn how to detect dozens of tricks to protect yourself and others. Learning can effectively begin by concentrating on the income statement and the cash flow from operations portion of the Cash Flow Statement. That's where the manipulators focus. Once you find two or three tricks you really have enough evidence that you don't want to put money in the hands of such con artists.

This chapter provides elaboration on a few of the most popular IFRS-based games that we've identified in previous chapters. They involve the two main neglected areas of financial reporting under IFRS: exaggerated profits and bloated cash flow from operations. A grasp of profit manipulation and cash from operations cons may be all that you need to judge a management's ethics.

By not requiring *cash* or cash equivalent receipts from borrowers, and instead by substituting vague IFRS words such as "economic benefits," a company's entire *actual cash picture* becomes uncertain. Under IFRS, companies can produce financial reports that can easily fail to alert investors that operating cash flow as well as overall available cash on hand is rapidly declining. The decline may be occurring because the company is paying dividends in excess of legitimate income/profit, awarding excessive management bonuses or suffering under other management manipulations. In the end, such companies become forced into bankruptcy because they have run out of money. Under IFRS much of a reported fat profit may be non-cash.

For example, IFRS permits non-real-estate companies, to increase appraisal "values" for buildings and include the inflated values under comprehensive income, which becomes equity. Unless the notes fully explain the procedure, lenders and investors have no way of telling whether the appraisal is based on faked discount/interest rates and whether the appraiser is fully independent.

Some tricks affect only profits, for example, some affect cash flow, others affect both. To get the full picture of a company's merits, you have to examine and put the pieces together yourself. Many analysts have not been adequately trained to be able to come close to coping with IFRS. Even more appear to have not tried to learn of IFRS's major deficiencies.

INCOME/OPERATION CASH FLOW ENHANCEMENT

Here are a few of the most common deceptions that we see in Canada to inflate income. Some of these tricks can also inflate cash flow from operations. But, without incoming cash a company can easily fail. IFRS can therefore be treacherous; non-cash "economic benefits" can be fantasies.

1 Revenue overstatements can be based on only a 50.001% assurance of cash collection. Some companies abide by higher standards than others. Investors must read the notes to financial statements carefully to comprehend which revenue standard is being applied. Nortel recorded revenue by showing an offsetting long-term investment on its balance sheet; no cash was involved. Castor Holdings increased its mortgages receivable; but negligible cash was received. National Business Systems "sold" to invented customers, who obviously could not pay. For all of these situations both profits and cash flow were being faked.

2   Expenses being reported as assets:
    A few of the Canadian favourites are:
    a   Eliminating repairs and maintenance expense by burying them
        within appraisal value increases, and showing a net effect figure.
    b   manipulation of fair value of inventory; write-ups and write-
        downs based upon management estimates; cost of good sold
        and amortization become affected, which affects income/profit;
        not cash inflow;
    c   cost of constructing facilities that includes management salaries
        and factory overhead, thereby lowering regular operating
        expenses and consequently overstating continuing cash flow
        from operations;
    d   recording a tax asset arising from losses, based on a 50.001%
        probability of receipt of the asset, in order to increase income
        after tax; no cash receipt;
    e   recording customer development contracts as assets instead of
        marketing cash outflows, which are expenses. Thanks to IFRS's
        variable treatment of interest, cash expenses can also be turned
        into non-cash expenses; again, cash decreases are allowed to
        vanish into the fog;
    f   including interest expense as part of assets under construction
        and development, instead of recording the interest-related cash
        outlay as an expense, because it bears little relationship to cur-
        rent construction; once more a cash outflow is not counted as
        a profit reduction.

Investors must always determine which of these and similar games
affects cash flow from operations. Repairs and maintenance and
minor construction of facilities, for example, are both cash outlays
that should be recorded as cash expenses.

To catch some of the above games read the "Accounting/Reporting
Policy" notes to the company's financial statements and watch for
vagueness, evasiveness, and similar. You can be given good clues by
non-descriptions. Also study the income tax note so that you can
determine what is non-taxable. A huge profit accompanied by small
income tax expense means that plenty of hot air could have been
included as income. (But, some exceptions could exist.)

BOOK VALUE NONSENSE

Some investors and analysts still compare a company's book value (assets less liabilities, roughly) to its market value in deciding whether to buy, hold, or sell a stock. But depending on the industry, the concept of book value under IFRS differs considerably from the same concept under old Canadian GAAP. Here are some reasons:

1 For such assets as land, buildings and equipment, IFRS could give management the option of reporting original cost less accumulated depreciation, which is the actual old GAAP book value. If fair value is higher than book value, management will likely use that figure in its financial statements. Investors should check its effects on book value, as defined by the particular analyst.

2 In reporting asset values, IFRS allows corporate management to record the "recoverable" amount, which it defines as "the higher of an asset's fair value less costs to sell and its value in use." If the company has its reasons to record a higher asset value, management will record a high "value in use" for the asset. (Much of IFRS's asset impairment words are easy to circumvent because of "value in use" and "recoverable value" looseness. (Consider the previously described "The Endowment Effect.")

3 IFRS allows management to use its own judgment to leave impaired assets on a company's balance sheet for a few years. As we've discussed, IFRS gives management wide scope to decide whether and when an impairment exists. Without regulations or sanctions, this abuse will become more prevalent over time in Canada. Annual asset valuations sound impressive, but in many companies the dollars should not be taken seriously.

4 IFRS has done little to stem the abuse by Canadian companies of the recording of goodwill and intangibles as a way to cover up over-payments of cash or shares for acquisitions and other management mistakes. As we have stated previously, investors must analyze how the cost of a corporate acquisition has been financed, and how costs have been allocated to assets and liabilities. Book

value is affected by expensing versus capitalizing on the balance sheet. Hence, what does book value signify under IFRS?

5 The revenue tricks used by management to inflate income can also decrease unfairly previously-created liabilities, arising from staged lawsuits, or unusual gains. Running the credits through revenue bolsters cash from operations; but maybe zero cash appears dependent upon which of the above methods are chosen.

As we have repeated, IFRS emphasis on the balance sheet invites management manipulation in industries where company value depends heavily on intangible assets and in resource industries where reliable asset values are not readily available. In these industries, book value of shareholders' equity under IFRS could easily be a corporate management fantasy. In short, the credibility of book value did not improve overall by the switch to IFRS from old GAAP.

OPERATING CASH FLOW IS VITAL

Failure to track sources of cash is not rational. As we've explained, cash flow from operations includes two segments: (1) cash income; and (2) changes in other than cash, for current assets less current liabilities. IFRS increases the number of available games in both segments. In our experience, too many analysts' reports ignore problems within cash flow from operations and the Ponzi schemes that go hand-in-hand. Investors are advised to give a high priority in learning cash flow tricks. Many of Canada's larger financial failures arose from neglect in tracking cash flow from operations. (See the Sino-Forest discussions.)

After the failure of Castor Holdings and other financial institutions, Canadian GAAP incorporated rules to help to prevent such collapses from occurring again. Sadly for Canada, IFRS did not adequately incorporate these rule changes. Investors have to determine for themselves the proportion of a company's reported operating cash flow that actually consists of non-cash or faked cash. In the case of Castor Holdings, for example, the company received hardly any operating cash flow, but it still had to expend cash to survive. To overcome this revenue deficiency, the company recorded a growing mortgage loan receivable on its balance sheet, instead of the bad debt expense that was warranted.

IFRS certainly allows companies to record clean cash-only operating cash flow on their financial statements and to exclude non-cash transactions and eliminate management's excessive or unrealistic optimism. But it also allows companies to muddle their operating cash flow calculations on the cash flow statement with net income equivalents such as non-cash amortizations and similar non-cash, non-operating adjustments.

As a consequence, investors have no choice but to examine income and cash flow statements carefully to uncover actual cash inflow from fake cash. They have to read notes to financial statements to identify non-cash and management valuation adjustments that have been dumped into the income statement. But, too often crucial information for adjustments can be lacking. If so, decide to invest elsewhere.

A strongly advised starting point is the operations section of the cash flow statement. Investors should look at the adjustments made to net income or net loss. In the case of Sino-Forest, for example, the company added a huge *amortization* expense to net income. Many other companies rely on bloating their income figure as part of their deception scheme for cash flow.

Having discovered such an adjustment, investors also then have to ascertain whether the non-cash adjustments to the balance sheet ended up on the income statement or in a separate category called comprehensive income, or something similar. Adjustments for period-end non-cash foreign currency translations, and for changes in the value of buildings (except for real estate companies) should not be included in the main income statement, and investors should be wary if they are.

For example, based on figures by a non-real-estate company recording its disposal of a building, we try to reconstruct the undernoted table. However, we have to be prepared to become frustrated because information may have been withheld from investors and creditors:

	Building Account ($millions)
Balance, December 31, last year	110
Additions (noted as "investments" in the Cash Flow Statement)	30
Disposals (noted under "investments" in the Cash Flow Statement; this should represent cash proceeds of disposal)	(5)
Loss on disposal (if large, this should be a separate item on the Income Statement; if it is not, where was the loss buried?)	(?)
Revaluation upward; management estimate, it seems	?
Balance, December 31, this year	175

We make the following calculation: $110 + 30 - 5 = \$135$, not 175. The two question marks in our table indicate information that we cannot easily find and have to search for. The loss (or possible gain) on disposal should be in the income statement, but is likely grouped with other items somewhere else. We look for something called "*Net* gains," which means that a gain and a loss could have occurred, and have been netted in total dollars. (Why then were they shown as "net"? To cover-up something?) We also try to ascertain whether a comprehensive income statement includes the increase in appraisal value or upward revaluation of the property. The $40 million ($175 - 135) probably does not represent cash flow from operations and should not appear on the cash flow statement. We want to find the missing $40 million.

If the $40 million was hidden on the income statement, we should be concerned, because it is not cash. Now we have to look at the income tax expense. If management has buried $40 million of non-taxable appraisal gain somewhere on the income statement, it should not have incurred income tax for the $40 million. If the company records a tax liability that does not seem to include the $40 million, a note to the financial statement should indicate why the company's income tax rate seems to have dropped this year.

All the foregoing requires considerable effort, and even then we may not succeed in distinguishing non-cash manipulation from cash from operating activities. Thanks to IFRS, the fake and the real may remain muddled, with the fake "buried at sea" forever.

Investors and analysts cannot make suitable assessments of a company when management mixes together cash, near-cash, non-cash and educated guesses in its financial statements. They need arm's-length, bargained *cash* equivalent flows to make discounted *cash flow* stock valuations and other calculations. The $40 million could be an unsolved mystery in too many companies.

At the very least, financial statements should provide information that shareholders can use to evaluate the performance of corporate management, at least according to the Supreme Court of Canada in its Hercules Managements decision. But when corporate management chooses the numbers, how can such an objective evaluation be possible? Clearly, the Hercules's attitude has been especially detrimental to advancing financial decision-making in Canada.

We can only conclude that IFRS does not come close to meeting the objectives of financial reporting described by the Supreme Court of Canada, nor does it meet the needs of financial analysts. For investors, IFRS leads to inevitable misinterpretations and misrepresentations and makes management cover-ups too easy. Canada took a major step backward when it accepted IFRS, with the major losers being savers, investors and creditors. The deterioration is ongoing.

SUMMARY

Perfection does not exist in financial reporting. But the closer the financial statements can come to minimizing speculative management-chosen values, the better off investors will be. A license to fog financial reporting through IFRS has to be prohibited, by abandoning IFRS.

A financial report on what actually happened during a financial period should contain historical material with as little management bias as possible. Most reports prepared under IFRS don't come close. Few of them contain enough unbiased current value information to create a useful balance sheet for investment decision-making.

It is vital that investors accept the concept that when times are tough, the magnitude of losses or lowered profits can be covered up by carefully chosen IFRS financial reporting, at least for a few years.

A question you must always ask yourself is why did the company that you are analyzing for investment purposes choose to report using IFRS? Why did they reject US GAAP?

31

Perpetual Ponzi Corporation

We are frequently asked: How long can a company last on bogus numbers? A quick reply is that Canadian investors and creditors do not act swiftly enough to these prolonged frauds. The ongoing con game in Canada is to use Canadian reporting weaknesses to produce fake profit and bloated cash from operations. In this respect, weak IFRS is a gift to financial manipulators.

Our general response to the duration of deceit is: survival of a company depends on several factors. If it can attract enough unsuspecting investors with a high but unwarranted dividend, for example, based on non-existent profits, then the schemers may perpetuate the scam for many years.

We qualify that response by explaining that each suspect company needs a minimal legitimate line of business to continue or it will exhaust its funds and go out of business. Companies that promise to develop a new product or exploit a rich ore body or bring to market a new drug once they receive the necessary government approvals can attract investors for several years, even if they eventually are forced out of business.

Combining a minimal line of business with creative accounting and reporting, swindlers can turn an ugly corporate duckling into a beautiful swan. Nortel, for example, attracted enough investors to boost its share price to $120 with audited financial statements that eventually had to be restated several times, and for several years. Unwarranted hope and its pro forma financial data, kept Nortel alive for many months longer than justified. Likewise, with Canadian investors routinely taking financial statements at face value, Sino-Forest could have survived for several more years if US analysts hadn't shone a light on the company's deceit. Business income trusts survived for 10 years or so by utilizing Ponzi-like capital structures.

Many semi-successful Canadian companies have used creative public relations and financial reporting games to elevate themselves into corporate super stars, squandering investors' money that could have been invested wisely elsewhere. The losses lowered the standard of living for average Canadians as declines in stock prices diminished their pension and mutual fund returns.

While these semi-successful companies attract almost no scrutiny from our securities regulators, their managements generate huge and unwarranted take-home pay through glorified Ponzi schemes and other forms of financial manipulation. When one of these companies fails, management moves on to another company where it applies the same types of tactics.

Such companies still trade on our stock exchanges and prey upon investors, often aided by glorified reports from suspect financial analysts. Too many "buy" reports from analysts can often be traced back to one source, being management's nonsensical financial reporting, which might also have been audited.

PRINCIPAL INGREDIENTS

If we place ourselves in the shoes of a financial scammer, we can identify the essentials necessary to carry out and prolong a securities swindle over a period of several years. These essentials include:

1 A stock exchange listing: Instead of starting from scratch, manipulators frequently obtain control of an already-listed but moribund company through a reverse takeover or similar arrangement. In return for shares issued by the listed company, the cheats transfer in assets, usually non-cash, of a private operating company. This company may be involved in a trendy industry such as wind-farming, sustainable development or re-populating endangered

species. With control of the listed company through owning 60% or more of its shares, the manipulators can now apply their creativity to attract more investors and raise the price of the stock.

2 To acquire as many new shares of the listed company as possible, the schemers arrange for a sometimes absurdly high value to be placed on the assets of the existing privately held company. Research in progress, for example, may be given a huge value, and not be expensed for five or more years.

3 To substantiate the high value of the assets being transferred to the listed company, the friendly business valuators provide the manipulators with exaggerated documentary material.

NEXT STEPS

Now the listed company has to attract investors and raise enough cash to:

1 Pay an attractive annual dividend: As we've shown, a manipulator may simply recycle investors' money, returning it to them in the form of taxable dividends.

2 Generate fat salaries, bonuses, and expense accounts for the management schemers.

3 Provide some cash to operate the company, perhaps inventing non-existent customers by renting post offices boxes and hiring cooperative lawyers and accountants, until the cheat can apply cosmetic accounting to the company's financial statements to attract a willing banker who will lend the company more money.

In the next stage the manipulators extend the cosmetics by:

1 Cooking the books to make the company look even more successful. As we've discussed throughout this book, IFRS enables them to overstate revenue, mislabel expenses as assets on the balance sheet, and similar.

2 Finding a stock underwriter who will sell more of the company's long-term debt and shares and arrange for friendly analysts to write "buy" reports about the company.

3 Using a portion of the company's long-term debt and equity to buy control of one or more companies that:

   a generate sales revenue, authentic or otherwise, and/or

   b have projects in progress such as wrinkle-shrinker cream or 3-D gaming, and/or

   c generate some cash, perhaps by selling their own manufacturing equipment and inappropriately recording the receipts as sales revenue.

4 With the acquisition of another company or two, the manipulation can be kicked into high gear. IFRS permits much of the purchase price of another company to be placed into intangible asset categories such as goodwill, where it can remain for several years. Meanwhile, the company records little or no amortization expenses, thus inflating its income figures and attracting even more investors, perhaps by hyping so-called new products in its development pipeline.

Tricksters can allocate the purchase price of an acquired company in several other ways, as well, to cook the books even further. For example, they can attach a low dollar amount to acquired inventory at the date of the acquisition. When the inventory is eventually sold, the company can record inflated gross profits, most of which arise from the low initial management-assigned inventory price. They can also create a high fake liability, which can later be reduced to increase profit. They can balance the books using a higher goodwill figure as a receptacle, including for expenses that may not be permitted to appear for years.

The more that IFRS-sanctioned manoeuvres are available, the longer the listed company can survive and dupe investors. Reality is that IFRS is especially permissive, and Canadian oversight is negligible.

Meanwhile, by selling more debt and equity in their listed company and using the proceeds to buy more companies, cheats can create financial turmoil and credibly argue that a pot of gold is just over the next hill. Such promises keep unsuspecting investors in line, as long as a high dividend yield arises from the grossly overstated profits and bloated cash flow from operations.

To prolong the life of a Ponzi scheme even further, the manipulators can set up a dividend reinvestment plan (DRIP). As the name suggests, a DRIP re-invests money in the company that would have been distributed to investors as a dividend. Investors receive additional shares, while the company can use the money in its operations. DRIPs are valuable for investors when a company is strong and credible. Weak or suspect companies use DRIP arrangements to reduce the cash dividend required to continue the life of a Ponzi scheme.

We've discussed in previous chapters the tricks that companies can use to prolong a Ponzi scheme, from covering the cash required for a dividend by selling assets and leasing them back or by recording income tax savings that later have to be repaid. Investors should be particularly wary of companies that pay out cash dividends for 100% or more of "reported income" that is heavily non-cash in nature, based, for example, on IFRS-sanctioned valuation adjustments. Included therein are frequent changes in current assets and liabilities (such as cookie jars).

In summary, many dozens of Canadian companies are taking advantage of loose IFRS. And there are more than a few bad guys. Huge salaries, bonuses, expense accounts, stock options and much more motivate them to keep a borderline company in existence for as long as possible. In purchasing these stocks, Canadian investors are simply not doing their homework, given the disturbing IFRS deficiencies and the more than obvious absence of Canadian investor protection.

DIVIDEND SOURCES

As we've said, investors must determine the main sources of cash that a company uses to pay for dividends. Watch closely for companies that recycle cash in amounts beyond what they legitimately earn from their regular arm's length transaction operations, from sources such as:

1 Bank loans; (these can be secured for a few years by pledging the best assets as collateral; but, the company can run out of quality assets to pledge.)

2 Sales of more shares and debt, often excused by the need for corporate expansion through acquisitions. The company then muddles the assets, revenues and cash flows from the newly acquired company with those of the parent company and uses the newly acquired company's cash flow streams to offset excessive dividend payments;

3 Grants from government and quasi-government bodies such as the Canada Pension Plan;

4 Cash reinvested through a DRIP or a similar arrangement;

5 Sale for cash of long-term equipment or disposal of a division of the company.

If it's any consolation to investors who have been tricked by these scams, supposedly wealthy people described in investment publications as super investors have been conned by these tricks. We often see their names in our forensic accounting documents after they've lost amounts of their cash.

Even in professional training courses for lawyers, financial analysts and bankers, we repeatedly hear participants utter misconceptions, such as: "The financial statements must be credible. They've been audited." As we've discussed, financial statement auditors simply do not provide the reassurance that people think they do. Period. End of story.

It is the well-designed financial statements, such as the income and cash flow statements, which validly measure a company's operations over time, and thus can tell investors what is actually occurring in the company. IFRS income and cash flow statements are not designed for investor use.

A balance sheet, on the other hand, is static, measuring conditions at a fixed date. It has the same limitations as a crude gas gauge that does not tell a car driver how quickly the gas is being consumed. IFRS-based balance sheets typically do not report earned-cash figures for a period but simply reflect management's dream for the future, or a few cover-ups. Canada's largest business failures tend to occur rapidly because the entity suddenly runs out of cash. IFRS can hide negative cash trends.

Investors may find some of the information they need in the notes to the financial statements and in the management discussion and analysis section of a company's annual report. Here they may find answers to such questions as:

1 When is the short-term debt principal balance coming due, especially the bank debt? The amount of dollars that will be renewed likely will not be made available.
2 Which interest rate is being charged on long-term debt? Same questions for short-term debt. Is it higher than normal, thus indicating that the bank thinks that the company is getting riskier?
3 Will the bank(s) likely renew the same amount and term of the borrowings? For how long? At what interest rate, and on which repayment terms? Mostly, this type of information would be skimpy, at best.
4 Which of the company's collateral security assets have been pledged to the bank(s)? Have any of the company's collateral assets not yet been pledged? Are they worth much? (Here is where many intangible assets can become a problem, because few buyers exist and their cash value can be low.)
5 How much bank and long-term debt exists compared to owners' equity (share capital plus retained earnings). Too much? Again, IFRS can obstruct analysis, because the fair value balance sheet could include speculative, optimistic valuation adjustments, while their balancing offsets are buried within owners' equity. As we've said, the adjustments can largely reflect management optimism instead of solid equity dollars.
6 Has the company issued convertible preferred shares or convertible debt? What are their terms? If conversion into common shares is not likely because the company's stock price has slipped down, dividends on the preferred shares and interest on the debt will have to be paid for some years. Both would put a drain on the company's cash.
7 Would you lend more money to this company, given what it already owes? Interest expense can pile up. Preferred dividends drain cash as well. An excessively high dividend rate can be

maintained only by the Ponzi-like technique of borrowing from others. (Thus, the cash must be traced.)

Similar questions have to be formulated to suit the specific situation. Some additional considerations are:

1 Does the cash flow statement show that long-term assets or divisions of the company are being sold to obtain cash and support the exaggerated dividend pay-out? If so, the end of the company could be very close. Sales of long-term assets are a desperation action. Cash gets generated by selling long-term assets. This bump-up into short-term liquidity often gets misinterpreted. Investors may think that the "bump-up" is favourable. It is the exact opposite. Sell your shares.
2 Do the required filings with provincial securities commissions show that management and some directors are selling their shares? How many?
3 Is the company's share price in decline? Do other movements in share volume indicate that insiders are unloading their shares because they know that the company's end is near? Friendly analysts could be issuing "buy" recommendations at the same time as their favourite clients get rid of their shares while they can still sell them at favourable prices.
4 According to provincial securities records, has the volume of short-selling in the company's stock increased. Short sellers who smell blood can drive the share price down quickly.

SUMMARY

Even before IFRS, Canada allowed Ponzi frauds and other schemes to operate for years. Only by doing your homework can you determine whether you're helping the scams to survive. Don't be fooled by companies that seem attractive because they're local and close to home. These companies deserve a closer look, as well. Their local flavour may be part of the hype, to relieve you of your savings.

Similarly, companies that are rapidly expanding by buying other companies should be placed on your suspect list. You should regard them as temporarily guilty of a Ponzi scheme until your analysis proves them innocent.

Overall, many public companies in Canada can be placed on a suspect list of being possible perpetual Ponzi schemes. IFRS is just too loose to be trustworthy and provides too many options and opportunities for the same transaction to tempt management into engaging in cover-ups. Bloating income and cash flow are made easy, because IFRS emphasizes a soft, alleged-value, approach.

Make no mistake. Vague reporting requirements will be chosen to make weak financial results and incompetent management look much better. Bringing IFRS to Canada was a dreadful decision because its deficiencies eventually will be revealed.

Visit the Canadian-based Ponzi graveyards before listening to hype from those who wave audited IFRS financial statements in your face. Financial nonsense is widely available in Canada, and is causing, and will continue to cause, large investor losses. Thus, Ponzis can survive for well beyond 10 years.

32

IFRS vs. Old GAAP

As we've shown in this book and our previous book called *Swindlers*, Canadian corporate failures that occurred prior to 2011 often involved negligence in preparing these pre 2011 financial statements. Well before 2011, Canada's financial reporting clearly needed much improvement.

Lacking improvements, investors were on their own to protect themselves against financial manipulation. Financial statement auditors had been relieved of most of that duty by the Supreme Court of Canada in the 1997 Hercules Managements decision. Governments, securities commissions, the courts, police and regulators also have continuously seemed disinterested in protecting investors.

After experiencing horrendous losses from the demise of Nortel and similar business income trust fiascos between 2000 to 2010, investors were left even more isolated when lawmakers took the advice of Canada's financial statement auditors and adopted IFRS. As has been detailed, IFRS has opened the door widely to financial manipulators in Canada.

We are now in the period before the next big storm. As our federal and provincial governments pass the buck, investors will have to educate themselves about the potential financial schemes allowed by IFRS, or suffer continuing losses. Inflating income and cash flow from operations is simply now out of control in Canada because IFRS permits such. Companies are pretending that they are successful. Tracing cash results through financial statements has become complex, and the fields are mined with explosives that few are detecting.

In this chapter we'll compare IFRS to its predecessor, Canadian GAAP, to show whether and how each reporting system addresses investor concerns. Large chunks of old Canadian GAAP still exist within private company reporting.

CANADIAN GAAP

Canadian GAAP had differences from US GAAP, and was "world's apart" from IFRS. Here are the main ingredients of Canadian GAAP:

1 It was made-in-Canada, primarily worded by Canadian external auditors, and only occasionally was drafted over the objections of a group such as real estate companies.

2 Transactions were largely recorded when an arm's length transaction occurred, at dollar amounts that had been negotiated with third parties. There were exceptions such as for certain resource enterprises, rate-regulated utilities and mutual funds.

3 A combination of concepts and rules were employed. The concepts were designed to be applied to situations not covered by the rules.

4 Historical costs, for inventory, land, buildings and equipment, and similar items arising from arm's-length transactions were being recorded on balance sheets.

5 A company's management and directors were responsible for choosing its reporting policies and principles and describing them in notes to financial statements. The CICA Handbook was the prime reference in determining what constituted GAAP. References from US GAAP were also utilized where deemed appropriate.

6 Canadian GAAP was anchored to a list of concepts that made manipulation of the income statement and operating cash flow statement more difficult, but not impossible, such as:
   - *Matching*, which stresses that, where possible, expenses should be matched to corresponding recorded revenue for the period to produce an income statement. While it can be

difficult to achieve in practice, matching cannot be down-played. Whenever income can be overstated to allow payment of dividends not justified by legitimate earned income from regular corporate operations, Ponzi schemes can flourish.

- *Realization,* (or revenue recording) which requires, wherever possible, the recording of dollar figures in financial statements that arise from actual bargained, arm's-length transactions. When corporate management is permitted to estimate revenue, for example, based on a possibly distant collection of cash, realization does not occur. Realization evidence was vital for recording revenue under old Canadian GAAP.
- *Conservatism,* which disallows the recording of profits based on anticipation of future transactions. GAAP needed proof before it allowed the recording of a profit. Management estimates were not sufficient, except for regular requirements such as for estimated bad debts.

7 Management had choices under old Canadian GAAP. For example, appraisal "values" could be utilized in limited circumstances; but, in general, over the years, details about the appraiser's methodology along with the person's name and the appraisal date had to be provided. Appraisals were the exception and were not commonplace.

8 Prohibitions were being added to Canadian GAAP, bit-by-bit, until about 2001. Financial manipulators could take advantage of GAAP, but GAAP presented fewer opportunities than IFRS. GAAP prohibited certain treatments and, unlike IFRS, did not give corporate management widespread ultimate responsibility for final decisions.

9 GAAP did not deal well with non-arm's-length transactions, because corporate management was permitted to define who were the related parties. GAAP was vague on whether fair market value had been determined and applied in self-dealing transactions. It also made it easy to adopt an arbitrary transaction exchange price when the buyer and the seller were the same person or entity. However, GAAP financial statements required both measurement in dollars and note disclosure related to these transactions.

10 Given that the alleged day-to-day users of financial statements in practice were investors and creditors, GAAP gave more importance to the measurement of income and operating cash flow. Under GAAP, income/operating cash flow dollars in industries such as merchandising and manufacturing usually arose primarily from arm's-length third-party transactions.

But as companies adopted more sophisticated financial reporting methods and as overall income was affected by changes in values, it became more challenging to separate cash and non-cash transactions.

Importantly, GAAP did NOT require the reporting of each balance sheet account at fair value. Emphasis was placed upon recording and reporting bargained arm's-length transactions, uncontaminated as much as possible by management tampering. Knowing what was actually earned in profits, to the extent possible, and which were the cash-like transactions (as opposed to management's hopes) were vital under GAAP for stock valuation purposes and to curtail Ponzi schemes.

After all, conceptually, the worth of a company today is based on what it will produce in cash flows to investors over the next several years. The same idea applies to bonds. Their worth today is based on the interest and returned invested principal that the owner will receive over time. Cash and cash-like amounts have to be known, along with roughly when the cash will be received.

In brief, GAAP focused on income and operating cash flow results occurring in the days between balance sheet dates (i.e., income; operating cash flow). The balance sheet refers to financial status on a specific date, allowing one quarterly or annual balance sheet to be compared to a subsequent quarterly or annual balance sheet to determine a trend line. GAAP did not regard two balance sheets, prepared months apart, as being sufficient for valuing a business. GAAP considered the transactions occurring between balance sheet dates as more important. It focused on measuring profit and its corresponding operating cash flows over a period of time. Among other matters, this made it much easier to keep track of suspected Ponzi schemes based on cooked books.

IFRS

IFRS departs from GAAP, bringing *significant* changes to financial reporting for public companies in Canada that elect to adopt IFRS:

1 IFRS does not regard as important the old GAAP starting point of requiring proof before recording the financial effects of arm's-length transactions; instead, IFRS allows unregulated management opinion about "values" to influence reporting;
2 IFRS emphasizes the balance sheet and does not emphasize the specific *details* of what happened between two or more balance sheet dates, i.e., for income statements and cash flow from operations;
3 IFRS abandons GAAP's reporting emphasis on the financial effects of following the historical costs of assets, such as amortization, being based on original cost; IFRS ignores conservatism in measuring income, and allows anticipating and recording future possible gains;
4 IFRS downplays GAAP's emphasis on concepts such as realization and matching, which require concrete evidence that a real third party, bargained transaction has occurred;
5 IFRS often allows one reported financial figure for a period that combines dollar amounts of the past, present and estimated future financial activities;
6 IFRS makes little attempt to limit invented management reporting choices; and
7 IFRS frequently does not require hard third party transaction evidence before financial activities can be ignored, or are recorded (e.g., estimated liabilities).

Needless to say, Canadian GAAP had its shortcomings, such as not requiring fair value verification for self-dealings. It also had difficulty handling soft assets and various fluctuating-value financial instruments. But its focus on operating results over a specific period rather than having to utilize one or two balance-sheet dates for decisions made it much more useful for investors to determine what was actually happening in a company.

All of this confirms that IFRS is absolutely *NOT* a continuation of the principles of Canadian GAAP. In fact, IFRS is *far removed* from Canadian GAAP in these important respects:

1 IFRS was formulated in Europe and the UK under a deadline imposed by the European Union. Prior to 2005, countries such as Germany, France, and the Netherlands, among others, had vastly different reporting systems and philosophies. Compromises were needed to reach a common basis for reporting across the EU. As a result, widely different reporting philosophies were literally forced into a less than cohesive system under the IFRS umbrella, thereby defying claims of world-wide uniformity.

2 A balance sheet "current value" or "fair value" approach was adopted, but the accepted definitions of "value" were variable. Refinements have occurred since 2005, but uncontrolled variations of "value," such as "value in use," and "recoverable value" as opposed to "net selling price" or other choices, are permitted by IFRS.

3 Although the users of the IFRS financial statements are purported to be investors and lenders, IFRS financial statements are certainly *not* close to being investor friendly. On the contrary, IFRS financial statements make it difficult, confusing and frequently impossible for investors and analysts to determine which are the actual dollar figures contained in aggregated expense accounts covering the past, present and future. Research, for example, to identify the specific arm's-length transactions that occurred in a specific period can be futile.

4 Companies with assets consisting primarily of goodwill, intangibles or hard-to-value financial instruments often cannot provide credible fair value information, because verified sources may simply not exist. IFRS proponents have to base their balance sheet on some measurements made over an arbitrary period that may distort the actual sale or use value of the assets. Historical cost, for example, could be chosen for one particular entity's property, plant and equipment. In contrast, a different entity could utilize "fair value" by applying management's variable estimates of what is fair in their eyes. The desired comparability

across companies that is allegedly sought by IFRS thus becomes fictional.

5 The intended purposes of an IFRS-based fair value balance sheet are not clear. By its nature, a balance sheet is prepared to reflect conditions at a particular time. A day later, a different fair value may exist, influenced by changing interest rates, raw material prices or other variables. Conclusions reached from comparing two IFRS balance sheets have serious limitations, because their information may not be close to being comparable. Historical cost compared to some combination of past, present and future IFRS costs results in confusion and uncertainty. Reliable operating statements such as income and cash flow from operations are essential to cross-check balance sheet value adjustments. But under IFRS, companies often do not provide the necessary data.

Management's hoped-for financial results as summarized in a current value balance sheet may interest investors. But, they really need to know how far management has *progressed* financially in the most recent financial period toward achieving these results. GAAP at least attempted to focus on what happened in terms of actual, bargained, completed transactions in the most recent financial period. IFRS, on the other hand, allows management to blend together its estimates of the "rosy" future with actual completed transactions, rolling forward recent losses to hide their magnitude and leaving investors in the dark about what actually happened. An example may be a write-up of a previous write-down of assets, such as inventory.

6 By not clearly mandating the reporting of fair value *measurements* for self-dealing activities, IFRS gives extensive latitude to corporate executives to engage in non-arm's-length self-serving transactions. They can acquire assets personally and sell them to the public companies that they manage, generating fat personal profits, without declaring clearly their self-dealing dollar effects in the company's financial statements.

7 When an IFRS reporting treatment does not produce results that appeal to corporate management, IFRS allows it to make a fairness exception. We have seen absurd applications of this exemption. A rogue trader, for example, lost eight billion Euros

through trading operations in the first month of a new year. By applying the fairness exemption, his employer recorded the loss in the previous year, with the approval of two large auditing firms. Who were the beneficiaries? Might bonuses or debt covenants have become a factor?

8 Exemptions are also made for first-time adoption of IFRS. For instance, companies can elect to utilize certain historical dollar amounts as they would have been calculated under Canadian GAAP. These historical figures and related expenses can linger for years in the company's financial statements, making uniformity and comparability difficult or impossible. If analysts don't understand or detect these exemptions, trend information in their reports can thus be misleading.

9 As we've discussed, IFRS allows the conversion of cash expenses into non-cash amortizations. What used to be called a cash expense is often now called a short-term asset on the IFRS balance sheet. This asset or non-expense is then amortized as a non-cash amortization expense item over two years, more or less, allowing the company to fake increased cash flow from operations and bloat EBITDA.

10 Faked assets combined with emphasis on the balance sheet under IFRS leads to abuse of income and cash flow financial statements. When cash expenses are artificially reduced, the effects on corporate business valuations based on cash flow can be huge.

11 IFRS allows many reporting alternatives showing much different dollar amounts. On many occasions, Canadian companies have included faked revenue within loan assets, such as receivables, requiring them to report huge losses in later years.

Under IFRS, with its minimal list of prohibitions, a company can fatten-up the balance sheet's manufactured goods inventory with non-cash prior-period overhead items mixed with cash or variable costs. It can also bloat its up-front profit because IFRS requires only minimal proof of profits from a long-term contract.

IFRS requires other costs such as those incurred for corporate acquisitions to be expensed and not included in balance-sheet acquisition costs. Yet it allows management to make other choices for valuations to offset acquisition costs and easily circumvent this supposed IFRS principle.

Financial (as opposed to management) accounting was originally designed to tell people which bargained financial activities occurred during a specific period. Attempts were made to curtail management optimism and pessimism and to prevent its self-serving financial manipulations from destroying the utility of the reported dollar amounts. These relatively uncontaminated dollar amounts could then be utilized for tracking management's progress in earning profits and operating cash flows over time.

IFRS has essentially destroyed this original goal of financial reporting by muddling:

1   Bargained, arm's-length, third party, cash equivalent types of operating transactions; with
2   Corporate management's hopes and dreams and cover-ups incorporated into their fair value figures, and lists of alternative reporting treatments.

SUMMARY

If financial reporting in Canada is not revamped soon, IFRS will cause huge investor losses through their pension plans and personal savings. Protection of investors and creditors has to be restored and enhanced. Lawmakers must act positively and not assume that IFRS will straighten itself out.

IFRS does not have a solid foundation on which to build. IFRS commenced as a compromise in 2005 and has deteriorated as it caves in to pressures to report faked income and bloated operating cash flows.

It would be especially frightening if the courts in Canada accepted IFRS as the applicable standard for reporting in Canada. The courts and our lawmakers all have to step up to the plate to re-establish credibility in financial reporting for investors and citizens of Canada. Procrastination will only compound the problems and thereby increase investors' and creditors' losses.

33

Government Neglect

For more than 80 years, since the 1929 stock market crash, no Canadian government has assembled the necessary talent, databanks and other resources to combat repeated securities scams in this country. Instead:

1 Canadian governments have repeatedly procrastinated. As we described at the beginning of this book, we see buck passing and obfuscation and a long list of feeble excuses from cabinet ministers that defy logic. Contrary to their claims, the system is not under control, and is far away from being even tolerable. Investors are being swindled out of their savings. The government could help, but it has chosen to do almost nothing to prevent the swindles from repeating.

While the government sits back and allows self-regulating organizations to allegedly police Canadian securities markets, it adopts a far more aggressive approach to collecting taxes. Tricksters defy securities regulators with near impunity. They wouldn't dare try to annually bamboozle the Canada Revenue Agency using the more aggressive IFRS games. In our experience, self-regulating organizations ignore the big, important cases and pay minimal attention to minor cases. Understandably, cheats regard the Canadian securities regulatory system with contempt.

Earlier in this century, we warned the government many times, for example, that some business income trusts were nothing more than Ponzi schemes. Yet, the government chose, instead, to consult self-regulating groups, which apparently provided different advice, which then allowed huge investor losses. Similar thefts are occurring as you read this sentence.

As we've discussed, the government has been warned time and again, not just by us, but by Supreme Court judges and US regulators, that self-regulation isn't working. In 1986, in the last judicial inquiry held in Canada into a major financial collapse, former Supreme Court judge Willard Estey said, "The auditors, on the documentary and testimonial evidence before the Commission, clearly failed to apply in their judgment on the fairness of these financial statements as prepared by management in the year 1984, and probably as well in the year 1983, those accounting and auditing principles and practices pertaining to the audit of banks." In more than 30 years since that damning observation was made, many more failures have occurred because more auditors failed to do their job. How many times does this have to happen before the government steps in?

About 10 years later, in the Hercules Managements case, Canada's self-regulated auditors argued against their own published statements, which they'd made continuously, about working on behalf of investors. They argued so strenuously that the Supreme Court of Canada accepted their contention that, in auditing financial statements, they had no direct responsibility to individual investors at all. Potential investors and portfolio managers therefore had nowhere to turn to obtain current credible financial data on a company. Such a court decision made a mockery of federal corporation legislation that required external audits of public companies.

In accepting the advice of our self-regulated external auditor organization, governments are abandoning responsibility and assigning full power to the very people who are heavily contributing in the first place to the financial problems. Without a strong, *clearly independent* financial oversight body in Canada, swindling is continuing to grow out of control. Only tighter standards can begin to prevent the deceit. IFRS probably was the worst possible response for Canada after 2008, but it was implemented anyway, in a scattered manner.

2 In pursuing their scams, fraudsters can draw from 80 years of success in swindling Canadians; police and government prosecutors have had much less success in pursuing and obtaining convictions against fraudsters. To turn the tables, enforcement and prosecution skills have to be acquired and honed, beginning now.

3 In pursuing tax-related cases, the government operates from a position of strength through the Canada Revenue Agency. Canada has no equivalent body to prosecute serious securities infractions, and doesn't seem to care. Meanwhile, corporate managers can rely on high-powered law firms to defend them against accusations of deceit. A crucial role of government is to step in when such power imbalances arise, to support small groups of investors against their well-financed opponents. Rarely does such government action occur. The repeated losers are individual Canadian investors. No one steps up to support them.

4 Without the assistance of the US Securities and Exchange Commission, (SEC) Canadian investors would have lost many millions more. The SEC has intervened time and again, in cases like Nortel and Livent, while Canada has sat back and allowed swindles to proceed. Some Canadian authorities argue that they don't want to adopt US legislation. We say, Why not? Perhaps the authorities would have to improve their behaviour. As it stands, Canada's current inept strategy plays directly into the hands of the financial manipulators. Money that should be invested in Canada simply leaves the country in loot bags.

Despite the financial calamities that we've described in this book, the government hasn't held an inquiry into the causes of a large financial failure for over 25 years. After the Nortel and business income trust collapses, a thorough financial investigation was obviously necessary. Yet, essentially nothing happened. As investors' losses pile up, our governments continue to turn for advice to the groups such as securities commissions and external auditors that have already abandoned investors. The losers? Investors, of course.

It doesn't have to be this way. In the US, the government saw the problems and parted company with its so-called self-regulating external auditors. Canada could do the same immediately, and utilize US GAAP until it develops what suits Canadian resources and beliefs.

RELATED ISSUES

No doubt, self-regulation can function in some situations. But in securities regulation, too much money is dangling within reach of potential cheats, and unmotivated self-regulated authorities cannot prevent them from taking investors' money. Nor will a national securities commission correct the problems, especially if the same people who currently occupy provincial securities commissions move to the new federal body, carrying with them the same attitudes of indifference.

The consequences are wide-ranging and include:

1 Pension plan plundering: The beneficiaries of some pension plans are suffering losses as a result of portfolio managers not being attuned to various financial statement and investment deceptions.

2 Minimal prosecution of stock promoters: Lies and false claims about the merits of certain security offerings and investment products are commonplace, yet prosecutions are rare. Boilerplate warnings of risk have to be ignored by judges who should detect the gravity of the thefts, and their consequences.

3 White-collar crime proliferates: Crime against innocent victims through financial deception is widespread while lawmakers adopt clichés about being tough on crime. The Criminal Code needs revising to mandate longer prison sentences for white-collar crimes. From the perspective of investors who lose their pensions and savings, financial manipulators cause much more human suffering than a common thief.

4 Illogical support of suspect businesses: Canada perpetuates the myths about resource-based countries needing looser regulations to encourage start-up entities. The myths are false. Without thorough risk disclosures, investors are the losers.

5 Inappropriate lobbying: Self-regulatory bodies prolong their self-interest by lobbying against tighter financial reporting controls, in effect supporting deceptive activities. In the US, the SEC has long provided input into US reporting standards and has introduced rules that complement and sometimes override the advice of self-regulated auditors. In Canada, as the Preface and Chapter 1 noted, the government simply rubber-stamps the advice it gets

from self-interested, self-regulated bodies having a history of ignoring financial schemes.

6 Biased governance oversight: Governments should not be relying on self-serving bodies as their sole source of information, as Ottawa did before adopting IFRS. Canada needs to improve its financial reporting talent base so that governments can turn elsewhere for advice than to biased public accounting bodies. The US rejected unconditional support for external auditors decades ago.

7 National Securities Commission: Such a proposed body does not appear to address securities industry and stock exchange abuses. Canada needs an independent, national *prosecutorial* organization to deal with investigations and prosecutions in these cases. Too much provincial securities commission time is spent on window-dressing instead of successful prosecutions.

8 Poor investor education: After the late 1980s, Canada stopped investigating unusual financial failures. Consequently, the public has never learned about the causes and consequences of these repeated failures. Lawmakers have never understood that Canada is not a safe place to invest or that investors have become easy prey for financial scammers, who are given considerable freedom to fine-tune their schemes.

9 Investor oversight bodies: Canada badly needs a strong, independent oversight body that is *not controlled* or influenced by the self-regulatory bodies currently in place. Canada has too many non-independent bodies that have been given false labels, and masquerade as supporters of investors. Our government deregulated financial reporting by rubber-stamping ill-considered IFRS. Why was the inferior nature of IFRS not comprehended? One inappropriate decision can only lead to further losses, unless corrections are introduced promptly.

10 Prosecution and regulatory body: Canada needs police specialists and prosecutors who have been trained in securities crimes, who receive opportunities for personal advancement and who choose a career in securities case analysis.

With their lengthy inaction our lawmakers have turned Canada into a haven for financial manipulators. Ill-informed and unsupported, investors in Canada have become easy prey for the people who would swindle them out of their savings. Instead of supporting investors, Canada's governments have abandoned them to protect themselves against tricks, swindles and outright fraud.

We hope this book will help investors to identify the risks and pursue the rewards of investing with more confidence. We deeply regret that the people who should provide investors with such confidence seem unwilling or disinterested in that responsibility. We hope they're listening if not to us then to the thousands of investors who have suffered losses as a result of lawmakers' neglect.

APPENDICES

Financial Statements Explained

This Appendix discusses each financial statement on a one-by-one basis for those who are not familiar with financial reporting practices.

The financial reporting of Sino-Forest Corporation (sfc) initially raised two major concerns:

1 Grossly overstated cash flow from operating activities (a form of cash profits); and
2 Unreported self-dealings, such as purchases and sales of timber products, wherein sfc itself was alleged to be both the principal buyer and the seller.

In this Appendix, we focus primarily on sfc's reporting of bloated cash profits from income statement operations. Financial analysts often rely on a company's cash profits, as reported in its audited financial statements, to help to estimate the value of the company's stock.

sfc issued its audited financial statements for the year ended December 31, 2010, in the Spring of 2011. They were the last audited financial statements published by the company before it collapsed. We have taken crucial numbers from these condensed financial statements to support our discussions in this Appendix of the major issues facing sfc.

Table A.1 Sino-Forest Corporation balance sheet (US$ millions),
December 31, 2010

Assets	
Cash and cash equivalents	$ 1,223 (B)
Inventory	62 (I)
Other current assets	794
Total current assets	2,079
Timber holdings	3,123 (A)
Other non-current assets	527
[Longer-life assets]	3,650
Total assets	$ 5,729 (F)
Liabilities and Shareholders' Equity	
Current liabilities	$ 756
Long-term debt	1,660 (C)
Other	63
	2,479
Miscellaneous	52
Shareholders' equity	
Share capital	1,261 (D)
Combined debt and equity issues	159 (E)
Other	329
Retained earnings	1,449
	3,198
Total liabilities and shareholders'	
equity	$ 5,729 (G)

Note that total assets of $5,729 (Line F) million equal total liabilities and shareholders' equity of $5,729 million (Line G). The balance sheet dollars have to balance.

The following points are critical to our analysis:

1 Timber holdings of $3,123 million (Line A) were displayed as long-term assets. That is, unlike the tree and related inventory assets of $62 million (which was available for sale in 2011) (Line I), the $3,122 million was supposedly designated as having long years of

usage, such as would be so for land and buildings or for future, not current, sales. In S F C's case, the $3,123 million would tend to indicate that the growing forest lands would be allowed to mature, and would be sold many years later. That is, S F C was being portrayed as a "tree farm" that allowed the trees to grow for several years, until they "matured," and were cut down and sold.

2 Cash and equivalent assets of $1,223 million (Line B) were puzzling. What were the "equivalents"? Where are they located? Further investigation ought to have occurred. Why so high an amount? What was the ultimate purpose or usage of this cash?

3 Long-term debt, whereby interest accumulates and has to be paid frequently, amounted to $1,660 million (Line C). If S F C were a long-term tree farm, why is the interest-bearing long-term debt of $1,660 million much higher than the share capital of $1,261 million (Line D)? Long-term, growing assets, ought to be financed with a large portion of shares or share capital, to avoid having to pay interest (or "carrying charges") on the growing trees.

4 Included with shareholders' equity is another $159 million (Line E), which we have labelled as a "combined debt and equity." A technical explanation would be too lengthy and would not be worthwhile given the existence of other major concerns within S F C. But, if we add the $159 million to the $1,660 million, a total of $1,819 of debt had to have been sold. Who were the lenders? Were the amounts "real"? Hence, more questions arise.

Overall, a brief analysis of just S F C's balance sheet by itself should have led to requiring fundamental answers to serious questions. Above all, precisely which related business operations were being conducted by S F C: a tree farm?; a broker?, or quick-sale enterprise?; more?; if so, who were the suppliers?, the customers?, in which countries?, which currencies? Also vital, was the matter of why the equity money had repeatedly being obtained from Canadians prior to 2011? Were any significant trading operations in Canada? (Probably not.) Any worthwhile job creation in Canada? It seems not. (Sadly, as the story unfolded, Canadians were revealed as being the prime victims of an alleged billion dollar fraud.)

It is always vital to determine why physical operations are located beyond Canada's boundaries, yet finance dollars are being raised in

Canada. Legitimate situations occur, especially when there is a mine or ore body in another country, or some similar scenario exists. But, over the years we have seen too many fleecings of Canadian investors, when the only Canadian connection to a company is the providing of money, but not jobs and other benefits, in Canada.

Unfortunately, as we continue our analysis and examine SFC's other financial statements, the inconsistencies and concerns get worse. How could the Board of Directors, teams of financial statement auditors over several years, securities commissions, underwriters/sellers of the equity shares, financial analysts, and many others have missed such glaring issues? For example, four sets of auditors in three different cities, in a period of about 10 years, somehow failed to adequately pursue obvious questions.

We continue to see SFC's-style of dubious financial reporting elsewhere; it has been a Canadian favourite for over 30 years.

When we turn to the income statement of SFC for 2010, we encounter a surprise (more clearly-stated, a "huge shock") concerning the nature of their operations. A condensed form of their "income statement" shows in Table A.2:

Table A.2 Sino-Forest Corporation income statement (US$ millions), year ended December 31, 2010

Revenue	$1,924 (A)
Cost of sales (i.e., cost to Sino of timber products that were sold)	1,252 (B)
Gross profit	672
Expenses:	
Selling and administrative	90
Amortization	5
Interest	128
Other, net of interest revenue	(6)
	217
Income before income tax	455
Income tax	71
	384
Other items	11
Net income	$ 395

SFC's balance sheet (Table A.1) contradicts the income/profit statement. The existence of nearly $2 billion of sales revenue (Table A.2, Line A) rules out our first belief that SFC was primarily operating a tree farm, with over $3 billion invested in *long-term* timber holdings. With its huge sales revenue, SFC resembles a chain of grocery stores with hundreds of thousands of dollars in daily grocery sales.

SFC's balance sheet and income statement therefore tell two different stories. Further research is thus needed.

Without knowing anything more about SFC, we would have to conclude, from its income statement, that the company actively trades timber holdings and products. Yet the balance sheet tells us that SFC has made a major long-term investment in timber holdings. Could SFC operate at the same time as a timber trader and a tree farmer?

This is one of the many probing questions that analysts and investors should have asked SFC's board, external auditors and stock underwriters, as well as the provincial Securities Commissions and the people who sold SFC's stock.

Now we turn our attention to the Cash Flow Statement (Table A.3). Whereas the income statement contains both cash and non-cash transactions, the cash flow statement focuses on three, and only three, major components of *cash* transactions:

1 Operating transactions (or, roughly the cash portions of the income statement's focus).
2 Financing (roughly sales of equity shares, and increases or decreases of long-term debt during the year).
3 Investing (roughly increases and decreases in long-term balance sheet assets, such as trees intended for harvesting in 20 or 30 years or longer).

Financial cheats most commonly manipulate a Cash Flow Statement by increasing cash from daily operations or "operating transactions/ activities" (Table A.3, Line B). They do this by inappropriately shifting dollars in and out of the financing and investing sections of the statement, and into Table A.3, Line B.

They do this because financial analysts partly value companies by assessing the strength of their cash flow from operations. Depending on the industry, they may value a company at six, eight or 10 times adjusted cash flow from operations. The higher the analyst's market value recommendation, or its hype, the more investors the company can attract.

Unfortunately for investors, companies can bamboozle analysts by manipulating cash flow from operations.

Table A.3 Sino-Forest Corporation cash flow statement (US$ millions), year ended December 31, 2010

Cash flows from operating activities:	
Net income	$395 (D)
Depletion of timber holdings, included in cost of sales	746 (C)
Depreciation and amortization	8
Other	(309)
Cash flow from operating activities	840 (B)
Cash flow used in investing activities:	
Additions to timber holdings	(1,359) (A)
Other	(44)
	(1,403)
Cash flow from Financing Activities:	
Increase in long-term debt	625
Other	56
	681
Increase in cash during the year	118
Minor items	3
Net increase in cash	$121

Two items on the cash flow statement require special highlighting:

1 Especially disturbing is that SFC did not refer to "additions to timber holdings" (Line A) as "cash-like" inventory purchases. It did *not* include this figure in reducing cash flows from operating activities. Instead, SFC recorded $1,359 million in "additions to timber holdings" under "cash flow used in *investing* activities." If SFC had labelled some or all of these "additions" as inventory for quick resale, it would have to have included what was sold as expenses with "operating activities," and "cost of sales" (Table A.2,

Line B). In this category, the $1,359 million would have reduced SFC's total cash flow from operating activities (Table A.3, Line B) to a negative number ($840 million minus $1,359 million = -$519 million). Applied to a negative dollar number, an analyst's valuation multiple would not attract many investors, to say the least.

2 SFC inappropriately recorded "depletion of timber holdings" (Table A.3, Line C) of $746 million as an *addition* to net income under "cash flow from Operating Activities" (Table A.3, Line B). The result was total "cash income" of $1,142 million ($746 million plus $395 million (Table A.3, Line D)). This didn't make sense. Cash had to be utilized to acquire the timber that was sold; but the cash operating cost *was ignored*.

When a company sells its long-term assets such as factory buildings and land, after many years of ownership, it may record gains or losses on its income statement, but they do *not* constitute revenue. The company is not in the business of selling its factory buildings and land every year. Revenue arises from selling products made in the factory or selling goods held as inventory in a retail store. A company cannot account for gains from selling long-term assets such as timber holdings as both cash-like revenue and non-cash depletion.

SUMMARY

What Sino did should have been easy to detect. We have written about Cash Flow Statement problems for years. Investors who noticed the unrealistic reporting actually had several years to sell their shares, because the inappropriate reporting occurred over many years.

Hercules Immunizes Canada's Financial Statement Auditors

Two appeals to the Supreme Court of Canada were made in the late 1990s involving alleged negligent financial auditing of companies that suddenly failed. The Court chose to hear the case of Hercules Managements but declined to hear the case of Victoria Mortgage. Both entities were public companies.

In the Victoria Mortgage case, the Appeal Court of British Columbia supported the contention that the company's auditors had been negligent in approving the company's financial statements, which were included in annual securities offering prospectuses. Debt securities were being offered to the public on a continuous basis. The case revolved around deficient financial reporting of delinquent mortgages leading to unrecorded losses and unfounded recording of interest revenue on the company's books. The deficiency enabled Victoria Mortgage to borrow money from lenders who alleged that they would have reconsidered their loans if they'd known the complete financial condition of the company. Since the case did not proceed to the Supreme Court, it has had only limited influence over subsequent court decisions, and may be restricted to Prospectus Offerings.

Whereas the court decision on Victoria Mortgage focused on financial statements that were included in an offering prospectus, Hercules dealt with annual audited financial statements.

In contrast, the Supreme Court of Canada ruled unanimously in the Hercules Managements' case that shareholders (and prospective investors) cannot routinely pursue actions against auditors who are negligent in detecting deceptions in a company's financial statements.

Some observers attributed the decision to the judges' lack of business expertise combined with intensive lobbying by representatives of external auditors in Canada, especially the then-named Canadian Institute of Chartered Accountants (CICA), and the CICA's role in being permitted to argue the case in court. Whatever the reasons, the Hercules decision has had especially serious consequences, for investors, which our lawmakers have since done little to correct. The decision merely added another card to the deck, which has been stacked against investors in Canada for almost a century. In the years after the Supreme Court issued its 1997 decision, lower courts in every province except Quebec adopted it. Similar cases that were already in progress were abandoned. Meanwhile, the news media paid little attention to these consequences, leaving many investors in the dark about the removal by the courts of yet another protection against fraud, that being permitted by external auditors.

Our experiences in holding educational seminars is that minimal attendees know about the Hercules decision. They usually assume that, as investors, they are protected by Canadian laws. Well, they are wrong.

BACKGROUND

Shortly after the 1929 stock market crash, the US moved fairly quickly to pass their 1933 and 1934 legislation, and to put resources into a Securities and Exchange Commission (SEC). The purpose was to protect investors against public companies that issued faked income and operating cash flow statements and bloated balance sheets. The SEC is not perfect, but, it has put the US light years ahead of Canada in investor protection. Canada's response to the 1929 stock market crash was essentially to do nothing. No equivalent to the SEC was formed in Canada, and the provinces have enacted only very weak rules. No one focused seriously on training securities regulators and virtually no one compiled records and data about financial crimes and swindles that the industry and investors could use to educate themselves.

Instead, Canada has allowed external auditors and accountants to regulate themselves, under varying degrees of provincial supervision but with almost no federal oversight. An "inadequate" status quo prevailed in Canada for decades. Combined with the introduction of IFRS into Canada in 2011–2012, investors now face extreme risks for certain types of financial manipulation.

In the early 1950s, Canada's auditors began to issue Bulletins, recommending how to report certain types of financial activities. Additionally, authors were engaged to write about appropriate reporting and auditing procedures. In the early 1970s, books appeared about what constituted Generally Accepted Accounting Principles (GAAP) in Canada. The Bulletins were superseded by the CICA Handbook.

From the early 1950s, auditor recommendations had to be sold to corporate executives. Compromises in wording had to be made. Canada's governments did little to make the sales job less onerous. Ottawa and the provinces amended their Companies Acts in the 1970s, but they basically supported the CICA Handbook's approach to financial reporting. But after Ottawa and the provinces passed the buck, the courts slowly began to discipline companies that failed to comply with the CICA Handbook.

In the early 1980s, accounting firms began hiring more external auditors based on their ability to attract paying clients. Forcing clients to adhere to accounting rules became less important than collecting the fee for the external audit. Once again, though, Canada's lawmakers did little to counter or reverse the observable decline in the commitment of external auditors to investors. As firms began to regard audits and related consulting assignments merely as sources of revenue, less and less investor protection became too intertwined. The concept of an auditor "gatekeeper" acting on behalf of investors and creditors commenced a multiple-year crumbling.

Through the 1980s and early 1990s, a rash of corporate failures occurred, including Canadian Commercial Bank, Northland Bank, Confederation Life, Confederation Trust, Castor Holdings, Standard Trust, and more. Each failure involved serious alleged auditing deficiencies. A subsequent federal inquiry into the two bank failures raised concerns with the quality of their auditing and led to changes in bank regulations and inspection.

The federal judge appointed for the federal inquiry into two Alberta bank failures stated in part:

The auditors, on the documentary and testimonial evidence before the Commission, clearly failed to apply in their judgment on the fairness of these financial statements as prepared by management in the year 1984, and probably as well in the year 1983, those accounting and auditing principles and practices pertaining to the audit of banks. The Northland Bank statements did not, on the basis of the information revealed in this record, fairly present the financial position of the bank at the 1984 fiscal year end, and probably at the 1983 fiscal year end as well. Accordingly, the auditors should not have issued their certificate of approval of these statements for 1984, and probably should not have done so for 1983. This is not an assessment of circumstances exercised in hindsight and based upon loan reviews after the appointment of the curator, but rather a judgment which must necessarily be passed on the basis of the record as revealed and known to the auditors by 31 October 1984.

The Hercules Managements decision by the Supreme Court came after the report of the federal inquiry had been made available. Despite the dismal record of Canadian auditing in the 1980s and 1990s, the external auditors retained their "self-regulation" status. Canada's solution to the financial failures was not to end self-regulation, but was to immunize external auditors from liability.

After the Hercules decision in 1997, the last straw came when external auditors began advocating for International Financial Reporting Standards (IFRS). IFRS gave even more leeway to corporate management to cook their books, while auditors who approved them remained practically immune from investor action against their possible negligence.

Meanwhile, external auditors continue to this day to issue reassuring bromides about their role in protecting investors. Here's what they stated for about 20 years up to 2010. (IFRS for 2011 onward is reproduced in part in the main body of the book, and surprisingly promises even more protection):

1 CICA Handbook, Section 1000.09:

Ownership of profit-oriented enterprises is often segregated from management, creating a need for external communication of economic information about the entity to investors ... *investors include present and potential debt and equity investors* and their advisers. *Creditors* and others who do not have internal access to entity information also *need external reports* to obtain the information they require. In the case of financial institutions, investors, creditors and others include depositors and policyholders. (Emphasis has been added in the above paragraph and those that follow in this Appendix.)

2 CICA Handbook, Section 1000.11:

the objective of financial statements for profit-oriented enterprises focuses primarily on *information needs of investors and creditors* and, for not-for-profit organizations, focuses primarily on information needs of members, contributors and creditors. Financial statements prepared to satisfy these needs are *often used by others* who need external reporting of information about an entity.

3 CICA Handbook, Section 1000.12:

Investors and creditors of profit-oriented enterprises are interested, for *the purpose of making resource allocation decisions,* in *predicting the ability of the entity to earn income and generate cash flows in the future* to meet its obligations and to generate a return on investment.

4 CICA Handbook, Section 1000.15:

Objective
The objective of financial statements is to communicate information that is useful to investors, members, contributors, creditors and other users ('users') in making their resource allocation decisions and/or assessing management stewardship. Consequently, financial statements provide information about:

(a) an *entity's economic resources, obligations and equity/net assets*;

(b) *changes in an entity's economic resources*, obligations and equity/net assets; and

(c) the *economic performance of the entity*.)

5 CICA Handbook, Section 1000.20:

Relevance

For the information provided in financial statements to be useful, it must be relevant to the decisions made by users. Information is relevant by its nature when it can influence the decisions of users by helping them evaluate the financial impact of past, present or future transactions and events or confirm, or correct, previous evaluations. Relevance is achieved through information that has predictive value and feedback value and by its timeliness

(a) *Predictive value and feedback value*

Information that helps *users to predict an entity's future income and cash flows* has predictive value. Although information provided in financial statements will not normally be a prediction in itself, it may be useful in making predictions. The predictive value of the income statement, for example, is *enhanced if abnormal items are separately disclosed.* Information that confirms or corrects previous predictions has feedback value. Information often has both predictive value and feedback value.

CONSEQUENCES FOR INVESTORS

What the external auditors for public companies stated for investor consumption over many years clearly was opposite to what had been communicated to the Supreme Court of Canada in the Hercules case. In addition, any misunderstandings by the Supreme Court were not corrected by lawmakers after 1997. Previous rights of investors were stripped away, with an extreme position being adopted by Canada's top court.

In brief, Hercules cancelled any rights to protection that prospective investors may have held before 1997. As the book describes, IFRS and Hercules combined, are devastating because they have essentially abolished nearly all protections for prospective investors. Major irreconcilable conflicts now exist.

Nevertheless, in Canada, nothing of consequence appears to be being planned by lawmakers. Investors must clue-in, and do so quickly. The Canadian investor protection system is close to non-existent, or worse, because the vast majority of Canadians do not realize that their savings are largely being managed by people who falsely believe that they can legally rely on audited financial statements.

Stock Market Rides

We encounter many people in Canada who believe that advocating for acceptable investor protection is a waste of time. They say it is not possible to protect humanity from charming snake oil salespersons, so we shouldn't bother. According to their reasoning, why have laws at all?

This short Appendix deals with the yet another example of a situation that ought to have been detected by Canada's alleged market regulators before Canadian investors lost billions of dollars of their savings.

Valeant Pharmaceuticals, under a previous name, had a history of buying companies and watching its stock price grow, and later fall. Warnings were ignored that the stock was too risky for many investment portfolios.

Our main focus in the undernoted article (reproduced courtesy of *Advisor's Edge Report*) was on the way that corporate officers and board members were being compensated. Were they motivated to function in the best interests of investors?

When our article was written, Valeant's stock price was over $300 per share. By publication date the price had fallen to around $225 per share. Six months later the stock price was under $40 per share. Despite situations like this, Canada's federal government continues to pass the buck. Is the suffering of losses of your savings just another cost of investing in Canada?

IS BLOATED EXEC COMPENSATION
PUTTING COMPANIES AT RISK?

How much an executive gets paid has always been a thorny issue for investors. Are some managers really worth tens of millions a year? How about hundreds of millions?

That's the current conundrum for Valeant Pharmaceuticals investors. The company's CEO, Mike Pearson, has earned compensation totaling $3.4 billion since taking the job in 2008. That equates to making the average Canadian's annual salary ($49,000, according to StatsCan) every 56 minutes. This might also be a conservative estimate. The total amount earned is open to interpretation based on share price, vesting dates, expected share price, and hold restrictions.

Besides an annual salary and bonus of $8 million, and executive perks, the bulk of Pearson's wealth has come from the granting of stock options, restricted share units (RSUS), and performance share units (PSUS).

The company hasn't granted Pearson any options since 2011, but he currently holds 4.9 million of them. Approximately 4.4 million are exercisable today and would net him $1.3 billion if he cashed in. The RSUS are granted as a form of equity matching. Valeant's executives are rewarded extra for holding onto their investment in the company. Pearson owns 580,000 RSUS, which are fully vested and worth $177 million as of August 2015. According to the company's proxy circular, matching RSUS and required hold periods are an effective and motivating retention tool (expensive as it might seem), especially for executives that have been "extraordinarily successful at the company and have built up significant net worth."

While the value of the options and RSUS are impressive, the majority of other-worldly compensation is actually driven by PSUS, which vest only when certain total shareholder return (TSR) triggers are met. The better the share price performance, the more they vest, sometimes up to 500%. That means five times the number of shares initially granted would be earned if the top growth target for share price is met. For instance, the company issued 450,000 PSUS to its CEO in January 2015, which could turn into 2,250,000 shares if the top TSR target is met over five years. This tranche alone could be worth

$3.2 billion. Pearson has also received generous PSU awards under previous employment agreements.

Potential Lopsided Motivation

The lopsided weighting of the plan toward a single metric (share price) can create questions about executive motives. Increasing EPS is typically an easy route to a higher share price, but there are different ways to boost EPS. It can be done organically, through better core performance, or through financial engineering. For instance, reducing the number of shares without an actual increase in earnings can raise EPS. This can be done by issuing debt and using the proceeds to buy back shares. Likewise, earnings can be bought through acquisitions. If those acquisitions are paid for with debt, EPS will see a boost and, most likely, share price will follow.

Since 2008, Valeant has made more than 20 major acquisitions valued at $30 billion. During that same period, the company has added more than $30 billion in net debt. As a result, Valeant's leverage has deteriorated. The company has gone from having no debt to supporting a balance sheet that is financed 82% with debt (or 4.6x debt to equity).

Further, that equity portion is tenuously supported by assets that are 84% intangibles and goodwill. Advisors should question whether Valeant's super-charged executive compensation plan has overemphasized share price return at the expense of mounting debt load. A similar problem exists with the company's annual bonus structure, which is based on meeting targets for revenue and cash EPS growth. Both are easily achieved through debt-funded acquisitions.

Counter Argument

Despite these challenges, the share price is increasing, and that's often what matters most to investors. As Valeant notes, the goal of the board is to align management pay with long-term share price returns, and to "richly reward" outstanding performance but shell out "significantly less" for below-average performance. In such situations, it's good to step back from a purely shareholder-focused view to look at the underlying financial health of the company from a different perspective.

The major credit-rating agencies generally regard Valeant's debt as BB- (three notches below investment grade). The debt side of the balance sheet rarely lies, and the signs are there for advisors to take heed.

Advisors Can Always Cash Out

Valeant has enjoyed a huge multi-year run in terms of share price, and advisors can be excused for wanting to take some money off the table. Huge debt loads can be unforgiving if markets turn, and the value of the intangible assets supporting that thin margin of equity becomes questionable.

The company's CEO, on the other hand, will have a much tougher time cashing out. Most of his current wealth is tied to agreements that prevent him from selling many of his shares until 2020. No one will likely shed a tear, though, if he ends up forfeiting a billion or two.

Acknowledgment: Reproduced courtesy of *Advisor's Edge Report*, October 16, 2015, authors: Al Rosen and Mark Rosen.

Mainstreet Equity Corp. Illustration

INTRODUCTION

Mainstreet Equity Corp. (MEC) adopted IFRS effective October 1, 2011 for its reporting year ended September 30, 2012. However, for comparative two-year reporting for September 30, 2012 and September 30, 2011, figures had to be prepared as of October 1, 2010, for use in its year end of September 30, 2011, its 2012 comparative reporting year.

The condensed (and without notes) balance sheets as of October 1, 2010, September 30, 2011 and September 30, 2012 show (in millions of Canadian dollars), using IFRS.

	IFRS		
	(in millions of Canadian dollars)		
	September 30, 2012	September 30, 2011	October 1, 2010
Non-current assets	$987	$912	$743
Current assets	76	7	6
	$1,063	$919	$749
Non-current liabilities	$465	$492	$417
Current liabilities	165	51	39
	630	543	456
Equity	433	376	293
	$1,063	$919	$749

The net profit/net income statements, in condensed form, for
September 30, 2012 and September 30, 2011 showed, in millions of
Canadian dollars, using IFRS reporting:

	IFRS (in millions of Canadian dollars) years ended September 30	
	2012	2011
Rental revenue	$66	$56
Profit from continuing operations	$15	$11
Fair value gains	$47	$75
Profit before income tax	$59	$86
Net profit	$56	$82

When we compare reported IFRS results to GAAP for the September
30, 2011 changeover year end (as published by MEC), the effects of
switching from GAAP to IFRS are especially informative (in millions
of Canadian dollars, both methods of reporting being audited). Which
figures should you trust, for investment purposes?

	Year ended September 30, 2011 (in millions of Canadian dollars)	
	IFRS	GAAP
Rental revenue	$56	$64
Profit/(loss) from continuing operations	$11	$(4)
Fair value gains	$75	$ Not Applicable
Profit/(loss) before income taxes	$86	$(5)
Net profit/(Net loss)	$82*	$(4)

*Observe that only $4,000,000 of income tax ($86 – $82 million) was
recorded. This is your clue that the $75 million of fair value gain was NOT
taxed, as is in accordance with tax legislation. Should we assume that if a
government does not elect to tax such an alleged gain maybe second thoughts
about the gain should occur?

MORAL OF THE STORY

Actually, several morals can be derived. Some are:

1 IFRS is hardly a continuation of old Canadian GAAP, as IFRS proponents have stated. Just examine the figures for income/loss. IFRS is a totally different measurement basis, based on a difficult-to-determine concept, or purpose. Much of IFRS bears a close resemblance to the types of financial reporting that was utilized leading up to the 1929 stock market crash.
2 Fair value gains are not the result of bargained transactions. They are management's estimates. Hence, what is their credibility level?
3 Both of the 2011 sets of figures were declared to be audited. What then does "audited" mean for investors? (Audited in accordance with a set of rules that could cause losses for investors?)
4 If it is logical to conclude that nothing of consequence changed in the MEC's business operations during fiscal 2011, why should the company's share price noticeably change upward? Do analysts and investors not understand the limitations in the IFRS numbers? Might greater problems arise from IFRS? Why should simply "counting a different way" lead to major share valuation changes? Are they warranted? Might some stock market players detect an opportunity to obtain gains from those who do not grasp IFRS's serious downsides?

Quite obviously more issues can be listed for debate. Educational limitations are clearly showing in this example; and MEC is just one of hundreds of Canadian company situations that could be illustrated, and analyzed.

Additional Reading/Viewing

The following sources have been mentioned to us as having provided useful background for investors.

PRINT

- Baines, David. Many columns written in the *Vancouver Sun*. (David has now retired from the *Vancouver Sun*.)
- Buell, Stan. Publications of SIPA (Small Investor Protection Association).
- Hunter, Douglas. *The Bubble and the Bear: How Nortel Burst the Canadian Dream*. Toronto: Doubleday, 2002.
- Kivenko, Ken. *Fund Observer* (newsletter).
- Livesey, Bruce. *Thieves of Bay Street: How Banks, Brokerages, and the Wealthy Steal Billions from Canadians*. Toronto: Random House, 2012.
- Morgenson, Gretchen. *New York Times* (weekend columns).
- Roseman, Ellen. Columns in the *Toronto Star*.
- Rosen, Al and Mark, *Swindlers: Cons and Cheats and How to Protect Your Investments from Them.* Toronto: Madison Press, 2010.
- Rosen, Mark and Al, *Advisor's Edge Report*
- Rosen, Mark and Al, Advisor.ca

TELEVISION/VIDEO

- CBC, *The Fifth Estate*
- CTV, *W5*
- Elford, Larry. (Videos)
- Global, *16 × 9*

Index